A JOHN CATT PUBLICATION

The N Middle Leader's Handbook

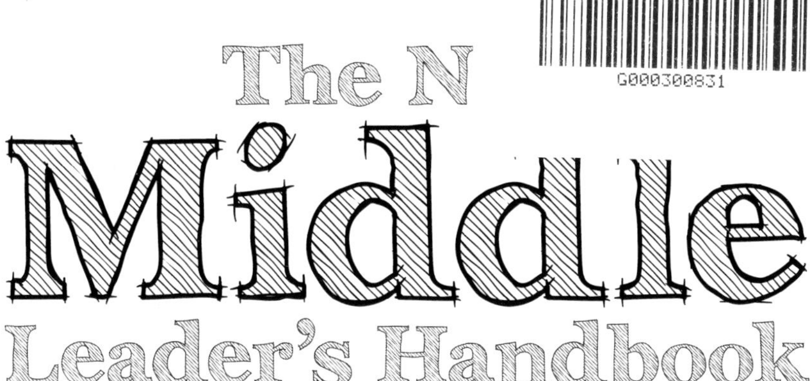

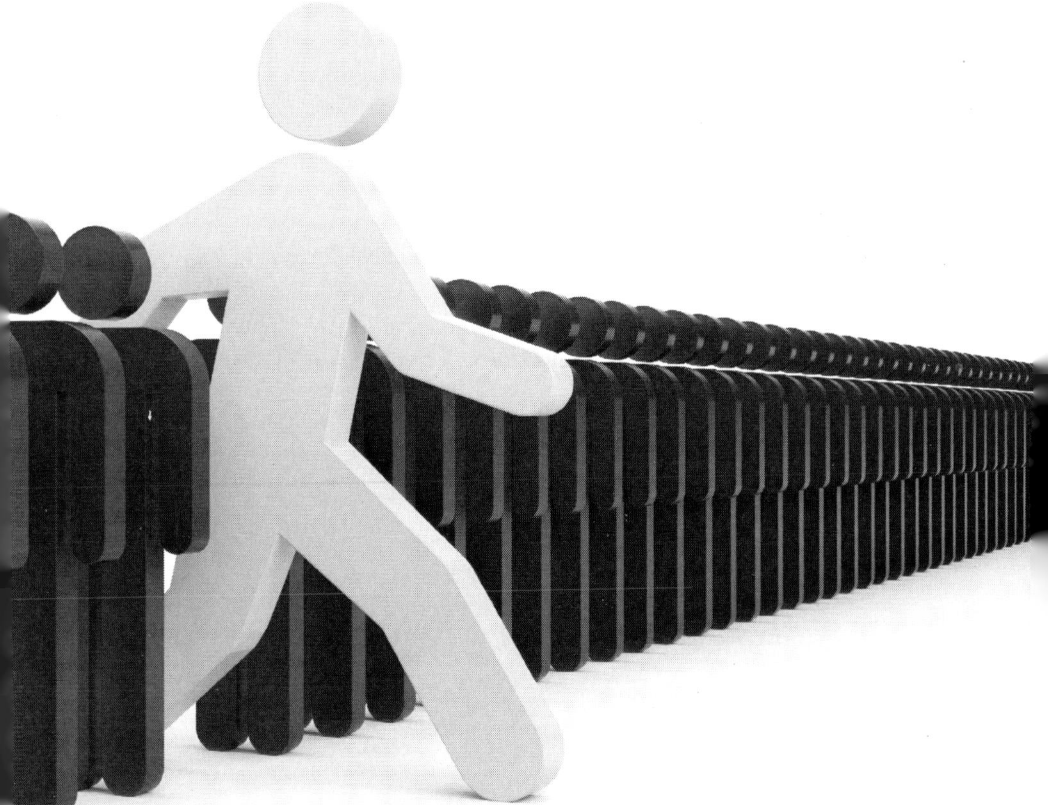

James Ashmore and Caroline Clay

First Published 2016

by John Catt Educational Ltd,
15 Riduna Park, Station Road
Melton, Woodbridge IP12 1QT

Tel: +44 (0) 1394 389850
Email: enquiries@johncatt.com
Website: www.johncatt.com

ISBN: 978 1 911 382 03 4

Set and designed by John Catt Educational Limited

Contents

Introduction 5

Chapter 1:
Applying for a middle leadership role 9

Chapter 2 – August:
Creating your vision and mapping out the year ahead 35

Chapter 3 – September:
Developing a personal leadership style and sharing the vision 73

Chapter 4 – October:
Leading Change, Organising people, Creating a Team 99

Chapter 5 – November:
Innovating in teaching and learning and monitoring the quality of teaching and learning 125

Chapter 6 – December:
Dealing with data 168

Chapter 7 – January:
Culture and Ethos 201

Chapter 8 – February:
Leading Professional Development – Developing A Coaching Model 218

Chapter 9 – March:
Managing Meetings and Time 247

Chapter 10 – April:
Enrichment and Community 264

Chapter 11 – May:
Preparing for review or inspection 286

Chapter 12 – June:
Designing a Creative Curriculum 301

Chapter 13 – July:
Reflection for Long-term Strategic Planning 313

Chapter 14 – August:
Results 335

Chapter 15:
Moving on to Senior Leadership 343

Acknowledgements 359

About the authors 361

Introduction

James says…

One morning in October or November of 2014, early morning, I think, most likely 5am or some ridiculous hour like that, I got in the car to traipse down to Nottingham to meet up with Caroline. This, for me, is always a source of anxiety. Not the driving, not the early mornings, not leaving my wife and babies, not even meeting Caroline. No, what makes me anxious is venturing outside of Yorkshire. Actually, West Yorkshire. Ok, outside of Huddersfield. I've never really seen the point. Don't get me wrong, I'm not narrow-minded, I'm far from parochial, I've travelled, very far and very wide. And anyway, as anyone from my home town will confirm, people from Huddersfield (especially my dad!) always find ways of coming together, bumping into each other on foreign streets, and being wholly unsurprised by yet another random intersection of lives, as though a gravitational fault-line has flickered between them, *Interstellar*-style, and drawn them together – an exchange of "Hiya, James", "Alright, Dave" being almost boringly commonplace and requiring no further comment.

So it's not even a fear of being alone or not among friends, or certainly the like-minded, that makes me like this. It's just, when I get home again, that's comforting because it's familiar, it's that abstract sensation of simply being *sure*. I'm certain this isn't a sensation unique to the people of Huddersfield – you'll feel like this, too, maybe, about your own hometown or about your work. Working in education in particular needs to have a strong element of consistency about it so that we can embed, cement and then build, and then change again when we need to. I certainly don't have an aversion to change (although, I once had so many consecutive nights of dreaming that my teeth had fallen out that a member of my form bought me a dreams analysis book to prove to me it was my subconscious telling me just this), but I need to feel that it is me, or my team, or my school as a whole, who is driving the change. So often in teaching, it isn't.

However, back to that journey south: meeting Caroline was pre-arranged, necessary, *contractual* even, since we were to run our course for ASCL called, 'How to be an Outstanding Head of English'. This has always been an inspiring course to run because of the times we could just stand back and watch as genuinely passionate, intelligent, funny people enjoyed their opportunity to freely share knowledge and experiences. Sometimes they griped, consoled and commiserated, comforted by the chance to be with others who simply understood, who 'got it'. They were grateful too for our advice coming as it did from two people actually doing the job, the practical nature of the day and the way they could return to school to immediately apply their ideas; the way they left feeling full of energy and determination. And so, in the car on the way there, it struck me that we should, y'know, probably write a book or something. I suggested as much to Caroline who always says yes to stuff like that. This impact that I knew our ideas were having on a relatively small scale could then reach a bigger audience, that maybe many more people could be helped to do the job of middle leader that bit better, more efficiently, more dynamically, more strategically.

I think we've managed that with this book. It's structured around your school year so use it like that if you wish, reading a chapter every month, or jump to the chapters with which you know you need help. It's a handbook so it's designed to be written in and scribbled on, and contains activities you can complete on your own or with others. It invites you to plan and reflect, to challenge and to question. It offers you methodologies and principles that we *know* work effectively and will hopefully work just as effectively for you, too. When we refer to Ofsted, we refer only to their criteria for outstanding because this book is aspirational and ambitious, like you must be if you're reading this book. It's small so you can carry it around. It's free from waffle so you can flick the pages and find the bit you need without wading through a load of blather. It works for you as a middle leader, whether you're already in post, imminently beginning the job or ready to apply, because it understands what a great job it is to have. Ok, you don't have control or influence over everything, but that's good because the role allows you the opportunity to gain senior leadership-like experience without any of the major responsibilities. You still get to teach loads. You get to work with other middle leaders who are, in my experience, universally lovely people. Finally, you get to establish your own feeling of certainty, through the strength of your own leadership, making going to work akin to that intangible sense of assuredness I talked about experiencing in coming home so that your days are as free of doubt as you can make them; planned, thought-through, with problems pre-empted, your vision unclouded, surrounded by people who share your motivation and sense of moral purpose. What better reward for your hard work than seeing a team functioning well together, results improving and children enjoying their learning, outcomes this book will help you achieve.

Caroline says...

Writing this introduction is unequivocally the most difficult part of the whole job so I have left it until the very end. One thing that strikes me as I read through drafts is that our voices (a little bit Yorkshire, a little bit sweary and always opinionated) are always perceptible and permeate the book. We sound just like we do when we're talking and I think that stylistically we have taken the right approach. I would love to sound like a wise academic and a person of great knowledge and endless experience, but I am not those things. Neither is James. We are bog-standard people. We work hard and have some experiences and ideas worth sharing. We have had some successes and we reflect continually, but that's it.

As James has said, this book is an amalgamation/solidification/consolidation of the work we have done together. The book has been brewing for sometime and its manifestation has been an organic process (I'm not happy with that phrase but it's a pertinent choice); we haven't invented a book to write, it was just there, waiting for us to sit down and do the work.

James is quite right in saying that I always say yes to suggestions like this, and I'm glad I did because I think that what we have produced will be helpful and practical and also that it will encourage reflection.

Please do, as you read the book and carry out the tasks, question what we say and argue with our ideas. Adapt what we have produced to suit you and develop ideas and approaches of your own. It was not our intention to produce a book with all the answers – mainly because that would be impossible. Our intention was a philanthropic endeavour with our focus firmly fixed on what would be useful and how we could help those doing a challenging but amazing job as middle leaders. We have been supported, coached and mentored by lots of people throughout our career journeys. As well as this we have been fortunate to observe and work with many incredible teachers and leaders from whom we have learned heaps. Hopefully this will be the case for you too – your learning and development as a leader will come from so many different people, places and writings. If this book contributes in any way to your learning and thinking, we're happy.

Chapter 1

Applying for a middle-leadership role

"Oh, it's delightful to have ambitions. I'm so glad I have such a lot. And there never seems to be any end to them – that's the best of it. Just as soon as you attain to one ambition you see another one glittering higher up still. It does make life so interesting."

– L.M. Montgomery, *Anne of Green Gables*

Why do you want a leadership role? What is compelling you to consider applying for a job as a leader? What is it about a leadership role that appeals to you? You probably have a number of motivations ranging from necessary practicalities, such as an increased wage, to a utopian daydreamy notion that you could "sort all this rubbish out". You could be a hero, rescuing your team from failure and leading them to success; or a champion of your corridor, storming the best results EVER known or a graceful luminary spreading your leadership wisdom. Or perhaps you just have the – frankly somewhat odd – feeling that you 'want more responsibility'. For many, it's a vague but pervasive feeling of being ready to take the next step on the ladder of your career. Whatever your reasons, this is just part of your career journey, one of its many phases; it may feel like a straightforward progression to some but like a gargantuan leap to others. We began this book with a question because asking yourself why you might want to be a middle leader is where we think you should begin.

Consider how you might answer the following questions:

- What will I gain professionally from becoming a middle leader?
- What will I gain personally from becoming a middle leader?
- How might the role differ from my current role?
- What could I bring to the role of the middle leader that will benefit both students and the staff in my team?

We should make an attempt to define the term 'middle leader' and offer some interpretation of the term in the context of a school or educational setting. We know that it is a position of leadership, management and of responsibility and accountability; but what sets this role apart from others? You will often hear people talk about the importance of middle leadership in an educational organisation. You may have come across the clichéd banality that describes middle leadership as the 'engine room' of a school and you will have heard the phrase 'leading from the middle' being bandied around in meetings and on courses. Senior leaders will talk about the need for a strong middle leadership in schools in order to lead and drive change and ensure sustainability – the middle leaders develop the skills to become the senior leaders. You may well have overheard a middle leader lament the enormity of their position and its multifaceted nature. The role of a middle leader in a school is both complex and varied and thus requires wide ranging skills and attributes. We digress though and what we actually need to offer you is a summary of middle leadership in one sentence, so:

Middle leadership is about creating and leading a team and constantly improving the quality of the work of that team.

Those are our thoughts – what do you think middle leadership is?

There is often much rhetoric about the importance of middle leadership and, when you are in the process of choosing an organisation in which to work, you will need to consider the value that the organisation places on middle leadership and the investments it makes in developing those leaders. You may already see yourself wanting to be promoted to middle leadership in your current workplace, a move which can have its benefits since you hopefully already have the practical knowledge of the school, the relationships you will need with key staff and the respect of the students. It will also be worth discovering and considering how involved middle leaders are in the strategic leadership of the school. Are they well supported and given autonomy at the same time? Are they viewed as pivotal to moving the school forward and making improvements in teaching, learning and progress? If you visit a prospective school, before or during an interview day, make careful observations to ascertain what extent all staff are encouraged to take on leadership roles. Do the staff appear to be supported in developing their leadership skills? Is there evidence that the school has an ethos of distributed leadership? Do middle leaders meet frequently and work as a team and are they supported – and challenged – by senior leaders? How much autonomy do middle leaders have? Are they encouraged to take risks and lead change? Don't be afraid to ask these kinds of questions on a visit or at an interview.

This chapter will consider the role of middle leaders in an educational setting and explore the skills and attributes that make a successful middle leader. You will be encouraged to reflect honestly on your relevant experience and on areas where you may need to develop skills or knowledge. We will also take a look at the process of selecting the roles for which you might apply, the process of applying and approaches to an interview day.

So, let's start to add some detail to our middle leader definition: "Middle leadership is about creating and leading a team and constantly improving the quality of the work of that team."

By leading a team, we mean: supporting, developing, challenging and holding accountable a group of people working in your field or area of specialism (*eg* pastoral/subject). A team could be any number, perhaps 3 or maybe 15 people, in size but this will vary greatly depending on the role and the size of the organisation. Leading a large team isn't necessarily more challenging and difficult than leading a small team, in fact it can be easier in some ways (it can be easier to motivate and inspire a bigger team while resistant or pessimistic staff get less airtime when there are more voices).

A middle leader is:

- responsible and accountable for an area or areas relating to and directly involved with teaching and learning
- responsible and accountable for the quality of the area/s on which they lead
- a link between their team and senior leaders and can influence both
- part of a network of other middle leaders
- a manager
- line manager
- coach
- mentor
- planner
- delegator
- listener
- problem solver

Take some time to consider what the role of a middle leader means to you. Talk to a middle leader about their job and the challenges it brings; ask them what they love about it and what they hate about it! It is likely that you are currently line managed by a middle leader – observe them in their role and reflect on what they do and how they do it. Seek out leaders and ask them questions – leaders don't belong to some mystical, invite only, covert leadership club with secret handshakes – they are fulfilling a role in an organisation and should always be happy to share their knowledge and experience.

James says...

The decision to apply for my first middle leadership post was an easy one, but that was the last easy thing about it because my first post was as Head of Year 8. Teaching Heads of Year will know where I'm coming from here – on an extra three free periods a week, I was expected to monitor the behaviour, attendance and well-being of an entire year group; I had to meet parents, carers and outside agencies or carry out home visits; I would go and support in lessons; I would hold meetings, plan assemblies, monitor tutor time; I would mediate between staff and students, students and other students, and even staff and other staff; I would shout, cajole, comfort, enthuse, laugh, cry and commiserate, mostly on a daily basis. And for the rest of the time, I taught English. So, yes, it was a hard year, but it was a great year, the year in which I learned how to be an effective middle leader (and no, that didn't come from the enforced enrolment upon the dire, and hopefully now defunct, 'Leading from the Middle' course). Taking up the role of Head of English the year after wasn't leaping from the frying pan and into the fire, it was more like a warm bath in comparison! By that point, such was my confidence, that my decision to apply to lead a faculty came not through a hunger for career progression or an increase in salary (in teaching? As if!), but because I really, really didn't want someone else to do it while I sat by, regretful, knowing I could've done things better.

Now that we have a clear image of the role of the middle leader in mind – if such a thing exists – we need to consider the skills, attributes and knowledge required to carry out the role successfully. Bookshelves in motorway service stations are awash with 'ultimate guides' to leadership and management and within their pages you will unearth myriad descriptions of leaders and middle leaders. Rags to riches tales will inspire you and you will discover that – in just ten minutes a day – you can become a virtuoso of leadership. You'll learn the secrets of success from global vendors of concepts and cars; purveyors of fibre optics or fashion. You can of course take a more academic route to your research on leadership but we recommend a judicious mixture of the scholarly and the mainstream. Hopefully, you have had opportunities to engage with some professional development centred on leadership and, as you move on to middle leadership, it will be important that you are supported in developing your knowledge of leadership and your leadership skills. Make sure prospective employers are keen to invest in developing their leaders. Most people learn about leadership through a combination of learning mediums. It is unlikely to be a neatly formed, linear learning journey; it will be a mishmash of learning and assimilation and a jumbled fusion of experiences. We believe that at the heart of understanding leadership are your astute and considered observations and deep self-reflection. File a folder labelled 'deep self-reflection' in an accessible compartment of your mind because we want you to come back to it many times on your leadership journey.

Every organisation will boast some amazing leaders who are inspiring and challenge others; find those people and watch them in action! When you consider the amount of time we spent observing others teaching and, of course, taking notes and discussing our observations during our training, it's somewhat odd that there are fewer options when it comes to observing leadership in action. I'm sure many of us observe – and no doubt critique – leadership on a daily basis so we could take a carefully designed approach to this to help us better understand leadership.

- Observe a leader you work with and take some time to reflect on what you like/dislike about their leadership styles and ask yourself why this is.
- How effectively does the leader interact with different people (*eg* students, parents, senior leaders and support staff)?
- What does their role appear to encompass and what do they do all day?
- How do they act and behave in different situations and with different people?
- How do they vary and adapt their leadership style?
- Imagine you're a leadership mentor and think about the advice you might give them to improve elements of their leadership.

Day in, day out we see leaders at all levels going about their jobs so it's worth taking the time to consider and reflect upon what we observe. We also think it's important to talk to leaders informally or perhaps arrange a Q&A session and have a more structured conversation. Ask someone in your school who has a leadership role if they would give half an hour of their time to talk to you about what leadership means to them. Make the effort to prepare some questions so that they don't have to do all the work. You might ask about their specific role, its challenges, their personal achievements or perhaps more generic questions about leadership.

As you observe and question leaders, you might find that you can begin to compile a list of what you perceive as desirable characteristics of leaders. We have created a list of core attributes that we believe are found in good leaders. It is by no means a definitive list and will vary depending on the setting in which you work (or intend to work). What would you add to or take away from this list?

A sense of purpose: The best leaders we have worked with are always going somewhere. This might be somewhere long term or an ultimate goal, but it's also just the way they do their day-to-day thing. They move and talk with a sense of purpose and resolve.

An explorer: We think that good leaders are open to exploration. They are eager to explore new avenues and possibilities. They might have a clear sense of their ultimate goal, but they are always aware that there are new things to see, do and learn along the way and they're open to their own new learning. Where there are problems, they probe and analyse.

Positive: On the whole, the best leaders are positive people. That doesn't mean that they are at all times smiley and amenable, bright and cheery, but their take on life is positive. The way they approach challenges and barriers is with the old cliché of a 'can-do' approach. You don't hear good leaders sighing and whinging.

Creative: We could write an entire chapter on creativity and creative approaches to problem solving, but the bottom line is that leaders create. They create all sorts of things: the right atmosphere for success, opportunities, challenges, great trackers, great resources, interesting and varied long term plans and, of course, hardworking and successful teams (of learners and of staff). A really good leader is not precious about their creations and encourages opinions, input and adaptations from others

A learner: Good leaders are learners whether they are working in an educational setting or not. They can be seen learning new skills and knowledge and delight in it. They're also comfortable with being seen to be learning. Leaders who lead us all to believe that they are infallible, all-knowing demi-gods don't impress anyone.

Great communicators: Whether they are supporting, building teams, chatting, praising, debating, presenting or explaining – they do it well. They communicate clearly and with confidence.

Organised: It's easy to get carried away on the tide of leadership and focus on the inspirational and creative nature of great leaders but the bottom line is that day-to-day management and organisation are integral to good leadership. Great leaders will be seen spinning their own plates, and ensuring that everyone else's plates keep spinning too. They will be there when plates break, fixing them, replacing them, asking why they fell and making sure nobody has too many or too few plates on the go at once.

Inspirational: We have talked at length about just what it is that makes a person inspirational. We have agreed that it is a combination of characteristics and behaviours, some of which are difficult to define and fugacious in nature. What inspires some may well be different to the traits that we find inspirational. Above all, leaders who are authentic and original inspire us. They forge their own path and have a healthy, but reflective and well-reasoned, disregard for trends and obvious choices. We are also inspired by those who focus on others. Folk who have an innate yearning to improve the lives of and help other people, in any way, are an inspiration. We are not inspired – or even mildly impressed – by relentless self-promotion thinly disguised as strategic school improvement!

So, having decided that stepping into a leadership role is the route you would like to take, how do you go about choosing a role or roles for which to apply? Sometimes these opportunities just present themselves to us; perhaps a Head of Department retires or a friend informs you of a post that is advertised in their old school because they think you might be interested. Maybe your life circumstances mean that you have to move to a new area and you consider taking on a new challenge in a new school at the same time. Sometimes, however, people just become jaded with their current role or setting and actively seek out a new challenge. You begin where everybody begins, on the TES Jobs website, searching for posts under the 'middle leadership' tab. You will, no doubt, have a selection of predetermined filters and criteria as you begin. You probably have an idea about the area in which you'd like to work, you know what your subject specialism is and it is likely that you have personal preferences about the type and size of the school, too. Once these obvious filters are out of the way and you have a selection of possible roles for which you could apply, you will need to consider more abstract elements and explore the less instantly tangible aspects. These are some of the questions we suggest asking and considerations that we think are worth making before applying for a post:

- What is the vision and the ethos of the school and how are they aligned with my own beliefs and sense of purpose?
- Who attends this school?
- Where on its journey would I place this school? Is it an outstanding school or a school that is on a journey of improvement? How might this affect my choice and my development as a middle leader?
- What is the achievement and progress of students like?
- What are the challenges being faced at this school?
- What appear to be the school's strengths and areas for development and how is the school addressing these?
- Do I like the general vibe of the school and can I imagine being happy working there?

These questions can be partially answered by carrying out a smidgen of online research. We may be stating the obvious, but doing this with a focused and considered approach is vitally important in finding a school in which you can thrive as a middle leader. Of course, you can only gain a fragment of the picture through research of this nature but it is an important starting point. We're pretty sure that there are people who have (for numerous reasons) skipped this stage in selecting a new organisation in which to work and ended up feeling unhappy when they find themselves working somewhere that just isn't for them.

Having identified a school or organisation in which you might like to work, you will also need to consider the role itself. There are countless titles for middle leadership roles and there are new and innovative roles and responsibilities being created constantly. You may think that a 'director' of a subject, Key Stage or area of learning is out of your league, but look closely at the job description and don't be put off by a job title that sounds like an influential, big-league role. Flashy job titles are designed to attract the best candidates. Look carefully at each of the criteria listed in the job description and ask yourself the following simple questions:

- Have I done this or something similar?
- Could I learn to do this?
- Do I want to do this?
- Might I be good at this?

Having ascertained that this is a role you could possibly apply for, look closely at the person specification. At this point, don't worry too much about there being a few gaps and some criteria that you feel you don't meet. We have rarely interviewed people who have met every single one of the criteria on the list of skills, knowledge, experience and qualifications criteria. Some criteria will not be negotiable, but there will always be others that have appeared on the person specification as a result of someone's vision of the ideal candidate for the post.

Advertised posts will usually have a list of skills, attributes and experience that they are looking for and then there will be the aforementioned, detailed person specification amongst the application documents. This specification should form the basis for planning and writing your supporting statement or letter. Again, we are stating the obvious, but applicants frequently ignore the specification when writing their supporting statement. Each application must be specific to the school and its requirements. As a pre-application activity, you can use a generic list as a starting point. We recommend using the table on the following page to record your own concrete examples of skills, knowledge and personal attributes and, very importantly, a comment about the impact that work or personal quality had.

Person specification	*Example from current or recent role*	*Impact on progress and achievement*
An excellent classroom practitioner		
Good knowledge of current educational developments		
High expectations of students / learners		
Enthusiasm and a sense of humour		
The ability to deal with difficult people		
Skills required to support and develop a team of staff		
A great team-worker		
Commitment to raising standards, achievement and progress		
Highly skilled at ... (insert your relevant specialism / job title)		
Experience of leading initiatives and / or teams		
Passion for subject area / s		

Person specification	*Example from current or recent role*	*Impact on progress and achievement*
CPD attended and / or led		
Commitment to enrichment		
Experience of using tracking and data systems to monitor students' progress		
Experience of mentoring or coaching		
Reflective		
Strategic		
Good organisational skills		
Resilient		
Flexible		
Do you possess vision? If you haven't created a vision in your current role, attempt to create a vision for the direction, improvement and leadership of a future team.		

The task you have just carried out will serve as an excellent way to focus your thinking prior to completing an application. When you begin an actual application, repeat the task but populate the first column with each of the criteria in the application form/person specification. Each row can then serve as a section/paragraph of your supporting statement or letter. Don't skip this critical stage; it is absolutely fundamental to a successful application.

Some organisations will ask for information about your experience and activities outside of work. This is an excellent opportunity for you to allow your personality to shine and also to demonstrate that you value – and can manage – a positive work/life balance. We don't want to patronise at all, but allow us to offer a few tips:

- Don't say, "I like to read" – too vague and fluffy. By all means talk about your passion for the metaphysical poets, mountain biking magazines or fan fiction, but for goodness sake, don't just "like reading".
- Don't make suggestions that you are super sporty when you don't even own a pair of trainers. Iron Man contests and triathlons are not for everyone and it really is ok if your passion is for a quiet, indoor activity. What will impress is that you do something other than work, something constructive that is, with your spare time (gigs and festival don't count as constructive pastimes in this particular context).
- Don't make things up! You may have seen some inspirational wing suiting videos on YouTube or know a guy who's into base jumping, but if you are not able to hold an informed and passionate discussion on a subject, don't include it in your application.

Draft and redraft your letter or supporting statement. Think carefully about your language choices and tone. Your vocabulary choices should echo (but not copy) that of the ethos of the school to which you are applying. Clarity of structure is important because your reader does not want to be fumbling around for information and finding it in an unexpected place. For individuals who will be reading great numbers of applications, having to read back and forth and impose their own structure on a piece of writing will be frustrating. Make sure that the task of reading your letter is a straightforward and simple process. Finally, it is absolutely imperative that your writing is proofread and that spelling, grammar and punctuation are accurate. In job applications, accuracy is non-negotiable and we don't think it is possible to be too exacting or meticulous. If you need help with this element of your application, get some!

Often, the first time you visit a school will be at an interview and demands on you will obviously be high that day. For this reason, it pays to prepare not only for the things that are expected of you – lesson to plan and teach; interview/s with various panels; tour of the school; data or in-tray task – but also to prepare carefully for collating evidence of the things you are looking for in a new role and school. In our fondness for lists, we have complied one here of some of the features that we would look for on a visit to a school, whether that's on the interview day or a less formal visit prior to an application. Use our list or compile your own to help ensure that your attention isn't focused solely on your own performance. Some of the questions you may get the opportunity to ask during the recruitment process, either when asked, at the end of an interview, the much dreaded "Do you have any questions?" or more informally as you tour the school and chat to staff and students. Some of the questions won't need to be asked out loud! You will answer them through observations that you make during your visit. It's common to feel uncomfortably self-conscious and scrutinised on an interview day; focusing some of your attention on the task of gathering information will help to alleviate the feeling that all eyes are on you. Here's our list of a few suggested questions:

- How is my arrival at the school managed? Who greets me and how do they treat me?
- Who do I meet during the day and which staff am I given the opportunity to talk to?
- Do I meet members of the team with whom I will be working?
- What do I observe about the general conduct and behaviour of students in classrooms and around the school? "Behaviour" should encompass students' enthusiasm for learning; their having fun; the way in which they speak to one another in and beyond the classroom and the respect that they show for their environment and the people

in it. Then look at the behaviour of the staff in the same way.

- How well is the school looked after and do the staff and students appear to be proud of their school?
- Are classrooms and other areas well organised and is learning and achievement celebrated through good displays?
- Is there visual evidence of a rich and varied curriculum and interesting enrichment activities?
- How well is my visit (whether it is a full day interview or an informal visit) organised and managed?
- How does the school invest in the professional development of its staff?
- How would I describe this place in three words?

Listing the questions that are important to you, before you arrive at a school, will help you focus on relevant aspects while you are there. It's easy to get swept up in the events of the day and to become paralysed by the pressures and demands. However, we really do think it's important that you find a school that is right for you. Don't allow the interview process to be a one-way street. Have high expectations and demands of a school, just as they will of you. Of course, it's important that you create a great impression (and avoid, in the process of asking questions, as presenting a pernickety or egotistical persona) and many of your questions will be best asked and answered through being sagaciously observant. Above all else, get a feel for the school and the area you will be working in. Finally (and we make no apologies for insisting you do this), ask yourself whether you feel positive vibes in this organisation. Schools have character and you either feel it or you don't – go with your gut instinct.

Let's look now at the demands that will be put upon you during the interview process. If you're applying for a middle leader's post, we can assume that you are a great teacher so our focus now will be on the interview/s and possible in-tray activities. Don't, however, neglect to plan and teach an amazing lesson if you want to be successful at interview!

Before you attend an interview day, spend some time making notes to answer the questions below. One of the most important aspects of this task is preparing examples that will serve to demonstrate your skills and knowledge. Obviously, since you are being interviewed for a new role, there will be certain things you have never done. Timetabling classes within a department, for example, might be something you know absolutely nothing about, so look at what you have done that required similar skills. The questions will of course vary from post to post, but each question will be linked to knowledge, a skill or a personal attribute. You may not be able to give an example of the task but you will certainly (if you've spent some time preparing) be able to give an example of a time that you used the exact same skill.

A useful formula to follow when you're answering many interview questions could be:

An example of a time you did this

The impact that it had (achievement and progress should underpin any impact you describe)

The learning that has taken place and your reflections and analysis

Based on the above, the impact you will have should you be the successful applicant

Think about how you might use this approach to answer the following interview questions:

How would you prioritise your workload and a work/life balance?

They want to know that you are organised and will deal well with pressure without constant intense support. They want a well-rounded individual with a healthy outlook in their work.

How would you support a member of your team who tells you they are having difficulties with an aspect of their role?

They want to know that you can be supportive of others but able to challenge people and hold them accountable. They want to know that you can coach or mentor where appropriate.

How would you deal with a member of your team who shows resistance to a change being made?

They want to see someone who can adapt their leadership styles and approaches. They want to know that you are resilient and determined. They want to know that you are not afraid of having difficult conversations.

How would you approach delegation and organisation of roles and tasks within your team?

They want to know that you can be pragmatic and efficient and also that you are adept at getting the best from people. They want to know that you won't adopt a micro-managing, control-freak approach to leadership, and that you will be committed to the development of others.

What would be the important considerations when timetabling and allocating classes to members of staff in the team?

They want to know that you can think practically and logically and perhaps that your attention to detail is good, too. They also want to know that you can think strategically. They don't care that you have never knocked up a timetable before – they are interested in your potential.

How would you develop effective cross-curricular links?

They want to know that you are a team player and a networker rather than someone who would like to create their own dominion and operate in isolation.

How would you raise the profile of your department in the school/locally/nationally?

They would like to see some creative thinking here and evidence that you have the confidence to forge new links.

What are the important considerations when designing and planning a curriculum?

They want to see some more creative thinking and they want to be sure that you have a deep knowledge of your subject area and progression through it. They want to know that while your focus is on achievement and progress, you care about innovation and enjoyment, too.

What are the important considerations when choosing qualifications/ exam boards?

They want to know that you will research methodically, seek out sound advice and consult others. They want to know that you will make sound decisions, stick by them and happily be held accountable for them.

How would you develop a range of enrichment activities designed to enhance the learning of all students?

They want to know that you will engage your whole team and provide enrichment opportunities that engage all students – not just the ones who can afford every trip. (See designing and planning enrichment activities.)

How would you develop parental engagement?

They might be interested to hear an innovative approach to solving this perennial challenge. They want to know that you will persevere.

Why this school/role?

They want to know that you have researched the school and they genuinely want to know what made you choose to apply. They don't need to know that it's close to your child minder or that you are applying indiscriminately for all possible roles within a 30-mile radius of your house.

What would you have brought to the department after a month/term/year?

They want to see that you have vision and ambition and the drive to improve and change. They want to know what you have added in your current role and that you will do the same for them.

What leadership skills and attributes do you have that would make you an ideal candidate for this role?

They want to know that you have some knowledge of leadership styles and that your own leadership style is emerging. They want to hear that you can adapt and vary your approach.

How would you motivate the staff in your team?

They want to know that you are motivational. You don't need to have the inane energy of a children's TV presenter or adopt a 'team star jumps' approach to motivating staff, but they do need to know that you can read people and understand what motivates them. They want to know that you will personalise your leadership style for each member of your team and that your aspirations and expectations will be high.

How would you improve the quality of teaching and learning?

Firstly, they want to know that you know that the first step will be KNOWING the quality of teaching and learning followed by a strategic plan that will be well-implemented, monitored and reviewed. They would probably like to hear that you are keen to work with other middle leaders to develop strategies.

How would you deal with an underperforming member of staff in your team?

They want to know that you are tough and that you will not shy away from the difficult stuff! They want to know that you will challenge underperformance by following their policies to the letter and that, as well as being firm and vigorous in your approach, you will be simultaneously fair, kind and supportive. They won't mind if you have never dealt with this in your current role, they just want to know that you have given this kind of scenario some consideration.

How could you improve our students' progress and achievement?

They want to hear your innovative and creative ideas but they also want to know that you have a pretty good relationship with data and that you're confident in using data to inform what you do. They will be pleased to hear that you have a scrupulous attention to detail and monitor and review enthusiastically.

How would you monitor the progress of students/groups of students taught by each of the members of staff in your team?

They want to know that you understand the principles of monitoring progress and that you will do so rigorously. They want to know that you are comfortable with holding others accountable.

How would you use data to raise achievement?

Now they want you to zoom in on data, they've heard some broad comments and now they want to hear some detailed examples of the ways in which you have used and will use data.

What were the strengths and weaknesses of the lesson you taught for interview (or a lesson you recently taught)?

They want to know that you can be reflective and honest and that you make accurate judgements about the quality of teaching and learning. If something went wrong, they want to know that you can deal with it and move on.

How would you ensure pupil voice has a role in improving teaching and learning in your department?

They want to know that you value students' feedback and that you will gather it and act on it. They would probably be keen to hear any creative approaches you would take to developing pupil voice in your area of responsibility.

How would you develop a team ethos?

They want to know that you understand the ethos of their organisation and that that your team or departmental ethos would be developed in line with it. They want to know that you understand the importance of vision and ethos and again, they would like to hear innovative approaches to developing a strong and coherent team with a shared ethos. They want to hear about how you contributed to a great ethos in your current role.

How would you support the professional development of members of your team?

They want to know that the development of others is important to you and that you will support others in reflecting on their practice and identifying their development requirements. They would also like to hear about your experiences of leading CPD or mentoring or coaching. They probably want to hear phrases like 'sharing good practice' and 'open door policy'.

How would you 'sell' changes to your team?

They want to know that you will deal well with the inevitable changes that will be imposed upon you and your team at some point. They want to know that you will react calmly and that your responses to such changes will be measured. They want to know that you are capable of steering a team away from gossip, grumbling or mild hysteria. With change that you lead and implement, they want to know that you will do so with conviction, enthusiasm and with your team alongside you.

There may well be questions relating to current developments in education. These may be general or more specific to your role. Be prepared to demonstrate that you can adapt to changes, face challenges and that you are interested and opinionated.

Most schools will use a student panel to interview middle leaders and they will probably engage seriously with the process – as should you! A good school will train students in conducting an interview and will work with them to devise the interview questions. You might expect to be asked questions about things like: dealing with poor behaviour; dealing with bullying; curriculum enrichment; homework and revision sessions; supporting students and engaging reluctant learners.

An in-tray activity might include a selection of urgent and important items, urgent but not important items, routine items, and non-urgent and unimportant items. A common task might be to put the items in order of priority and, more crucially, explain how you might deal with each item. Additionally, more and more schools are asking candidates for middle leadership positions to undertake a work scrutiny and feedback on their findings and impressions. Another common task set for prospective middle leaders is a timed data-based activity that you're asked to carry out at some point during the interview day. You are likely to be provided with some data (either for a Year Group or Key Stage) and asked questions such as:

- Based on analysis of the data, what would you suggest as three key issues/areas for development?
- What strategies or interventions would you put in place to address these issues/areas for development?

They want to know that you can analyse data and use it to inform your strategic planning. They want you to have the ability to identify serious problems, trends, and underperformance of groups, and perhaps flaws in the data or problems with the way in which the data is presented to you.

Practise carrying out in-tray and data tasks prior to your interview. Ask a colleague to set a task for you. A current middle manager or senior leader will be able to help you with this and offer you some post-task guidance. In carrying out a data task, don't be afraid to offer radical and innovative ideas for intervention – show that you are a creative thinker and not afraid to try something new. Try and demonstrate that you can balance innovation with simple and conventional approaches. During data and in-tray tasks, you can demonstrate your ability to think big and think creatively as well as an ability to give attention to detail (tweaking the everyday) and implement small but potent changes.

Besides the interviews, teaching a lesson and an in-tray or data task, you will be spending a fair amount of time learning about the school; this is likely to include a tour of the school and opportunities to meet members of staff. There may well be some waiting time too, particularly if there are a number of candidates being interviewed. So, what are the key factors to consider in the way you present yourself throughout the day? At this point, we recommend looking back at your list of attributes that make a great leader (or use ours) and think about how you can demonstrate these attributes as you walk around the school, meet with various people, interact with other candidates during lunch or coffee breaks as well as in the interview. It may be stating the obvious, but you must look the part. We suggest a "look like a manager, behave like a leader" approach. By this we mean dress impeccably and professionally. Be sharp, be slick, be flawless but don't be tempted to accessorise in some manner that you believe will demonstrate your 'fun-loving, creative character'. There is no place for nail art, novelty socks or any form of evidence that you adore Sonic Youth or Metallica. You should be particularly sensitive to the context of the school here, especially any religious or cultural considerations. Do let your creativity and character show in the classroom and in interview, but not through what you wear. We are not suggesting that you adopt this approach to the rest of your working life… but this is an interview. Be warm and open; behave in a confident but not arrogant manner; show enthusiasm and ALWAYS smile.

There will be opportunities to ask questions throughout the day as well as in the interview. Things that you see and hear during the day will prompt some questions, but you should also prepare questions in advance. Base them on your knowledge of the school by all means, but try to ask questions about things that really interest you; it's always obvious when someone is feigning enthusiasm for something about which they couldn't give a toss. Similarly, questions that have been designed to impress are always detectable and somewhat cringe-worthy! You and the other candidates might have the opportunity to ask questions as a group; don't be tempted to compete with them by asking a deluge of demanding and elaborate questions. Of course, don't sit in silence. Ask a couple of well-considered questions. We suggest keeping the questions during the school tour light in nature and prompted by information, displays, resources and activities. Ask questions to show genuine interest in what you see. Reserve the 'big' questions for your formal interview. Prepare a balanced set of questions, ensuring that some are very specific to your role while others focus on the ethos or development of the whole school.

Here are a few questions that we think might be worth asking:

About the role you're applying for:

What are the key areas for development for the (insert role/job title here) team over the coming year?

What might be the greatest challenges for me in this role over the coming year?

What are currently the most successful aspects of the team?

(You may also want to ask a specific curriculum based question, but be careful not to ask something so subject specific that nobody in the room has the answer. You won't ingratiate yourself by trying to appear smart.)

About you and your development:

How does the school support the professional development of middle leaders?

How does the school support career progression of middle leaders?

(We would ask about 'the school' rather than saying 'you' to avoid making an individual feel like they're the one being interviewed.)

About the whole school:

What are they key areas for development for the school over the next year/five years?

What are the school's recent successes?

Does the school have a coaching or mentoring programme in place for staff?

On the tour I noticed (insert noticed thing here), could you tell me a bit more about it?

When I met (insert person here) they mentioned (insert mentioned thing here), could you tell me about the impact this has had on learning/progress/behaviour/achievement?

You can adapt any of these questions to suit the school, role and circumstances, but they might serve as a useful core set of questions to ask.

We think that it is useful when preparing for applications and interviews to reflect honestly on your strengths and achievements and to contemplate what motivates you. What are the strengths of your character? What are your finest skills? What is it that you are knowledgeable about? What are your greatest achievements in your current role, other roles, outside work? And what motivates you and makes getting out of bed a total joy each morning? Don't shy away from talking openly about yourself and endeavour to be comfortable sharing your achievements, successes and passions.

Strengths	*Achievements*	*Motivations*

Caroline says…

I actually quite like interviews. I'm not lying – I genuinely enjoy the process, the challenge, meeting new people, and the whole prospect of a new role and challenge. To me an interview is like a day out where I get to dress up in a best outfit and chat with interesting people. I've never been able to relate to those people who are crumpled in a sweaty heap of nerves and stuttering monosyllabic answers to questions with a facial expression that says "I would rather be anywhere than here". What's not to like about an exciting day out? I genuinely believe that you should treat an interview day as though it were a fun day out. Plan to enjoy the whole day and then do so. And make that enjoyment visible to everyone you encounter during the day.

Chapter 2 – August

Creating your vision and mapping out the year ahead

"Vision is the art of seeing the invisible."

Jonathan Swift

Ok, you've managed to land yourself the dream middle leader role and, by now, you may well have realised the enormity of the task you are facing. The August before you begin your new role is a golden time. If you're the kind of person who likes to be sequestered away doing all sorts of introspective contemplation largely undisturbed, then you will be in your element. Hopefully, you will find time during this period to have a holiday yourself and will take the chance to unwind before you begin September at a hundred miles an hour. But now, in August, while school is closed to students, your school should be peaceful and relatively empty – there'll be the odd workman knocking about repainting the staircase, but most of the staff, save the SLT most likely, will still be on the beach (and quite right, too!). In this chapter, we will consider how best to use this most valuable of months. This is your opportunity to get to know the geography of your school and establish your own classroom or base (or even office, if you're lucky enough). You can begin to plan how you will distribute leadership across your team and start to think about the links you will need to make within school and beyond. You will also face the essential task of analysing results (crucially, not officially *your* results, but those you have inherited from your predecessor). This is also the time when you can begin to formulate your vision for your new department. Finally, you will need to decide upon a marking and assessment policy that works in tandem with your whole school marking and assessment policy, so you'll give some deep thought to how you want this to theoretically look and how it will work in practice.

So how do you go about getting to know your new school when there's barely anyone in it? The condition and appearance of the classrooms are an ideal place to start. Have a good nosy around. Consider wall displays. If student work is on the walls, check dates or names and year groups to see if it's recent – a bit of detective work might be needed here. Look at what state it's in, too – curling paper, faded backing, dangling borders, graffiti, those awful, black-bordered motivational posters, you know the ones, with a lion or an elephant or a bloody dolphin and some quasi-spiritual phrase urging you to "dare to dream"…could all point to potential issues around pride in the job, workload, student behaviour, time management or even subject knowledge, things you will need to address.

Now look at the teacher's desk or work area: what does this workspace have to say about that member of staff? Be careful not to make snap judgements – some of the greatest teachers we've worked with have desks that look like a hoarder's back bedroom – but do tentatively decide upon a few appropriate adjectives. Especially make a note if any copies of the following DVDs are present on the desk – *Elf*, *Santa Claus the Movie* or *The Grinch*. This person clearly writes off the last week before Christmas. Any department office or workspace needs to be carefully looked at as well as they could give you some indication of the level of organisation that exists in your team and the way in which they work together on a daily basis; if your impression is a negative one, then there's work to be done here, although we would advise against any large scale chucking out – someone somewhere will be very upset that their favourite resource has ended up in the bin, no matter how unused or dusty it appeared to you. Lay the ground work for this in the coming term, but leave any departmental cleansing until Christmas of your first year at least.

Next, turn your attention to the layout and physical condition of the rooms: are desks in rows or grouped; are there enough desks and chairs to accommodate all the children; are they all the same or an assembled, random collection of styles and colours; are health and safety considerations being adhered to, especially in Secondary science, PE or technology areas; do doors open with an irritating squeak; do windows have effective blinds; is ventilation good enough; is there electrical wiring all over the place; what's the flooring like; does the technology work? How about the corridors? Are they welcoming and reflective of the department? Is there a consistent corporate style across school that you will need to adopt?

Finally, consider the treatment and state of resources: are student books and folders stored in good order by the teacher; are texts in good condition, free of graffiti and fitted with plastic covers; look at the state of equipment such as stationery or other subject-specific equipment like badminton rackets, poster paper or frying pans; can all scissors be accounted for (seriously, if you don't have a policy on the safe use of scissors, get one); do the glue sticks all have properly attached lids?! Again, make a mental note.

Additionally, insist on being given full access to your new school's ICT systems – you need usernames and passwords setting up now, not in September, so push for these to be established as soon as possible.

You should be gathering a pretty clear picture by the end of this tour, but feel free to use the checklist below to record your observations. Copy it as many times as you need for the number of rooms you want to write about.

Item	*Room*	*Room*	*Room*
Display			
Teacher's desk			
Layout			
State of repair			
Resources			

A good idea might be to compare all your observations about rooms and the corridors with other areas of the school. Go for a wander and find yourself some good practice. Take pictures even, and use them to illustrate your standards and expectations to those in your team. If there are issues surrounding the supply or availability of suitable furniture and resources, get the ball rolling on this now by speaking with the finance team or the school's business manager, sounding them out about investing in new tables, chairs, teachers' desks or cupboards. Anything in disrepair that could be fixed by the caretaking staff should be tackled now also. If ICT issues need addressing, do this now, introducing yourself to your ICT support assistants and giving them plenty of opportunity to fix what's broken or upgrade what's out of date. Anything that can be completed before the first day of the autumn term is a bonus.

The best way to ensure that rooms look great is by modelling the ideal through the design and organisation of your own workspace. If you have a classroom, it needs to be the exemplar room, although determining the standards for rooms and workspaces across your team is best decided *by* the team. Demonstrate through the design of your classroom how you expect others to follow. Here are some basics to get you started:

- Strip all display boards and replace with fresh backing paper and colourful borders, possibly even assigning one board to each class you teach at Secondary (if you're a Primary teacher, you're probably already a whiz at display. Move on to the next tip!). You could also save yourself a display board, preferably near your desk, so that you can display key documents like your long term plans, assessment calendar or department meeting schedule – more on creating these later.
- Next, use as many surfaces as you can to begin creating inspiring, interactive and imaginative subject-specific display: try glass pens for writing on any windows you have – key dates in history, common mathematical formulae, the structure of a plant cell – for instantly striking display; string a washing line across your room and hang from it mini paper t-shirts adorned with connectives (ensuring you've had that essential ladder training, obviously); festoon your door with the names of Shakespeare's plays, the

countries of the world or key French vocabulary; or buy some of those cheap, blank artist canvases from The Range or equivalent for a simple, week-one, student-generated display on whatever topic you're about to do – they're big, bold and look brilliant hung around your room.

- However you prefer to organise your tables and chairs (we prefer mixed groups of about four), ensure that, wherever a student sits, he/she will be comfortable and their view of you, the board or any other displays won't be blocked.
- Decide how you'll want to store student books, folders and any other resources you will require, and ensure everyone else does it this way, too. If this means investing in sturdy, plastic storage boxes, then so be it. This uniform approach will also simplify your scrutineering of marking – more on this later.
- Insist on seating plans, but leave the rationale behind the plan to individual teachers – as long as the rationale is a rational one. "Because they're best friends" doesn't fit into this category.

The key message you should take from it is the necessity of putting the hours in now, while you can, so that your classroom and any associated systems and processes are in place from the outset. You can't underestimate how much a rubbishy looking room will generate a negative perception of you. Resolve to keep up your standards as well, building the need to monitor their maintenance into your Quality Assurance routines.

It's imperative that you get a handle on your budget, carefully deciding now how you will allocate your capitation across the year. Look at when you will have periods of real expense (copying for mock exam season, stationery orders and so on) and find out how photocopying and printing are charged at your school. If possible, designate individual, monthly allowances for copying and printing to each member of your team to keep a grip on the spending. If you work in an Academy, then your financial year will most likely run from September so you will begin the term with a healthy balance in your budget. However, in most other schools, the financial year will run from April so your capitation could already have been eaten into in the previous summer term, especially if your predecessor became a little de-mob happy and really loosened the purse strings. When it comes to ordering goods and resources, have a carefully structured system that means you and you alone sign off on any purchases and that, when orders arrive, they are checked carefully by an elected member of staff. Don't worry that this might make you appear controlling – good! At the end of the day, you are probably working on a tight budget and are accountable for how your funds are spent. Waste or profligacy are unacceptable so go a step further and design a tracker for keeping a close eye on the cash. It is too laborious for you to be keeping this manually up to date; once again, assign the task to someone else like a departmental PA or other member of the support team. But obviously build checking it into your routine – once a month should suffice.

Although you may not have a clear and full idea of who your team exactly are yet, you should at least know their names and their varying levels of experience. Who is an NQT? Who is a RQT? Do you have any Lead Teachers or Lead Practitioners? Who is on UPS? Do you have any TLR holders? Is anyone on the Senior Leadership team? What about support staff? If you're unsure, go and find this out. It's going to be critical for when you come to thinking about effective delegation and, one step further, distributing leadership responsibilities.

Write your team's names and their respective points on the pay scale in the table on the following page:

Team member	*Point on pay scale*

You may be extremely competent at delegation, allocating tasks naturally and trusting others to deliver. Or you might be one of those people who freely admit to being poor at delegation. There may a whole gamut of reasons for your reluctance to assign responsibility for tasks to other team members. You may not like to relinquish control – after all, final accountability will always lie with you. We're probably all guilty of this. You've got to this position because you do things well, you do things right, you do things on time and you do things the way *you* imagine they should be done. If you are ever stung by someone singularly failing to complete a task the way you envisioned it, consequently completing it yourself, you must resist the temptation to stop delegating and take on too much yourself. This often happens to middle leaders. You shouldn't feel guilty making demands about the standards you expect from your team. Yes, there's definitely work to be done in September communicating these standards to individuals you entrust with different responsibilities. Indeed, you could make a case for your team to decide upon the high standards they need to set for themselves. But for now, while you're in your introspective contemplation phase, decide for yourself what needs doing, who could do it and how it should be done.

Here's a list of ten responsibilities that we think are common to most schools and that do not necessarily have to be directly led by a middle leader. It's not exhaustive by any means, but it's a good place to start. Add more of your own at the bottom if there are specific foci that will need your attention in the coming year. Tentatively write the names of your staff members from your previous list above who could take responsibility for leading each responsibility. Pay particular attention to which tasks you will assign to a second in department, if you have one:

Responsibility	*Staff member*
Managing the transition between Key Stages	
Display	
Homework monitoring	
Coordination of curriculum enrichment	
Implementation of the literacy policy	
Implementation of the numeracy policy	
SMSC (Spiritual, Moral, Social and Cultural) development	
SEND students	
More able students	
Community links	

An approach to delegation you must resist is to hand out tasks as and when they become a priority. By this we mean those jobs that arrive on your desk and that you then hand to someone else to do – end of term rewards lists, incomplete data monitoring, missing student reports, parental complaints, an enrichment trip or competition... The reason for this is threefold. Firstly, ask yourself if you want the perception others have of you to be disorganised and, well, a bit crap. Secondly, you will find this to be an inefficient way to operate, most likely creating more work as you end up micro-managing the various jobs that your team are undertaking. You won't be handing them the freedom to decide strategy for the tasks you give them. Also, because of the haphazard way that these tasks will inevitably arise, you will have no control over workload which will come in peaks and troughs. Thirdly, it will, in the long run, de-skill your team in the ability to independently lead. They will end up waiting expectantly for you to give them things to do. It won't matter that when you do give them jobs they complete them magnificently because that is only part of the intended effect of delegation. You want the job to be done well, but you also want your staff to become leaders within your team, taking the onus away from you having to do the constant dishing out of jobs.

The smart way to ensure your team fulfil their potential to be leaders is to spend some time this August thinking strategically about how you are going to distribute leadership responsibilities. This is distinctly different to simple delegation. At its core, the distribution of leadership is about developing leadership capacity within your team, freeing up your time and energy and minimising your direct involvement in a whole range of areas. It will mean that succession planning starts right now – if you ever do leave this post, your hard graft won't instantly dissolve since you'll potentially have developed your replacement among the members of your team. And it will also mean that you have people who can deputise for you – when you're on a course, if your kids are ever ill, when you're interviewing for new staff all day. This won't happen by magic or because you've decided right now that that's what you're going to do. You will need to identify the skills of your staff, their interests and their abilities, and you will need to invest time in a personalised approach to developing their talents. Some straightforward ideas for starting out:

- Communicate key outcomes and teach your team how to go about setting these themselves from a whole range of available evidence – statistics, interviews, observations *etc*
- Discover the hidden talents of your team and exploit them. Find out: who's an ace at public speaking and could deliver a great pitch at open evening; who's approach is methodical and meticulous and could assist in organising your exam entries or who can see the opportunities in new media for responsibly promoting your department and engaging your students.
- Talk regularly with your team about the qualities of leadership. Share with them Ofsted's ideas of subject leadership (as discussed in Chapter 3). Discuss their own ideas about the qualities of a good leader and draw up a department code of behaviour for leadership that everyone will aspire to. This will come naturally to some people, but for others it might need to be explicitly taught.

When you finally get time with your team in the new term, the allocation of responsibilities and a shared methodology around how these will be approached should be high on your agenda. We strongly suggest that you should try to arrange meetings this August with any members of your team who are TLR holders or hold any other position of responsibility for which they're paid. They need to have an understanding of your vision for the department and a share in its creation. We'll consider this in more depth soon after we have looked at August's most crucial job, results analysis.

But before we move on, it's worth thinking about devoting one morning this month to how you can proactively create links within and beyond your school, either in person or via email, that will be beneficial to you and your team. Your ultimate aim here is the creation of your own network of colleagues that you can call on for support. In no particular order, here are some ideas:

- The SENCO – a vitally important person who can give you reams of information on the students in your new school as well as the policies and procedures unique to your school. Also, find out about the deployment of support staff and their effectiveness. If you're reading this and you *are* the SENCO, then think about how you should be planning to meet all other middle leaders, either individually or as a group, to communicate your vision for SEN in the school.

- The library – hopefully, your school has resisted joining the worrying trend for giving up the library (this is happening all over as schools look to cut costs, often blaming their under-use, but we can't think of anything more myopic than taking a library away from children. If it's dysfunctional, fix it, don't shut it!). If so, meet with the library staff and discuss how you could utilise this resource – as an extra classroom, as a place for small group work, as a reward for students' hard work, as an evening venue for meeting parents when launching an initiative…
- The Pastoral team – find out who does what and where you can find them. Are they scattered all over school or do they all reside in one office? Look at what support they can offer you on a day-to-day basis, but also how you can reciprocate, especially important since there quite often seems to be a divide between the pastoral and academic teams in schools. Highlight how much you believe in a team philosophy; for example, if you are in a Secondary school, arrange to meet with the Head of Year 11 to discuss the potential career pathways of the more able students in your subject.
- Your SLT link – here, you will need to garner a clear understanding of the school's expectations of this role. Think carefully about what you will want from your SLT link (they'll be thinking about what they want from you!), agree on the frequency of your meetings and, if possible, agree on the focus or agendas for these meetings well in advance. Good things to ask them to support you with are: dealing with difficult staff; joint observations of staff; tackling extremes in student behaviour; data analysis and intervention planning and assisting with your quality assurance procedures, helping to check marking and assessments. They are unlikely to be a specialist in your subject so ensure you are ready to explain, justify and defend decisions you make with your informed knowledge of your curriculum and course content.
- The Middle Leadership team – this is another resource that, when working together well, can have a real impact upon a school. Too

often, MLTs are a disparate bunch struggling to juggle the demands of their team below with the diktats from their SLT above, and their meetings are characterised as a group of people sitting down for an hour, making lists of jobs they are being instructed to do. Introduce yourself to the members of your MLT and find out the characteristics of this team and the way in which it is expected to function. Be conscious that you should have a strong shared purpose and establish, with others, that much of the work of the team needn't be done in isolation, offering to pool resources and talent. Push for your MLT to autonomously lead its own meetings, too, and broadly plan out the focus for each of these for the coming year in your first meeting together.

- The other schools in your area – this includes as many equivalent post-holders as you can find in as many equivalent schools as you can find, Primary or Secondary. If you are in a Secondary school, look to make contact with your Primary feeder schools – but it might be a good idea to coordinate this with your fellow middle leaders so as not to inundate them with messages of introduction and invitations to participate in outreach. Depending on the strength of your Local Authority's advisors and on how proactively they bring middle leaders together to network, why not investigate forming your own network or federation to share ideas, resources, solutions to problems and subject specific knowledge?

There are undoubtedly others with whom you will need to make links (the exams officer, your data manager, the ICT support staff), but for now these should be enough to get you started and ensure you will start work in September with an increased profile among your colleagues. Aim to make a good impression (no cheesy jokes!), be professional in your manner, language and even your dress if you're meeting people in person (okay, it's August, so maybe not a suit, but also definitely no shorts and flip-flops) and demonstrate your eagerness to collaborate without loading yourself with too much extra, diversionary work. Collect your lists of names, email addresses and phone numbers and, with those outside of your school in particular, maintain semi-regular contact – not so much that you appear overly keen or needy, but not so little that, when you do get in touch, it doesn't appear you're only doing it because you want something.

In this next section, you may discover that the contacts you have made among your MLT will prove very useful for successfully completing your results analysis.

Results Analysis

One of the most high-profile tasks that you will instantly have to undertake in your new role is that of results analysis. Since this task is so high-profile, and may even involve the requirement to present to the whole staff on the subject on the first day back as we've seen in some schools, you will have to get it right – both in the conclusions you draw from your analysis and in the tone you take in your reporting of them. If the thought of this is already going to cause you sleepless nights, we suggest dipping into December's chapter on data which will provide you with many of the mechanisms and approaches you could use to completing this successfully. As you will discover when you read on, it is vital that tracking systems for your subject or area of responsibility are accurate and do what you want them to do. A decent spreadsheet that will allow you to drill down into the previous year's results needs to be created first. This is what it needs to be able to tell you:

1. What did the students achieve and what progress did they make?
2. What should they have achieved and what progress should they have made?
3. How accurate was forecasting?
4. Who has over-performed/underperformed/done as expected?
5. Can you identify any patterns or trends?
6. Which 'groups' of students have done well and which haven't?

For each of these, you'll then need to ask, "Why?" Your list of results won't automatically tell you this so you'll need to dig deeper, asking questions and discussing with staff some of the narratives behind the numbers:

1. What did the students achieve and what progress did they make? Why?

   This question is going to lead you into discovering so much

about all areas of your work: which teachers in your team are the most effective or work best with particular groups of students or year groups; which parts of the qualifications were taught the most effectively; whether the curriculum is suitable and provides appropriate preparation for student assessments; was staffing an issue that year and is it going to be again and were there any issues with the quality of teaching?

2. What should they have achieved and what progress should they have made? Why?

   Here, you should spend your time comparing student performance to target grade. You will need to find the percentage of students meeting and exceeding target grades by subject and teacher. Ensure you have a clear understanding of your school's targets system – where do they come from and how are they calculated? Don't pay any attention to anyone telling you that the targets were impossible or over-inflated; they might have been, but so what? The targets are the targets and you have to work with them. You have to trust that their calculation is rational, sensible and fair.

3. How accurate was forecasting? Why?

   If you are brand new to the school, this might be a little more difficult to answer without a lot more digging. The key to accurate forecasting is ensuring there are many opportunities for staff to standardise their assessment of student work and moderate the work produced under the guidance of their colleagues. Find out if this took place and, if so, how often.

James says...

A simple mathematical way of comparing the forecasting of your team is to find an average figure for their accuracy. Do this by comparing the forecast grade to the actual grade. If the forecast for a student was one grade higher than their actual grade, then give this a score of 1. If it was one grade below, give it a score of -1, and so on. If they were the same, the score is 0. Add up all your 1s, -1s, 0s and divide by the number of students in the class to find the average. Any score close to 0, say 0.11 or -0.2, shows broadly accurate forecasting, but anything above 1, either plus or minus, could indicate a problem with a teacher's ability to predict students' grades, either because they were overinflated or

massively pessimistic. Be careful not to draw final conclusions from this without considering other factors like the whims of the exam boards in deciding where the C/D boundary might lay this year.

4. Who has over-performed/underperformed/done as expected? Why?

   You will probably end up producing long lists of students here which you should use to support upcoming discussions with the members of staff who taught them. Listen to their reasoning and focus on how effective their intervention activities were, suggesting alternatives for the coming year if they appear to have been fruitless. You should discover the strengths of your team in these discussions, too – are they inspirational to boys, can they challenge the more able, do they succeed with the least able? For a much more detailed consideration of intervention, see Chapter Six.

5. Can you identify any patterns or trends? Why might these be significant?

   It is important to look at how results have progressed over the last three years so that you can give your current data some context. If this year has seen a real leap in results, why and how has this occurred? If this is another year of decline, what will need to be done to halt the slide?

6. Which 'groups' of students have done well and which haven't? Why?

   Look for differences and gaps, especially any gap between disadvantaged and non-disadvantaged students as identified by their FSM status. Ask why for each of them. Expressly look for how you compare nationally. For GCSEs, you can do this by looking at the JCQ website and downloading a PDF that will give you national statistics for your subject and break them down by gender. Consider using the following list, it's pretty comprehensive:

   - Gender
   - Ethnicity
   - SEND status
   - More Able

- Form/Tutor/Year group
- Free School Meals status
- Pupil Premium
- Prior attainment (KS1, KS2, KS3 or previous year's end of year result) – usually broken down into low/middle/high attainers
- Summer born children
- Looked after children

In the Primary sector, your results analysis is going to involve a root and branch breakdown of the previous year's results, whether it is internal teacher assessment or the results of external, standardised tests, or both. If you are a subject coordinator, this is your opportunity to assess the full, current position of student progress and achievement in your subject, and thus determine the actions you are going to take to address shortfalls in particular year groups or in any of the groups from the list above. You should be producing a report for each of the teachers that summarises your findings and gives them easy to digest information that can then inform their intervention planning (again, leap forward to December's chapter on data for some more good ideas on what you could be doing here). Be wary of being too personalised in your analysis of individual teacher performance if you are new to the school; you don't want to cause upset or offence in your first meaningful action in charge. Maybe you will be given some meeting time in which to put forward all you have found out. If so, pick and choose from the reporting structure suggested below for Secondary colleagues for ways to put together your findings.

Similarly, Secondary schools will have received GCSE and/or A-Level results in August, but there will also be a whole raft of data to analyse from end of year teacher assessments of the year groups who didn't sit exams during the previous summer. It is common practice for middle leaders here to have to meet with the headteacher or another senior leader early in September to report on the performance of students and staff in their subject area or year group. Make no mistake, your headteacher *already knows* how your students and staff performed; part of the purpose of this meeting is to determine whether *you* know, too. Be prepared. Cover as many bases as you conceivably can. If you work through our six questions above, you should be ready to produce a thorough and comprehensive analysis. Submit your report in advance of the meeting, and we don't mean that morning – this is really important as it demonstrates how much you're on top of this, and why you should aim to complete it as fully as you can before the term starts in September. There may be an agreed *pro forma* or school-specific way of presenting your findings so check on this in advance. If not, then you could use the following basic structure which will be a common format in every school:

1. **Trend**: Look at a three-year trend of improvement across all your subjects and in all performance measures. Add a commentary afterwards that explores issues and celebrates successes. Bullet points should be fine. Maybe even offer a tentative Ofsted judgement.

2. **National Context**: For each subject, compare to national averages, calculating the differences between the achievement of your students and those nationally (all available online) and add your own bullet-point commentary afterwards.

3. **Team Performance**: In tables, present a more detailed breakdown by subject and teacher of those meeting and exceeding target grades and include key performance measures, residuals and forecasting accuracy.

4. **Groups**: Next, look at the performance of key groups of students. Tables of figures should be fine again, but it is in your commentary where you will demonstrate your handle on the issues. This is a really important section since it could throw up areas of focus for you in the coming year, too – if white British boys underperformed for you this year, might they again?

5. **Other Year Groups**: Summarise the end of year data for other year groups, but probably not in as much depth. You could include here how you intend, through the distribution of leadership, to address performance in these year groups.

6. **Next Year**: Briefly talk about next year's KS4/5 cohort including some headline figures.

7. **Intervention**: List your early ideas for intervention.
8. **Action Points**: Summarise 3-4 action points as a result of your analysis that will feed directly into your development plan.

Check your document thoroughly, especially the accuracy of your maths. If possible, try and meet with another middle leader, someone who has been in post for a while, and ask them to verify your analysis, particularly whether it will pass muster with your head and whether it compares favourably with those produced by other middle leaders. With all the work you'll have put in, you could expect it to walk these tests of its integrity, but take any suggestions seriously.

This task should, by the time of its completion, have fully focused you on a very important aspect of your role – raising the attainment of students in your school – but your task in September is going to be presenting a vision for your department that encompasses so much more than just this. Let's look at how you could go about doing this now.

Writing a development plan and creating a vision

By the end of this section, you should aim to have a clear idea of the format your development plan will take, the methods you will use to generate its content and how you will communicate your final vision to the rest of your team.

A strong development plan will allow you to get on with your job safe in the knowledge that the tasks you're completing are essential pieces in a giant jigsaw which, when completed, will basically be your vision for the department. But that analogy is a poor one, right? Because you won't complete it. You'll fit many pieces together, yes, but the idea that there will be a definite end point to any development plan in totality is a mistake, and too many schools arbitrarily decide that all development plans need to be one year in length when, in actuality, some of your targets will stretch way beyond that. Certainly, by the end of your first year in charge you will want to be able to demonstrate real impact on a number of different areas (the book you're holding in your hands is, of course, structured around that year), but a strategic approach would take a different tack, instead inviting you to plan for what lies beyond this first year, in three, five or seven years time. After all, seven years could be the length of time some students spend enrolled in your school (definitely in a Primary school, and in Secondary schools with a Sixth Form), so why not plan with the progression of those students in mind? If this seems onerous now, because you've walked into a team where results have collapsed or the curriculum needs a complete overhaul or your team's idea of effective display are those terrible motivational posters we were on about earlier...don't worry. These *will* need your attention immediately, but in the background you must begin the process of long term strategising. We're going to walk through this process now. We've made suggestions and taken informed decisions about the methods you could adopt. We've tried not to be too prescriptive since your school may expect you to work within a framework of their devising. But this is your development plan so endeavour as much as you can to make this document personal to you and your team, in its format, in its substance and, firstly, in the ways you go about generating its contents.

Caroline says...

If I am completely honest with regards to my first development plan, I don't think I really knew what I was doing. If I recall correctly, my first development plan had plenty of ambitious plans and ideas, but lacked much detail concerning implementation and monitoring. I was lucky, I had lots of support and advice and I guess I had the tenacity required to draft and redraft my plans. I am great at thinking creatively and producing possible ideas, strategies and ways of making improvements, many of which are good ideas and prove to be effective BUT (and this is a huge BUT) my attention to details, logistics and practicalities can be awful. Knowing this weakness is good because it means that I no longer implement any kind of plan without consulting a colleague whose attention to detail and logistics is flawless. Identify your weakness in creating plans and get support from someone who has your weakness as a strength.

If I were to give one word of advice to somebody writing his or her first development plan, it would be: consult. Consult your team, consult other middle leaders and consult senior leaders. A development plan is not all about you – you should involve your team in its creation, as you will with its implementation. Make it a document of shared creation in

which everybody involved has invested in and will care about as the plan is put into action.

There is (almost) always an Inset day on that first day of term in September in which you will undoubtedly be handed some time, a few hours or so, to spend with your new team. Subject coordinators in Primary schools might be handed some time specifically for their subject as part of whole school training. This time is going to be crucial for two reasons: firstly, this is the perfect time to generate the contents of your fledgling development plan; secondly, you will be able to collect valuable intelligence on the personalities and working methods of the team. You will be able to discover:

- Who in your team is accurate in their judgements.
- Who is able to articulate the areas for development.
- Who knows what should be done about those things.
- How well the team works together.

We suggest that this meeting should involve all members of your team, not just the staff who hold a TLR or other position of responsibility, and you should try to plan as much of the structure as you can – how long each activity will require, who will work with who, what materials you will require and at which point. Additionally, in advance of this meeting, you will need to make it clear what is going to occur and what you will be expecting from the session. Ask them to bring with them up to **three ideas for areas for development** for the department, subject or team. State that the format of this meeting will be interactive, an opportunity to share experiences and beliefs. State also that it will be developmental, collaborative, that, by the end, there will be the beginnings of visible change. Hold the meeting in a suitable room, one where there is chance to move around and work in groups. In no way must the meeting become consumed by admin tasks outside of your stated agenda – no questions about classroom keys, timetable changes, rooming issues, naughty children or ICT meltdowns. These need to be dealt with way in advance of this first day back so pre-empt any of these distractions by telling your team this, perhaps promising them 15 minutes at the very end of the day to clear up any last minute questions, quibbles or concerns or just dealing with it all by email. By ring-fencing this time in this way, you will shield your intended aims and outcomes from any internal interference (or it could be external – the SLT might attempt to hijack your agenda with apparently crucial tasks of their own. Resist at all costs!).

At the beginning of the meeting, take a risk by asking the members of the team to grade the department against the four Ofsted categories (Leadership and Management; Teaching, Learning and Assessment; Personal Development, Behaviour and Welfare; Outcomes for pupils (as of September 2015)). They could do this on mini-whiteboards or post-it notes, and they could do this discretely, too, if necessary; ensure that **you** at least get to see their judgements and make a record of them if they don't feel comfortable sharing with the whole team, in itself a clue to the working relationships of your team. Depending on the experience of the team, you could provide them with the Ofsted descriptors for good and outstanding in each category to help guide their assessments. Anything outside of these descriptors is obviously RI, and hopefully there will be no need to examine what inadequate looks like, but be prepared anyway. We said this was a risky activity, after all. Worst case scenario? One embittered, disillusioned and resentful teacher hijacks your festival of positivity and damns your work before it's already begun by giving grade 4 in every area. But don't worry, that's unlikely to happen. If they will openly share their judgements, and you've got to expect they will, you should then draw out what they think their gradings mean for the department, expanding on the numerical score to hear their evidence and their views.

Next, they should have the chance to share the areas for development that they've brought with them and ask them to write these on post-it notes as well, identifying which they believe are short- or long-term targets, and adding any more that they could have thought of in the meantime. Why not then attach them to large sheets of paper that you've pre-prepared around the room and headed with each Ofsted category? You can then take these collected ideas and give them to four groups, instructing them to examine what has been written to see which ones are similar or could be categorised together. Ideally, you should end up with a relatively small number of targets in each Ofsted category if your team are in general agreement.

In this next task, start to think about what your team's responses will be like to this first activity by making a judgement on each category and then drafting up to 3 areas for development as you see it now. This is very much a preliminary activity since it's based on your current perceptions. Try to go for one target which deals with the situation right now, one which you will need to address over the coming year and one which is much longer term, say over three or five years.

Leadership and Management	*Teaching, Learning and Assessment*
Grade	*Grade*
Areas for Development:	Areas for Development:
1.	1.
2.	2.
3.	3.

Personal Development, Behaviour and Welfare	*Outcomes for Pupils*
Grade	*Grade*
Areas for Development:	Areas for Development:
1.	1.
2.	2.
3.	3.

Look back on what you've written above when you have carried out the same activity with your team. It will demonstrate to them that honesty, transparency and a shared strategy are central to what you do. How close were you to their ideas of what needs to change, develop or improve? If they were way out, what will you take from this? Were your own perceptions misplaced or has it shown you that your team are misinformed? Did your ideas correlate completely with those of your staff? Whatever the final result, it should have been a valuable process up to this point.

The next stage is to begin considering who could successfully lead or contribute towards each target, although you as the boss will take ultimate responsibility for their completion. Ask them which of the targets they see themselves naturally drawn to, based on their interests and skill sets. Your development plan will link closely to performance management targets (appraisal, review, whatever you call it in your school). Explain that you intend to use this as part of the performance management process so that there will be a measure of accountability to their work over the coming year towards this target, although any coaching process will be kept separate (see Chapter 8). To that end, it will be especially important to word these targets carefully so that they are measurable and achievable. Have a go at drafting them in the meeting together, but ensure you explain that you will be taking them away for your own fine-tuning, and also have a go at deciding how you will measure whether they have been successfully completed. Give them this to do next, asking for some concrete ideas on:

- How they are going to achieve it.
- By when will it be achieved.
- Who will take responsibility for different aspects of the target.
- How you will know you have been successful – what will have changed in your department? How will an outsider walking into your team be able to see your vision in action?

Discuss this together as a group and encourage them to debate and challenge the content. This is as much about their ownership of the development plan as it is yours so you are looking to generate a sense of investment in the vision. Be clear that you will be expecting to revisit this plan regularly throughout the year and that you require everyone to maintain their own evidence files for anything on which they take the lead or in which they participate. The monitoring and evaluation of each target is crucial so plan to revisit them regularly to maintain their high priority. A sure-fire way of doing this is to tie in your development plan to your department meeting schedule, something you absolutely must write in advance. Calendar the theme of each meeting and ensure that everyone in your team knows that they will be expected to take the lead on anything that is their responsibility in the development plan.

James says...

As a Secondary Head of English, I found pre-planning the agendas for our team meetings for the coming year one of the most liberating moves I ever made, ensuring that meeting planning was never last minute,

content was never arbitrary and the focus was always on the priorities of the team (priorities they themselves had identified). It took careful consideration, it took time and it necessitated me spelling out some important, rigid principles, namely endeavouring to stick to the allotted time we were given, usually an hour, and allowing absolutely nothing else to be added to the agenda by anyone (as well as a ban on AOB, a catch-all category for moaners). Topics were closely matched to the development plan and the staff in charge led the meetings, quite often jointly with myself or other teachers in the team. If there's one thing you absolutely must do this August, do this!

Your final move will be to physically create your finished product, quite often a grid of some kind. This has to be a working document, not something you print and file away. Make it accessible to your team and expect them to revisit the plan from time to time, adding evidence or updating progress. You could decide to create something more visual than a grid, an electronic presentation, for example, which everyone is able to display as a constant reminder of the aims of the team. Again, you decide on its format so that the document is personal to you, although be prepared to adopt the school's preferred format if necessary.

Creating a marking and assessment policy

First, a rant.

In the eighties and nineties, when we were at school, and as far as we can remember, the only things our teachers used to write in our books were perfunctory phrases like, "Good work", "Well done" or more likely "See me!" They'd 'tick and flick'. But that's rubbish, isn't it? It's simply not good enough. If Ethan and Amna and Jessica and Patryk had spent ages on their homework, if they'd got full marks in a test they'd spent the best part of a week revising for, they wanted more than that. *Today's* students want, indeed expect, more than that, and quite rightly so. What they don't want, and it is a sentiment shared by their teachers, are ridiculously over-complicated marking procedures invented to satisfy some imagined Ofsted pedant. They don't want their books given back to them endlessly so that they can write how they 'feel' about the grade they got for their essay on Hitler's rise to power. They don't want their Gothic horror story peer-assessed by someone with no clue. They don't want to get told off for annotating their Textiles research in green ink because it should have been in bloody purple. And they absolutely do not, under any circumstances, want to spend any lesson time writing empty phrases like, "I will revise more next time" or "I now understand how to multiply integers" or some other banal, boring cobblers (in red ink) that wastes five minutes of a lesson, when they could be *actually* multiplying integers, *practising* the skills they claim to have learned or *developing* the knowledge they've been made to clearly state they know.

And breathe…

As part of your development plan, under the banner of 'Teaching, Learning and Assessment', you will most likely have included something about marking – that you want it to be purposeful, timely and genuinely effective. These are all worthy aspirations. But by focusing on marking only, is your target too narrow? Let's start this section again:

Creating an effective feedback policy

While teacher marking in books does indeed have to be purposeful, meaningful and all that other stuff, it is not the only way in which teachers provide guidance to their students on the work they produce, the way they respond to the teacher's comments, the standards of their behaviour or their rate of attendance and punctuality. Look at this, by no means comprehensive, list of all the ways teachers provide feedback to students (and, of course, your whole school marking and assessment policy). If you have anymore, jot them down underneath:

1. Written feedback in exercise books at the end of a piece of work, including giving ways to improve and extend.
2. Verbal feedback in lesson time.
3. One to one verbal feedback on a piece of work or assessment after the lesson.
4. Parents' evenings.
5. Student reports.
6. Questioning.
7. Praise.

8. Sanctions.
9. Extension activities and enrichment opportunities.
10. Informal discussions between teacher and students.

What we're suggesting is that you should be creating an ethos of effective feedback; that there are a whole suite of techniques and strategies that, when used together and when used consistently, will enhance the teaching and learning that takes place in your team in real, measurable ways against a range of performance indicators. Consider these as 'marginal gains', the techniques popularised by Dave Brailsford and his team of gold-winning Olympic cyclists (look it up if you're unfamiliar with it – it's an interesting philosophical concept that has a host of uses in an educational setting), gains you can make in strengthening quality of feedback. For each of the ideas in the list above, you will need to create your own policy or your own set of expectations, preferably in conjunction with your team. Their involvement here is imperative since it virtually guarantees their tacit agreement to follow through on everything you put in place. If you can't find time on your first INSET of the year, make it the focus of your first team meeting or at least plan to do this as early as possible so that your team starts the year on the front foot, implementing all your initiatives quickly. Teething problems will be identified quickly, too, giving you a chance to sort them out. There'll be consistency from the outset, which will make monitoring the impact of your feedback strategies much less demanding (see Chapter Five for more detail on how to go about doing this efficiently and effectively).

In tackling each of these, we're going to go in reverse order so that we finish with marking and assessment. Along the way, we've also included the relevant snippets from Ofsted's outstanding criteria for Teaching, Learning and Assessment (Ofsted School Inspection Handbook, September 2015) so you can see where our advice fits in to their framework:

10. Informal discussions between teacher and students.

This is essentially about building relationships, about finding the time in your day to chat to the kids in your school about their performance in your subject or their behaviour and attitude. Are we suggesting you instruct your team to do this? Can you teach your team to do this? Probably not, since this is about personality as much as anything, but you can model this behaviour, especially for NQTs and trainee teachers. Show them the benefits of engaging informally but purposefully with students, providing them with brief and positive feedback on their work and their contributions. As a new middle leader, and most likely a new member of staff in the school, this will bring personal benefits, too, since a side effect will be raising your profile among the student body. It might be stating the obvious, but it is essential you get the balance right here: too informal and you risk losing credibility and authority; too formal and you come across as aloof and unfriendly. We all know teachers who fit into each category – don't be one of them!

9. Extension activities and enrichment opportunities.

In providing feedback to students, encourage your team to find opportunities to set extension activities, to seek out enrichment opportunities beyond the classroom walls (see Chapter 10) and to have a sound knowledge of what is happening across the curriculum in your school for students to explore on their own, with their friends or with their families – providing a list of dystopian novels for your advanced Y10 readers, suggesting climbing all over some of the monumental structures at the Yorkshire Sculpture Park, creating a playlist of essential eighties hits for them to stream on Spotify or encouraging them to take a different shaped or sized ball to the park this weekend. This is as much about raising aspirations and broadening horizons as it is impacting on the progress students make. Targets that your team write in student exercise books are an ideal place for these to appear, and make a change from targets confined to simply redrafting or developing the work they've done, although these are perfectly worthy too. Again, doing this is all about building relationships and is another small step to creating a culture of high quality dialogue with students. Our hope is that you don't find this concept patronising. We have both worked in schools of high social deprivation but also of high aspiration, and have seen first-hand the power of extending and enriching a student's experiences in school and beyond. Tailor what you say to your particular school, but be sure that what unites all schools is their students' thirst for knowledge, a thirst you can go some way to quenching with imaginative and creative opportunities like these.

8. Sanctions.

7. Praise.

Any sort of progressive thinking on both sanctions and praise by you and your team will inevitably be hamstrung somewhat by the need to tie your policies to those of your school. This isn't a bad thing – you want your team to follow school procedure after all – and it doesn't stop you from getting creative again, as long as you set some basic expectations. Prioritise praise is our advice. If your school employs an electronic system of recording sanctions and praise (say, SIMS or Sleuth), then set an expected ratio of ten entries of praise for every one sanction. If a member of your team ever has to call home about the poor behaviour of one student, ask them to mirror that phone call immediately afterwards with one to a parent whose child has been positively angelic – not only will that student be glowing the next time s/he comes to class, your team member will be in a better mood than if s/he'd just been making that first phone call home. And when you get to the end of each half term, you must write letters home – proper, effusive, formal letters that pour praise on students and their efforts, that can be framed by parents and celebrated at home. Ensure you collect any and all feedback from parents, too, as evidence of your impact.

6. Questioning.

The ability to skilfully question students does not, sadly, come naturally to some people, but without it there is a gap in a teacher's opportunities for feedback to students. Similarly, questions *from* students should be encouraged, too. Consider how often this actually happens in lessons and why it should be more prevalent. All questions will lead to dialogue, discussion and debate, once again extending and enriching the teaching and learning experience. Listen to how your teachers question students: do they ask open questions that demand extended, justified answers; are they able to guide students to explore deeper meaning, consider alternatives, question the conventional and do they praise original answers or celebrate new insight? In recent years the assessment of speaking and listening, English teachers will concur, has been side-lined, despite many people agreeing that excellent oracy is a fundamental part of being an excellent student. We'd take this further and say that the ability of teachers and students to fluently ask and answer questions that deepen understanding, that mean that feedback is placed at the centre of classroom practice, is an even more significant indicator of excellence in both teaching and learning.

> *Ofsted says: 'Teachers demonstrate deep knowledge and understanding of the subjects they teach. They use questioning highly effectively and demonstrate understanding of the ways pupils think about subject content. They identify pupils' common misconceptions and act to ensure they are corrected.'*

5. Student reports.

The reputation of the student report has suffered in recent years with some schools even deciding to abandon the written element altogether. This is a shame, but it's far from surprising. Common complaints directed at reports are that they are poorly written, blighted by empty, cut-and-paste phrases, that they take too much time and energy, require endless checking and are rarely understood fully, let alone read thoroughly, by parents. If you work in a school that has chosen to retain reports, however, you and your team need to decide now to make your efforts the best in the school since fluent, erudite reports full of genuine insight and guidance can have, in our opinion, a significant impact upon a student. Think carefully about how you want the content and style to reflect what goes on in your team's lessons: avoid waffle, technical jargon or teacher speak that risks alienating parents; maximise praise, but be realistic and honest; avoid surprises so that what is being said builds upon any other contact made between school and home in the past – reports are not the place to reveal a student is likely to fail an exam in a month's time; make descriptions of curriculum content sound fascinating (since it is!); insist on technical accuracy, and implement a buddy system within your team for partners to swap and check each other's reports; and ensure they are personalised and individual, reflecting the teacher's knowledge of the student – where their learning has come from, where it is now and where it should go next. Reports are a powerful tool for building bridges between school and home, too, so ensure they are used to enlist the support of parents, either by actually asking them directly, or indirectly through your team's clever use of praise and flattery. Parents should be falling over themselves to support you if they believe you think as much of their child as they do.

4. Parents' Evenings.

If you set about them in the right way, there is joy to be had at parents' evenings. Honest. Like reports, there are potential issues. At their worst, they are three hours of identical, regurgitated complaints, peppered with inaccuracies (ever known a teacher clueless as to the identity of the child sat in front of them?) and delivered in a monologue. You need your team galvanised from the outset on these so that they are a mutually supportive event, packed with information and ending with real agreement on next steps. It may already be school policy, but if not, encourage the students themselves to attend the evening; their presence will make for a more useful and productive meeting than if they were sat at home waiting expectantly for the evening's verdict. Go armed with props such as exercise books, teacher markbooks and best work (a mini-display would look great here – put aside one you do for open evening to save time) to dazzle parents with the quality of teaching and learning that goes on under your stewardship. Endeavour to hold the meetings in classrooms so that all these resources are easily to hand, and buddy up members of your team so that inexperienced staff have helpful eyes and ears close by. Finally, ensure all meetings end positively with firm handshakes and even firmer promises to keep in touch.

> *Ofsted says: 'Parents are provided with clear and timely information on how well their child is progressing and how well their child is doing in relation to the standards expected. Parents are given guidance about how to support their child to improve.'*

3. One to one verbal feedback on a piece of work or assessment after the lesson.

2. Verbal feedback in lesson time.

Verbal feedback is a key element in your suite of techniques – it's one of the easiest to promote among your team since it's meat and drink to any good teacher. But it's also very easy to get verbal intervention wrong, or at least in its frequency or tone: too much and the teacher becomes a nuisance in the classroom, interrupting when it would be better to let students just get on, but too little and you risk leaving students to drift, probably leading to misbehaviour and disengagement. It needs a focus on specific aspects of student practice, areas where they have done well and areas where they need to improve, and to avoid general praise. We have also seen a verbal feedback ink stamp being used by teachers…and we've also seen them misused. Properly deployed, teachers can use them to indicate in student books where verbal feedback has been given followed by time for the student to write a brief response, and then demonstrate how that feedback has had a positive impact upon their work. But abused, they become the ONLY method of feedback used, with stamp-happy teachers peppering books with their brand and giving no time for students to act upon what's been said (if anything *was* actually said). If you choose to implement such a stamp, make explicit your expectations for their use and watch out for anyone claiming their ink has dried up by October – they're most likely overusing it.

Ofsted says: 'Teachers check pupils' understanding systematically and effectively in lessons, offering clearly directed and timely support.'

1. Written feedback in exercise books at the end of a piece of work, including giving ways to improve and extend.

The sudden elevation of written feedback in exercise books to its current high status took some people by surprise which is, well, surprising, since it's obvious, isn't it? We started this section by reminiscing about the eighties and nineties and our own experiences of our schooldays, how derisory the marking in our books had been (and they're still there, in the loft, unmarked, if you'd like visual confirmation) and how insulting that was. There is a need to understand that providing written feedback to students is not an add-on, it's not an additional chore. This written feedback IS teaching, it IS learning. It is planning, it is professional development, it is the job you do. It's not extra or superfluous. Placed at the centre of your practice and the practice of your colleagues, written feedback, and the other nine types of feedback we have postulated, is utterly essential to impacting upon progress and achievement. It is not overstating things to say that getting this right for your students is a moral duty, such is the weight of evidence suggesting it's efficacy in schools. Let's look at some key principles, specifically for written feedback, that we believe you should adopt. We hope they are broad enough to encompass all subjects and all key stages:

- It has to be regular and timely – one of the most heart sink exchanges you will hear in a classroom goes like this: "sir, have you marked our homework yet?", "no, sorry…". And we've all been there. You didn't buy that bag for life from Sainsbury's so you could give your marking a different view for the weekend, lugging it home, sticking it in the hall and then lugging it back again on Monday. Ensure you and your team turn those books around, not by killing yourselves (and your relationships, and your family life, and your social calendar) with gone-midnight marking sessions, but by operating sensible procedures that alleviate or remove pressure. For example, insist: that books are marked only every two weeks; that, in the planning process, longer, extended tasks are designed for students and that it is these alone you expect to receive a full teacher mark; that you provide students with a rough book and a neat book with the latter being the only one where full written feedback takes place while the former is for notes, sketches, spider diagrams and all the other tasks students do that normally end up receiving a cursory tick and flick. Anyone who appears to be buried under a mountain of marking needs to be helped, to be shown ways to mark smarter and more efficiently. This guidance and support from you is essential, and you cannot wait for a round of monitoring to pick up on where someone is struggling. Have your eyes and ears open for this from the off.
- It has to be central to classroom practice – as ex-Heads of English, we have spent hours, and even days, marking work only to see a class quickly glance at our efforts, look at how they did and move on. This is depressing. There is nothing wrong with spending time,

lots of time, in class having students respond to your marking, not with some guff about how they enjoyed it or what they will do next, but with real reflection and real action – redrafting, improving, working together to create something better, learning facts, statistics, dates, methods, even spellings and testing each other on them. But then hang on, rewind, rewind to before they handed the work in because you should also be insisting that time is given over to them checking, rechecking and improving their work before it lands on the teacher's desk, ensuring they *own* their work, its successes and its mistakes alike. Ensure your team can train their students to effectively peer-mark, too. Contrary to what some people may think, it isn't a replacement for teacher marking, merely another string to a teacher's bow and can be an effective learning strategy for both assessor and the assessed.

- It has to be consistent – choose a pen, let's say green, and stick to it. Green's good since students won't, or shouldn't, be writing in green so the teacher's written feedback will be visible and distinct, but don't get hung up yourself on this use of colour – its only real purpose is to highlight quickly where marking is taking place. In your monitoring, you need to be carefully reading personal comments, sensible targets, real dialogue, humour and evidence that the teacher really knows the students they teach. If you want, have another colour (how about red?) for peer-marking. And that's it. No more colours. Don't let anyone impose another colour for literacy marking, or one for students to use when redrafting. *What* is written consistently is your focus, not whether a colour code is being followed. Finally, consider whether you might introduce a large sticker of some sort that focuses on standards of presentation – anything beyond this, which should be a consistent list across all work, becomes restrictive and prevents that more open, extended dialogue you are hoping to encourage.
- It has to offer ways to improve and extend – the teacher needs to write achievable targets that are acted upon, preferably immediately, or set extension work that allows the student to develop their knowledge or skills on a topic. Ensure teachers personalise these as far as possible. Use questions beginning with 'why' and 'how' so that

answers are open-ended and expect explanation and justification, or specifically direct students to the location of extra work, extra information, extra depth to their study. Have them use the time in lessons, as we stated above, to both complete the activities and to mark them. Remember, giving written feedback IS teaching – don't let anyone tell you that you shouldn't be marking in class when you should be teaching (unless the books belong to a different set of kids!) as this is akin to Orwellian double-speak.

James says…

Whether you want your team to give grades for classwork and homework is up to you. Dylan Wiliam and Paul Black in 'Inside the Black Box: Raising Standards Through Classroom Assessment' (GL Assessment Ltd, 1998) posited the theory that doing so can be counter-productive, that a student, upon receiving her/his assessed work, looks only at the grade achieved and does not consider the comments and targets. Personally, if that had been me at school, I would have been gutted not to be told how my efforts stacked up against the criteria I would ultimately be judged upon. I say, leave it up to you to decide and even try it both ways. Your students will soon tell you which way they like best anyhow.

- It has to be uncomplicated – if you need a fiddly, double-sided A4 checklist of sixteen tick-boxes to monitor your team's marking, you've overcomplicated things. Anything like this draws attention away from examining the *effect* of the marking and onto an admin check, looking at the basic completion of the marking. Keep things simple (this very list is a good place to start) so that when you come to monitoring you need only ask two questions: 'Have the books been marked in the way you all agreed they would be' and 'Is it having an impact upon progress and achievement?' That's it.
- It has to be personal – while you may have just read a big list of all the things your team's marking should look like, there also needs to be some room for a teacher to put their own personal stamp on their marking. Some of the best written feedback we've seen feels like it's coming straight from the lips of the teacher who wrote it since it oozes with their personality and humour. Good, genuine dialogue between teacher and student should be encouraged and,

while you must insist upon excellent presentation, spelling and grammar from your staff, there is nothing wrong with a bit of good-natured fun in what they have to say.

Ofsted says: 'Teachers provide pupils with incisive feedback, in line with the school's assessment policy, about what pupils can do to improve their knowledge, understanding and skills. The pupils use this feedback effectively.'

...and...

'Pupils are eager to know how to improve their learning. They capitalise on opportunities to use feedback, written or oral, to improve.'

Look around your school for examples of good practice in all areas of feedback and pinch it if necessary – the students will appreciate the consistency, too. Use your team to decide upon your collective approach to feedback and distribute the leadership of particular areas where you can. Finally, work out the monitoring procedures you'll put in place – see Chapter Five for comprehensive guidance on how to do this.

So, a very busy August awaits you, and here's you imagining you were on holiday! Be assured, putting in the hours now will pay dividends. The next chapter will explore how you will go about sharing your completed development plan with your team and, further, how you will determine your own personal leadership style so that, through reflection and examination, you can successfully implement your vision.

Chapter 3 – September

Developing a personal leadership style and sharing the vision

"If you have good thoughts, they will shine out of your face like sunbeams and you will always look lovely."

Roald Dahl, *The Twits*

It is the beginning of the school year and September is often the month that marks the beginning of a new role. We love this season of new pencil cases and stationery; it's not quite the end of summer and it's not quite the beginning of autumn; it is the season of new shoes and blank pages and endless opportunities. In the world of learning and education, this season holds more promises, possibilities and potential than your average springtime. If you are new to a middle leadership post, this is the time where you find your feet, get to know your team and the job and, crucially, it is when you begin your journey as a leader. You will make vital impressions on those who you will lead as well as other leaders in your school.

This chapter, and the tasks within it, will help you consider and focus your initial approaches to leadership and plan the journey on which you will lead your team. We will also guide you through the process of getting to know your team and working towards making a reality out of the vision that you created in Chapter 2.

James says...

It's difficult to talk about yourself and your own leadership style without sounding pompous and arrogant, two character traits you won't find in truly effective leaders anyway. That isn't to say you won't find them in leaders (look at most politicians), just not the effective ones. I reckon I am principled and conscientious. I think long and hard before making decisions. I'm not precious or territorial, and encourage others to take responsibility and leadership roles. I practise what I preach, especially in the classroom. I'm organised, I meet deadlines, I don't cancel or postpone without a very good reason. I offer time, support and resources without demanding reciprocity. I understand that people have lives and families beyond school, that pupils are just children and come from often difficult backgrounds, and that both staff and students need you on your game all the time, even when you're under the weather, under pressure or under a mountain of marking. I delegate and trust others to succeed or fail at tasks. And I don't ask anyone to do anything that I wouldn't be prepared to do myself.

Leadership Styles

It's not the case that a leader has a single style of leadership that they utilise unswervingly; an effective leader will use many leadership styles and shift between them flexibly and almost imperceptibly. An experienced leader knows how and when to adapt their leadership style in order to get the required results and outcomes. Whether leadership is a learned set of skills or is an innate characteristic that one is born with, is an oft-debated topic with some claiming that great leaders are 'born not made' and others convinced that anyone can learn to lead. We think that there are some natural qualities – the characteristics that we're born with – that are fundamental to good leadership. You can study theory of leadership and you can learn and practise and be trained in the skills of leadership, BUT your personality is what it is.

We are not here to repeat theory and tell you things that you can discover for yourself, so we recommend that you spend a little time doing some light research on the following leadership styles:

- transformational leadership
- moral leadership
- distributed or participative leadership
- adaptable leadership
- coercive leadership
- coaching leadership
- authoritative leadership.

It's easy to imagine that a loudly confident, authoritative and charismatic character will make a great leader, but would you want to spend much time in meetings where everybody was like that? There are those assertive leaders who ardently stride their corridors oozing charisma. You can see them, practically perspiring power and leaving a trail of influence behind them as they sweep through the building. Leaders like that can be truly amazing, but we think that there are also amazing leaders who move quietly with an unassuming manner and a soft voice. You might find them engaged in quiet one to one conversations or frequently working alone. They might not engage in small talk with you, but what they say will be a comment of value or a considered response. In a crisis or moment of chaos, such leaders emanate calm. We have, of course, created two stereotypes to illustrate a point when, in reality, there are infinite ways to lead successfully. What we think that you should be mindful of is that there is a lot to learn about leadership and you should be prepared to embark on a huge and exciting process that will involve learning new theory and new skills. We're not going to use this chapter to delve deeply into theories and models of leadership; for that, you will need to consult other, more academic tomes and we strongly recommend that you embark on a programme of professional development to guide and support your learning. So, where might you find that training? It seems that the government intends to invest in training for leaders and that that training will be developed by 'the best' multi-academy trusts. The Department for Education's "Educational Excellence Everywhere" White Paper (March 2016) sets out the government's plans for improving education. Over the next five years, it commits to the development of *'new voluntary National Professional Qualifications for each level of leadership, to better prepare new leaders for the full range of leadership roles. These new qualifications will not be mandatory, but instead will set a 'gold standard' against which licensed providers can develop their own innovative programmes for leadership development'* and to *'launching a new Excellence in Leadership Fund: this will encourage the best MATs and other providers to develop innovative ways of boosting leadership in areas where great leaders are most needed'.*

For now, though, our aim is to guide you through some useful practicalities that will support you in your early days as a leader.

Caroline says…

I don't have a particular leadership style, I use different ones with different people or for different purposes, but underpinning them all, I think, are optimism and enthusiasm. I'm sometimes stupidly optimistic and I'm aware that I am prone to exuding – often-unwarranted – enthusiasm; a bit like a small child who has eaten all the blue Smarties. I'm conscious that my way of being could be a source of major irritation to others so I have learned, over time, to rein in my zealousness and develop my ability to be serious, guarded, reflective, measured, quiet, cynical, concerned or questioning as and when there might be a more appropriate response or approach than whimsical optimism and enthusiasm. I could tell you about the ways I get organised and plan strategies and hold people accountable and slip seamlessly between being authoritative and supportive, but I don't think that I shine in those areas. I just have a (generally) positive outlook and I'm excited about working with people and the possibilities and ideas and opportunities that we can generate. Would it be acceptable at this point to quote Roald Dahl? Good, because I believe it is possible that glittering eyes are an important feature of a good leader.

"And above all, watch with glittering eyes the whole world around you because the greatest secrets are always hidden in the most unlikely places. Those who don't believe in magic will never find it." Roald Dahl – The Minpins

I'm not all eyes of glitter though; I am opinionated and sometimes stubborn. I'm a starter rather than a finisher; full of creative ideas and easily bored when it comes to implementing the details. I can be impatient and don't suffer fools gladly. My manner is possibly a bit abrasive at times and I have not yet mastered the work/life balance thing.

Leadership is neither simple to define or to carry out. It is a multi-faceted entity and will require countless different approaches, some trial and error and much practise. As we have said, a skilled leader might morph seamlessly between leadership styles and conjure up the perfect model of leadership as situations demand. This isn't something anyone learns to do overnight. When you've read this chapter and completed the tasks, it's imperative that you get to grips (at whatever level you feel is appropriate) with some leadership theories. For now, however, we want you to carry out some observational activities.

This time we want you to consider two leaders (real ones that you work or have worked with) and observe what they do/did. Ideally these two leaders will have very different characters and styles. It may be that you believe one is more effective than the other, but try and adopt an objective approach to the task. Look at each of the leadership 'behaviours' and make notes on your observations of the two leaders in relation to these areas.

Leadership actions & behaviours	*Leader 'A' observations*	*Leader 'B' observations*
Creating a vision and sharing it with others		
Developing people		
Communicating with clarity and conviction		
Creating / designing / redesigning systems		
Managing the day to day running of the organisation		
Inspiring people		
Empowering people		
Challenging people		
Supporting people		
Encouraging collaboration		
Modelling behaviours in order that others adopt them		

Leadership actions & behaviours	*Leader 'A' observations*	*Leader 'B' observations*
Embracing change		
Encouraging risk taking		
Tackling obstacles		
Holding people accountable		
Making difficult decisions		
Questioning		
Reflecting		

It is unlikely that you will be able to answer or make notes on every one of those actions and behaviours for your two leaders – there are bound to be gaps, but that doesn't matter. What is important is that you exert some effort in reflecting on the effectiveness of what you observe. This is a task that you can carry out over time and repeat at a later date. Many of us find it easy to make sweeping judgements about leaders and to come to our own quick conclusions, perhaps offering advice from our armchairs, and that's fine; it's an inescapable human trait. However, it will benefit you greatly if you take the time to observe and reflect objectively. If you can create the opportunity, it might even be helpful to observe leaders working outside education in a sector or area that is unfamiliar to you.

It's all very well watching other leaders lead, but you will be keen to get stuck in to doing some leading yourself. You can't lead without there being someone or something to lead so we will begin by looking at the people in your team and the way they might perceive you as a leader. What do they want and need from a leader, both collectively and as individuals? You probably don't know your team brilliantly yet, but you can begin by exploring what you would want and need from a leader. What qualities do you want to see? How do you want them to treat you? What kind of support do you want them to offer? What impact do you want them to have on the work that your team does?

By visualising and considering what matters to people when they are being led, you can take a step towards visualising yourself as a leader and embodying those behaviours and characteristics. Some of the qualities that we might like in a leader may be less obvious and we might be unlikely to list them despite the fact that we need them. For example, it is helpful to have a leader who ensures we meet deadlines and never lets them slide, and a leader who challenges us to think differently and try new approaches can be great. We might not ask for these qualities in a leader because life is easier in the short term if we don't have to meet deadlines and learn new things or change our thinking.

Below are some of the leadership characteristics that your team might be expecting you to have. How will you demonstrate these qualities and attributes?

Qualities and attributes that my team are hoping to see me display in my leadership	*Ways in which I might demonstrate these qualities and attributes*
They want me to be open about mistakes I make and they want to see me put things right	
They want me to be accountable	
They want me to make difficult decisions	
They want me to have high expectations	

Qualities and attributes that my team are hoping to see me display in my leadership	*Ways in which I might demonstrate these qualities and attributes*
They want me to be honest, reliable and trustworthy	
They want me to have a clear vision, know where we are going and how we will get there	
They want me to be knowledgeable about our subject / area / specialism	
They want me to be organised and efficient	
They want me to have a friendly and cheerful demeanour and a positive outlook	
They want me to support them	
They want me to help them develop professionally	
They want me to communicate clearly	
They want me to create a strong team	
They want me to listen to them	
They want me to value their hard work and encourage them to have a good work / life balance	

There are also the measures of leadership prescribed by Ofsted and you might find that the Ofsted grade descriptors for leadership and management (those we think relevant to a middle leadership role are listed below, from the Ofsted School Inspection Handbook, September 2015) of a school are a useful tool that can provide structure as you reflect on your practice. They are also, crucially, the criteria against which leaders are judged in an inspection so really they are worth understanding. The ones below are the descriptors for 'outstanding leadership and management' – which is what you're aiming to be part of in your school. Your leadership will not, of course, be judged in isolation, but look at each of the criteria and consider the ways in which you will contribute.

'Leaders and governors have created a culture that enables pupils and staff to excel. They are committed unwaveringly to setting high expectations for the conduct of pupils and staff. Relationships between staff and pupils are exemplary.'

Can you create a culture that enables staff in your team and students to excel?

Will you set high expectations?

Will you actively ensure that good relationships are fostered?

'Leaders and governors focus on consistently improving outcomes for all pupils, but especially for disadvantaged pupils. They are uncompromising in their ambition.'

Achievement. Progress. Everybody. Simple. How is this central to your role and the work of your team?

'The school's actions have secured substantial improvement in progress for disadvantaged pupils. Progress is rising across the curriculum, including in English and mathematics.'

Progress. Everybody. Simple. How is this central to your role and the work of your team?

'Leaders and governors have a deep, accurate understanding of the school's effectiveness informed by the views of pupils, parents and staff. They use this to keep the school improving by focusing on the impact of their actions in key areas.'

Do you know your data well? Is it accurate? Are you using it to improve? Are the rest of your team using data effectively too?

'Leaders and governors use incisive performance management that leads to professional development that encourages, challenges and supports teachers' improvement. Teaching is highly effective across the school.'

Is teaching highly effective in your area? What are you doing to improve it? Is your performance management effective? Are you developing your team effectively?

'Staff reflect on and debate the way they teach. They feel deeply involved in their own professional development. Leaders have created a climate in which teachers are motivated and trusted to take risks and innovate in ways that are right for their pupils.'

Are you creating this climate? Are you ensuring that reflection, debate and sharing are high priority activities?

'The broad and balanced curriculum inspires pupils to learn. The range of subjects and courses helps pupils acquire knowledge, understanding and skills in all aspects of their education, including the humanities and linguistic, mathematical, scientific, technical, social, physical and artistic learning.'

Do you offer an inspiring curriculum?

'Pupils' spiritual, moral, social and cultural development and, within this, the promotion of fundamental British values, are at the heart of the school's work.'

Are you supporting the school's work in this area?

'Leaders promote equality of opportunity and diversity exceptionally well, for pupils and staff, so that the ethos and culture of the whole school prevents any form of direct or indirect discriminatory behaviour. Leaders, staff and pupils do not tolerate prejudiced behaviour.'

Are you contributing to this ethos?

'Safeguarding is effective. Leaders and managers have created a culture of vigilance where pupils' welfare is actively promoted. Pupils are listened to and feel safe. Staff are trained to identify when a pupil may be at risk of neglect, abuse or exploitation and they report their concerns. Leaders and staff work effectively with external partners to support pupils who are at

risk or who are the subject of a multi-agency plan.'

'Leaders' work to protect pupils from radicalisation and extremism is exemplary. Leaders respond swiftly where pupils are vulnerable to these issues. High quality training develops staff's vigilance, confidence and competency to challenge pupils' views and encourage debate.'

Are you supporting the school's work in these areas?

Knowing yourself

Look at the descriptors of an outstanding leader. Which describe you? Grade yourself – using 1 for amazing and 5 for awful – and give a couple of examples and/or areas for development in each box.

Circle your grade

I have created a culture that enables pupils and staff to excel. 1 2 3 4 5	Relationships between staff and pupils are exemplary. 1 2 3 4 5	I am uncompromising in my ambition to improve outcomes. 1 2 3 4 5
I focus on consistently improving outcomes for all pupils. 1 2 3 4 5	I use incisive performance management that leads to professional development that encourages, challenges and supports teachers' improvement. 1 2 3 4 5	I have a deep and accurate understanding of the school's effectiveness. 1 2 3 4 5
I have created a climate in which teachers are motivated and trusted to take risks and innovate in ways that are right for their pupils. 1 2 3 4 5	I promote equality of opportunity and diversity exceptionally well. 1 2 3 4 5	Our broad and balanced curriculum inspires pupils to learn. 1 2 3 4 5
Pupils' spiritual, moral, social and cultural development is at the heart of what we do 1 2 3 4 5	Work to protect pupils from radicalisation and extremism is exemplary. 1 2 3 4 5	Safeguarding is effective. 1 2 3 4 5

In Chapter 2, we took you through a process of getting to know your new school and in this chapter we have looked at what your team want/need from a leader. Now let's focus our attention on getting to know the department you'll be leading. Begin by planning a simple audit of the area you are leading. You could see the process of leading an audit as your first opportunity to do some actual leading. The audit will give you a lot of useful information, but the way in which you introduce and implement the audit, and what you do with the results, could play a big part in you establishing yourself as a leader. As far as the audit is concerned, what you want to know is:

- How is this team currently performing?
- What are their strengths and areas for development?

When you have this information and insight, you will be equipped to plan efficiently. Think about the information you need and whether some of that information is readily available or whether you need to ask further questions and gather further evidence. Be clear about the intended outcome of your audit – why are you carrying it out and what will happen with the results? Consider the audience and format of your audit. Think carefully about how you sell this to your team. It may be that some of the information can be found easily by looking at data. Further questions could possibly be answered by your line manager or another member of the senior leadership team. Some questions you will need to ask your team. You might also carry out informal learning walks and look at students' books.

In order to obtain an overview, the following tool might be helpful. We have put together a table of the key areas a subject or department leader might have responsibility for. You can adapt this to your specific role and team.

So how should you use this tool? It depends on your team and only you can gauge or predict their willingness to carry out a task like this (or any possible resistance they might show). You will have to decide the best approach. Our first suggestion would be to allocate some time during a meeting, give each person in your team a copy of the table and ask them to rate each area in the box. They could rate it on a one to five scale with one being "We are amazing at this" and five being "We have serious work to do in this area". After they've done this (and get them to do it as a quick task, no right or wrong answers, just an initial response) discuss each area together, compare the scores given and consider why they were given. The next step might be to make a list of suggestions for developing each area (even if an area was scored one by everybody!). Try and keep it simple, perhaps just two or three suggestions. Record ideas and use them to inform your next steps. It's important to note that collecting and recording suggestions from your team, while a positive thing to do, is pointless if you do nothing with them. Agree a date to come back to this and, when you revisit it, you can prioritise tasks and list actions that need to be taken. Don't overwhelm people. Don't try to do everything at once.

Simple audit:

Student achievement	Student progress	Use of technology	Planning
Teaching	Coaching and mentoring	Classroom: organisation, layout, display	Resources
Curriculum	Creativity	Pupil voice and independent learning	Data, tracking and intervention
Communication within the team	Marking	Meetings	Enrichment activities

To see what this might look like in practice, let's take marking as an example. Imagine everybody gave it a score of 3 or 4 and, in discussion, agreed that marking had being identified as an issue because:

- Staff are unsure as to which pieces of work are 'assessed pieces' in each unit of work.
- Peer and self-assessment is *ad hoc* and there isn't a standard protocol for teacher comments on these pieces.
- Marking for literacy is inconsistent.

Having identified issues, the team then work on what's needed to move forwards. Sometimes there is a simple solution: an assessment grid that staff complete and students stick in their books or perhaps a list of assessments created. Sometimes you will be able to create a resource for your team that will save them time and make their job easier. It's ok to do this – in fact, it's a good thing to do. Help them out, take the lead, make their lives less complicated and tasks easier to carry out.

You could approach this task by asking your team to reflect on the positives, the negatives and questions they might have. Providing a frame for negativity and questions is an excellent way to avoid a free for all moaning session... Here are a couple of examples (one from a subject team and one from a pastoral team):

Positives	*Negatives*	*Questions*
Key Stage 4 results have improved every year for 5 years	Progress of FSM has taken a dip over the last 2 years	We used to have a spare classroom and we used it for small group intervention which was led by our TA - can we do that again?
Attendance at parents' evenings has increased by over 50%	The number of students who are late to lessons after lunchtime has increased by 30%	Can we set up a new working party to look at updating our rewards system and making it more consistent and cohesive?

As soon as possible, get your team together during a scheduled meeting and have a frank discussion about where they are at that current time, but keep it light-hearted because you are trying to gain an overview, not scrutinise the work people have been doing before your arrival. You might discuss the different things you will be looking for in an audit. Perhaps as a team, score performance in different areas, make brief notes about the reasons why a score was given and write down some initial thoughts about how each area could be developed.

Area	*Comment about current situation*	*How might we develop this?*
Student achievement		
Student progress		
Use of technology		
Planning		
Teaching		
Coaching and mentoring		
Classrooms		
Resources		
Curriculum		

Area	*Comment about current situation*	*How might we develop this?*
Creativity		
Pupil voice		
Independent learning		
Data, tracking and intervention		
Communication		
Marking		
Meetings		
Enrichment activities		

It is important to know your individual staff well, too. The sooner you get to know them and understand their needs and motivations, the sooner you will be able to lead them as a team towards your vision. In the early stages of your role as a middle leader, aim to learn as much about your team as possible. Piece together a detailed picture of individuals and their relationships with each other and the wider school community. This is no easy task and requires you to be a good listener and a careful observer. It might be helpful to use the table below to jot down notes on members of your team. We have used this task during training courses with experienced middle leaders and it's surprising how often they discover that they know very little about the people they are leading. In particular, people find that they are well aware of an individual's day-to-day performance in the classroom and the state of their classrooms, but they have never considered what motivates them, their personal leadership styles or their preferences for the ways in which others lead them. All these are things you should consider when getting to know your team. Some things you can find out quite easily – look at a tracker, some results or classroom display and organisation. Other things are more challenging to discover and you won't learn them over night. So, how do you learn this stuff? We wouldn't recommend a questionnaire or an in depth, one to one interrogation of each member of your team. We would, however, recommend being a personable and open leader; openly share your own strengths and areas for development and as you are modelling honesty and transparency, your staff will feel more comfortable with behaving in the same way. Creating a large, perhaps A3, table like the one on the following page will enable you to develop a clear picture of your knowledge about your staff. What's even better is that it will provide you with an overview of your team and their strengths. You could get carried away with highlighters and traffic light the whole thing to indicate the strengths, weaknesses and areas for development within your team – the level of detail you go into is up to you. Leading a team always requires being able to see the 'big picture'. Imagine – a member of staff believes that they need – as a matter of urgency – to attend a course on AfL; the belief is based on a very small picture that is their own perception of their needs. Your role is to understand a much bigger picture; in this instance, aspects such as professional development of the whole team, departmental priorities, budgets, timescales and so on. We should mention here that the completion of this activity is for your own benefit as a leader; it's not a piece of work that you should leave lying around!

Know your staff table

Area	*Member of staff*	*Member of staff*	*Member of staff*	*Member of staff*
Teaching				
Learning & progress of students				
Achievement of students				
Creativity and imagination				
Subject knowledge				
Quality of marking				
Strengths				
Recent successes				
Interests				
Meeting deadlines				
Resistance to change				
Appearance of classroom / work space				
Use of data				

Area	*Member of staff*	*Member of staff*	*Member of staff*	*Member of staff*
Planning				
Intervention				
Contribution to enrichment activities				
Use of technology				
Contribution to the team and the vision				
Keeps up to date with relevant educational developments				
Their response to my leadership				
Approaches I may need to take in leading or managing this person				

As is always the case, the areas suggested in the table are just our suggestions. Tailor the table to fit your team and your particular role. Use the scoring approach if that works for you or jot notes. We'd do both; the scoring approach makes it easy to identify patterns and gaps. Making notes will help you consider ways of developing your team or, at the very least, identify gaps in your knowledge. It is important to adopt an open and inquisitive approach to the whole process. Never, under any circumstances, try and prise information, thoughts or feelings from individual staff members. Big questions relating to the direction of your team and the vision should be asked to the whole team. The worst thing you could do is show yourself to be in any way sneaky or untrustworthy in your methods. Don't fish for information like this – your team talk to each other when you're not there, but as a rule you should talk to them as a team. Of course, there are times when you should and will talk to individuals, but team stuff should be talked about as a team. Essentially, what we are saying is that it's really important that you show yourself to be an open, honest and trustworthy leader right from the beginning.

Don't expect to be able to gather all of this information on your first day. It will take time and you should see it as a task that needs regular review. Be wary of letting it become an open-ended task without a deadline though as such tasks – and we know this from experience – rarely meet with a conclusion. Without finalising these information-gathering tasks, it will be difficult to plan next steps and move forward.

Having spent some time reflecting on your own leadership styles and skills, and through meeting with your team and observing and listening, you have gathered information that will be crucial in your strategic planning for the coming year. Ask yourself the following questions:

Have you articulated your vision?

This is a crucial step and the way in which you do it is important too. Avoid articulating a vision too early. You may have a vision of the perfect Science department, but we think that a vision needs to be relevant to the setting, organisation and specific context. Of course, some elements of the 'pipe dream' department should be present in the vision that you articulate to your team, but make it a vision that is firmly rooted in reality if you want to maximise the chances of getting your team to buy into it.

Have you gathered information, data, ideas, thoughts and feelings?

You should ensure you've spent time looking at qualitative and quantitative data, observing people carrying out their jobs, asking questions and, most importantly, listening carefully.

Have you allocated time to think, meet, plan?

It may sound obvious, but one of the most important things you can do as a leader is organise your time. If you don't do this and if you don't allocate yourself specific slots where you think and plan, it won't happen. Or it will happen, but on an *ad hoc* basis – you'll do all your thinking and reflection while you're driving, showering or shopping and you won't be able to make notes or give thinking/reflecting your full attention. You might find that if you just let your thinking and reflecting happen like this, thoughts will repeat themselves on an endless loop. Allocate yourself thinking/reflection slots and keep the whole process neat and tidy. Obviously, epiphanies that take place in the shower, sudden realisations in the cereal aisle and flashes of inspiration on the M25 are not to be scoffed at, just do not rely on them as your sole means of reflecting and thinking. Planning time to meet with individuals might be partially beyond your control due to school calendars for departmental meetings already being in place. However, as far as you possibly can, plan time that you can spend with your team whether formally or informally. We both confess to the fact that we plan and rehearse conversations in our heads, testing out different approaches and outcomes and envisioning the responses of others. This approach might sound a bit weird, but it can be useful.

Being a strategic leader

Unless your educational background includes some study of business, this whole notion of strategy may mean little to you. Ok, we know what strategy is in relation to playing chess or one of those never ending soldier board games. We know that elite athletes and top footballers do strategy, but what does 'strategic' mean in the context of middle leadership?

To be strategic simply means to be looking ahead and planning at the same time as analysing what is going on in the present and perhaps the past. In business, strategy is used to make as much money as possible, but in education the reason for being strategic is to improve everything (ultimately this might mean to improve achievement and progress) and be great at what you do.

We know what leadership is all about; being a strategic leader means having powerful long-term plans and bringing your team along with you. You can, of course, operate strategically as a team as well.

In this task, reflect on how strategic you are and areas in which you might need practice or support. As usual, make notes on each point; give examples and comment on how well you think you do each thing.

Signs that you are being strategic

I am knowledgeable about the current political landscape and how it affects our organisation

I have a deep understanding of the contexts in which my organisation operates

I can balance the day to day operational stuff with having a long term view

I am able to see the bigger picture

Signs that you are being strategic

When planning, I look at the possible short term and long term impact of carrying out actions

My team is able to have strategic discussions and meetings

I question things - including my own ideas, beliefs and approaches

I'm adaptive

Signs that you are being strategic

I'm good at spotting opportunities that might lead to improvement

When I have planned strategically, I can actually make it happen!

Chapter 4 – October

Leading Change, Organising people, Creating a Team

> *"Everyone thinks of changing the world, but no one thinks of changing himself."*
>
> Leo Tolstoy

> *"I feel confident imposing change on myself. It's a lot more fun progressing than looking back. That's why I need to throw curve balls."*
>
> David Bowie

Years ago, we were both on the same leadership course, possibly in Swindon. At one point a presenter shared a slide which stated: 'Don't water the rocks, they won't grow'. Neither of us can remember whether the presenter was commending or condemning the statement, but we have an awful feeling that he was suggesting the best approach to dealing with those who are resistant to change is to ignore them and concentrate your energies elsewhere. Our advice, years later, is that you should absolutely, categorically keep watering the rocks and expecting magic to happen.

You have now been working in your role as a middle leader for about a month and, no doubt, the month has been a steep – but hopefully enjoyable – learning curve. You have spent time reflecting on your own and others' styles of leadership; you have been getting to know your team and making lots of plans. You will find that these processes are ongoing and we recommend looking back at the notes you have made on leadership, your department, and the individuals that make up your team. This chapter will explore the notion of change and what it will mean to you within your organisation and your team. We will examine the ways in which change is a powerful tool that you, as a leader, can use to drive forward your vision.

Many people working in an educational setting are not that impassioned by the concept of change. They like routine and the familiar. That's why they stayed at school. Perhaps that's a cynical over-generalisation or perhaps there's an element of truth in it. Teaching is not a profession where you find yourself waking up in a different hotel room every morning; you don't rush through unfamiliar airports being greeted by unfamiliar faces; you don't journey a different motorway every day to meet people whose names and faces are new to you; you don't walk into a treatment room with absolutely no idea what you will find in it and you don't take huge risks with money or save lives. We are not dissing this amazing career in any way whatsoever, but most days you wake up in your own bed; you take the same journey to work; you greet the people that you work with on a daily basis; you walk into rooms with a fairly good idea of who will be in them and what they'll be doing and if you take a risk, the relative impact of any failure will be minor. Indirectly you will certainly change lives but not with the immediacy of a heart surgeon. You will have successes, but without the associated risks faced by a mountaineer ascending Everest.

It's imaginable that, perhaps unconsciously, those who work in education have chosen to do so, in part, because of the familiarity and the routine it provides them with. That's not to say they are not passionate about teaching, learning and innovation and we are not suggesting that everyone working in education loves a pedestrian and routine work life. But it is worth some consideration when you plan changes that you want to make. It is not the changes themselves that need to be your prime focus. It's the people with whom you work that are central to the process of change. They can be the drivers and catalysts of change; or the barriers to change taking place or they can be the change itself.

The people in your team are what we are focusing on in this chapter, rather than the policies, strategies, initiatives and systems that you might change. Those elements do, of course, change constantly but what we want you to focus on is your people and how they can adapt to change, make change happen and even thrive on change.

Sometimes change is a nightmare. Bring to mind an initiative or policy that has been thrust upon you in the last few years. Perhaps a change to exams or testing that impacted your work or a system change over which you had no control and were not consulted on.

Change and effect	
Describe the change that was imposed?	
How was the change introduced?	
How did you and people around you respond?	
What did you and others think or feel? What reactions did you observe?	
What did people say about the change?	
What was the positive impact of the change - for students and for staff?	
What was the negative impact of the change - for students and for staff?	

It's fair to suggest that reactions to imposed change may have been fairly negative; staff will have identified obstacles and barriers to implementing the change. Some may have felt worried or annoyed. Ultimately, the initiative may have been adopted and embedded, its impact may have been measured and its quality assured. Eventually, the change may have dispersed into the ether, making room for exciting new initiatives and changes. Often a general response to change is a collective "Eff off and let us get on with our jobs", particularly where those impacted are not involved in designing the change.

As we focus on the people in your team, we can explore ways in which you can work with them to initiate changes that will benefit both staff and students. You will want to make changes and change is inevitable so ideally you will form a team of people who respond positively to change; who are comfortable with adapting when change occurs; who learn to initiate change and who are open to changing themselves.

The strategic changes that you might make primarily require leadership rather than management. Some types of change need to be managed however, particularly where there is a need for a smooth transition from current state to future state. For example, your school buys new PCs, they need to be installed and some re-rooming needs to take place. Someone – or possibly a few people – will manage this process of change and if they do their job well, they will manage it in such a way that the impact on staff and students is only positive. Everyone will have new and accessible PCs to use; the re-roomed staff will have had their belongings carefully moved and they will have been consulted throughout the process; timetables and room booking systems will have been updated; signs on doors will have been changed and students will have been notified. This is *change management* and at times your role will involve some managing of change. Think about the changes that will happen that are beyond your control. When these changes occur, it is important that you react to them and manage them in a way that ensures the impact on your team is minimal. You're paid to deal with that extra stress and hassle and we think you should see making life easy for your team as an important part of your role. If you're told that the maths rooms will all be re-carpeted and lessons will have to take place in DT rooms for a week, deal with it. Manage it. Be an organised and proactive manager because managing is important, too. In fact, a well-managed and slick operation is a vital foundation on which you can build your leadership. Nobody wants to be led by someone who's perpetually flailing under an avalanche of paperwork or someone who's never entirely sure what day it is or someone who never remembers to attach the attachment. Running an organised department frees up time and space to focus on the big things, the things that really matter. If you leave a desk clean and tidy at the end of the day, it is so much easier to start work the next day focusing on the real challenges. If you're not already, we highly recommend becoming a devotee of all things colour-coded, filed and ticked off. Be a highlighter and post-it junkie. Allow yourself to be enchanted by spread sheets, organiser apps and colour-coded calendars.

So, what is exactly is this 'change' thing?

In the context of middle leadership, change is basically doing things differently in order to bring about improvements in achievement and progress in order to develop a creative, innovative team that has a positive ethos and functions effectively. As we know, sometimes changes are imposed upon us (a new system of data collection brought about by senior leaders or changes to GCSE exam entries brought about by exam boards or ministers for education) and sometimes we initiate change as leaders and encourage our staff to do the same. While, for the most part, the changes we decide to make as leaders should be designed to impact positively on students' progress and achievement, there are times when change for the sake of change can have a profoundly positive impact. For example, a department has taught a comfortable and effective scheme of work since its inception in the early 90s and, although it is still fit for purpose, the resources are tired and teachers are tired of teaching it. In this instance, making a change and teaching something new would be a good change to make for a number of reasons. Staff might be invigorated by the change and, through creating a new scheme, they will feel some ownership of the work. Students will be inspired by the new and exciting learning opportunities so they become more engaged and motivated; this makes the teachers feel successful and thus a happy cycle has begun. Sometimes an initial change is needed to kick-start the process and change feelings; try and be wise in your choosing of that initial change.

Let's imagine a most hideous and dire approach: you introduce a 'new' scheme of work from your old school (replete with your old school's logo and names of its staff) and ask people to start teaching it because it is the best scheme ever and at – insert name of your old school which NOBODY in your team wants to hear more than once – literally everyone made 8 levels of progress. It may well be a fantastic scheme of work, but that will be irrelevant because you will have *imposed* the changes, your team won't own them and they will hate you for this. It is probably worth saying, however, that in an RI school or Special Measures school, where planning is perhaps weak or almost non-existent, imposing a SOW from your old school might be the best thing you can do.

Where you identify need for changes to be made – whether it's developing a new enrichment plan or implementing a new curriculum or just amending the revision timetable – you need your team to be on board and to react positively to these changes. The first thing you should do is model the ideal reaction to change and show your team exactly how you would like them to respond to both types of change – enforced change and planned change. If necessary, plan and stage model reactions to change and then enact them in front of the staff who most to need see them!

Caroline Says:

Once upon a time, a few months into a school year, schools were told by the DfE that they could no longer enter students for English/English Language GCSE with two different exam boards. Well, they could, but only the first exam sat would count in the schools' results. At this point, many Heads of English were entering students for English in June of Year 10 and November and June of Year 11 in varying combinations of entry dates and varying combinations of exam boards. They were, of course, doing this to maximise the chances of success for their students and their schools. The sudden change meant that plans for their exam entries, for what were their current Year 10 and Year 11 cohorts, needed to be hurriedly revised. So, how did the middle leaders affected respond to the changes imposed?

- ***Some may not have had a chance to respond – senior leaders may have made a decision about exam entries for them.***

- *Some will have felt panicked and worried, shared their panic and worry with their team, deliberated and procrastinated openly, made a decision and then panicked openly about the decision they'd made.*
- *Some will have sat down, done some research and considered the options. They will have consulted their line manager and other sources of advice. Based on all the knowledge they'd accrued, they will have made a decision that would be best for the students. At necessary stages of the decision making process, they will have informed their team about what was happening. They will have shared the information clearly and succinctly. Any panicking and ranting will have been done out of sight and hearing of their team.*

The third method of dealing with imposed changed is the best one, but likely goes against the way we might naturally react. It requires a calm and measured approach and it requires – to a degree – that you shoulder the burden of change alone. It is also an effective way of dealing with an imposed change. If you choose to rant, deliberate and panic publicly, your team will assume that this is the preferred method of dealing with change in your department. If, at a later date, you decide to make some significant changes, don't be surprised when members of your team similarly rant and panic!

The Importance of the Vision in relation to change

In order for change to happen successfully, you have to first have a strong vision. If the vision is clear, has been communicated well to your team and they have bought into it, they will more readily accept any changes that will move them towards that vision. Even if the changes are difficult or challenging or tedious, where people are committed to the vision, they will sense the purpose and need for the change. If your vision states that, 'Pupil progress at Key Stage 2 will be the best in the country', staff will find it totally acceptable when you suggest developing brand new trackers that will make monitoring progress easier and more effective. Be clear about the vision you have shared and development plans created, and link changes to the ultimate goals of the department or team.

Why change is good for your team

Developing a strong ethos of change encourages new ways of thinking and fosters a positive view of problem solving. If you can develop a team that generally reacts positively to change and immerses itself in the process of transformation, the team will become practised at planning and implementing change and doing things differently. People can learn to embrace change and, if you have staff who are resistant to it, it's your job to help them shift the way they view change. Don't forget what we said about having solid, well-organised, consistent day-to-day systems as a foundation on which to make change. Those day-to-day 'definite things' provide security for your team and when people feel secure they are more confident about trying new things.

Without change, people and systems stagnate so, in organisations that embrace change, the atmosphere is exciting, forward-facing and full of possibilities. Teaching and learning and the associated routines become stale and spiritless if they don't change on a regular basis. For students and staff alike, routines and systems are vital, but change is also hugely important because it invigorates, inspires and energises and – if nothing else – prepares young people for real life in a world that is bursting with change.

Change offers new opportunities, for both staff and students, to develop skills and knowledge. For the staff in your team, having the opportunity to lead or implement a change is a fabulous opportunity for professional development if you adopt this approach. Its shared leadership will mean that change contributes to the construction of a sustainable and motivated team. Change is a great tool at your disposal; its existence provides you with the means to provide opportunities for people to experiment, take risks, be creative and to succeed and shine.

We think that it's a good idea to plan a variety of changes; changes of different sizes and shapes. Plan modifications so small that they can happen quickly, with positive impact that is instant and immediately perceptible. Also, plan ambitious transformations that are substantial, that will take time to implement and even longer before the impact becomes evident. Where change will take place over a longer period and the impact may not be seen for a couple of years, it could be helpful to map a timeline of change: a simple chart that provides a visual representation of when the change will happen and when the intended impact will be seen.

It's important to celebrate successes of change and this can be much more impactful if someone in your team (other than you) has led the celebrated change. Celebration of people's success will help you make the change ethos something that your team buy in to and want to be a part of. It's a cliché, but success breeds success.

Next, we would like you to create a list of changes you would like to make and the possible impact they will have. Think about the reasons you have for wanting to initiate changes; which could range from "Progress is poor" to "It looks untidy" and anything in-between. And it is totally acceptable for an impact to be something as banal as "It will look nicer". This list isn't your definitive list of change initiatives; it is a set of possible changes for you to contemplate and to kick around as thoughts for a while.

Change ideas	*Why is there need for this change?*	*What impact will the change have?*

Responses to change

As a leader, you will encounter a variety of responses to the different changes that are introduced and you will need to consider how you will address and deal with each of these responses. In Chapter 3, you completed the 'Know Your Staff' table; it may be helpful to revisit (and update if necessary) the section on resistance to change at this point. Know which of your staff embrace change, which question it, which grumblingly accept it and which resist it outright. Accept that some people need to have a moan and give them a platform on which they can perform their wailing if necessary, but only dedicate a small window to this moaning process. The departure of a dearly cherished long-term plan does not necessitate full-blown mourning and the skipping of thirty copies of a poetry anthology from the dark ages does not require lengthy lamentations in the tea room. Consider carefully the approaches you need to take with individuals when implementing changes; utilise your emotional intelligence!

Someone who is wildly enthusiastic and adopts every change you fling at them may seem like an ideal person to have in your team. But – do they ask pertinent questions about the purpose and relevance of changes? Do they work to embed changes made or move quickly to the next change? Some people are fabulous at starting new things, but not as proficient at finishing them. While their enthusiasm for all things new is an attractive characteristic, be wary of aligning yourself too closely to those who are starters but not finishers. Know who they are and support them where they need to develop the skills required to embed or complete projects. In the same way, that person who appears to be the curmudgeonly, obstinate grouch may well ask pertinent questions and be skilled at considering all possible eventualities.

What about a member of your team whose default setting is 'resistance' mode? We have all encountered the person who says: "Well that won't work because..." at every opportunity. We have seen these resistors sat, arms folded and brow furrowed, at meetings. They appear to take huge delight in pointing out obstacles and faults. These proudly intransigent folk are universal beings and you will, without doubt, have to contend with one or more of them at some point. Why are some people like this?

It's important to consider why a person is so resistant and perhaps try and understand the circumstances that led them to being so. Remember what we said about watering the rock! Have they worked in an organisation where change was badly managed or led? Are they tired of change that is constantly imposed upon them? Perhaps they have never had an opportunity to lead change? Are they scared of the way changes might set them up to fail or increase their workload? Do they just genuinely like things to stay the same? Asking the right questions and understanding what motivates people is the first step in dealing with resistance. Frequently, fear will be the cause of resistance to change and fear is easily dealt with if you're prepared to patiently offer time and support.

James says…

If asked to identify the biggest change I've had to handle, it probably wouldn't be anything lobbed at us from the DfE, but more likely those times when you're facing a virtual exodus of staff from your team – someone's having a baby, someone's moving to Germany, someone's going to teach in a prison, someone's got a promotion. All of these things happen, but when they happen all at once, and only a month before you were encouraging your excellent student teacher to apply at a local rival because "We just won't have any vacancies", you might be tempted to crawl into the store cupboard with a flask of coffee, a woolly blanket and that Game of Thrones box-set you've been meaning to watch. And that did happen to me (not the crawling into a cupboard bit), albeit for more mundane reasons than I gave above. This was April, close to exam season, close to the deadline for handing in your notice in order to be in your new school in the Autumn term. Who did we know who might apply? What sort of field of candidates could we expect, given the paucity of quality we'd encountered when we'd advertised previously? How could we, as a team and as a school, be proactive in our recruitment methods? We did recruit and we recruited quality, but the key was not to leave it to chance. You have to go on the offensive, selling you, your team, your pupils and your school through every medium you can think of. Network, get a bit cheeky and contact anyone you know with itchy feet, phone up training providers and ask them if they've got a great trainee. A bit of good luck wouldn't go amiss either.

Barriers to leading change

When you plan changes it is essential that you are mindful of possible barriers and obstacles you might encounter. We think there are three common key barriers that might hinder your leadership of change:

- The first type of barrier is any created by an individual in your team. These barriers are not all created by the 'perpetually resistant' character. Sometimes staff are sick and tired of changes that have been imposed on them or too much change that appears to have happened for the sake of it. Sometimes, a usually enthusiastic person is put off by change that has been badly managed or led or initiatives that are not well embedded and fall apart. Being part of a change that is unsuccessful or that made more work is bound to make even the most optimistic person a little cautious. Don't avoid dealing with this type of barrier. It can be hard to have difficult conversations, but pessimistic and parochial outlooks have to be challenged and changed, one way or another. Each situation and person will call for you to adopt a different approach.
- The second barrier is sustainability – you make a change with good intentions and in essence it's an excellent change that will have positive impacts. The change hits the ground running and your team are on board. It's all going so swimmingly well that you decide to initiate another change. You are successful and feel like a pioneer of change and leadership – you can change the world! You implement your next change and the first one is forgotten; it fades into oblivion while you're introducing your new great change. We are familiar with this eventuality – it's happened to us and it's probably somewhere on every leader's list of fails. Sometimes it's absolutely fine if a change you made fades in importance or disappears entirely. While this might be the case where change was planned for the sake of change, usually it's not fine and is an indication that change has been poorly led or was unnecessary in the first place. Strategically planning for change and its leadership will help you to avoid this. Start with the obvious questions: Why is change required? What will the change be? When will it take

place? How will it happen? Who will lead it? Who will look after it and monitor it? When you've considered everything, map the changes out across the year.

- The third barrier to be aware of is lack of support from senior leaders for your implementation of change. Senior leaders are powerful drivers of change within your organisation. Ensure you consult with them when you plan changes and enlist their support. Something as simple as your initiative or change getting a positive public mention from a headteacher can be enormously helpful. Ask senior leaders for advice too – they will undoubtedly have some to offer.

The process of leading change

Kotter's 8 Step Model (for Accelerate's 8-Step Process (2014), visit www.kotterinternational.com/the-8-step-process-for-leading-change) is a ubiquitous and popular change model and just one of many that you could utilise when you are leading change or planning to lead change. Use the commentary that we have contributed – usefully we hope – to each of the eight steps and consider how this model might support you in your leadership of change.

Step 1:

Establishing a Sense of Urgency

Our comments:

How do you establish a sense of urgency? Firstly, you need to identify the things that need to be changed. This might be a daunting task for those of you who think – rightly or wrongly – that absolutely everything needs to be changed. Creating an overview of possible changes might be a good place to begin. We suggest completing the following table (it contains possible areas in which change could be identified, but adapt it where appropriate) in order to focus your thoughts and enable you to consider which changes can be made quickly and easily, and which will take longer and require more planning. Think about whom you might involve in this task and at what stage:

Change Area	*Quick fix*	*Long term / transformational*
Change Area (adapt / add to suit your leadership role)	What requires change? (be as specific as you can and say why it needs changing, why it's not fit for purpose any more)	What requires change? (be as specific as you can and say why it needs changing, why it's not fit for purpose any more)
Ethos of the team		
Meetings and communication		
Student progress and achievement		
Display		
Teaching and Learning		
Curriculum		
Homework		
Tracking and intervention		
Planning		
Resources		

Change Area	*Quick fix*	*Long term / transformational*
Change Area (adapt / add to suit your leadership role)	What requires change? (be as specific as you can and say why it needs changing, why it's not fit for purpose any more)	What requires change? (be as specific as you can and say why it needs changing, why it's not fit for purpose any more)
Quality assurance and monitoring		
Students' attitudes to learning		
Rewards systems		
Extra-curricular and enrichment		
Engaging stakeholders and community		

Typical inclusions might be:

- A need to change the curriculum in order to improve pupil engagement and motivation as well as progress and achievement at KS3 (long term).
- A need to update all classroom and corridor displays to reflect students' current learning (quick fix).
- A need to implement changes to attendance rewards and sanctions to address falling attendance (could be quick fix, but embedding and revising the change will be longer term).
- Having established what needs to change, how do you create a sense of urgency? It is important that, in creating a sense of urgency, you don't scathingly dismantle the previous achievements and hard work of your team. The unit of work on the life cycle of a butterfly may be badly dated and somewhat irrelevant in this

decade's curriculum, but somebody in your team may have spent a few weekends producing it and think it's fabulous. Be tactful and be kind in discussion and action, but do talk about the need for change. Spend a lot of time talking about change, but spend a lot of time listening to others' ideas and thoughts, too. Encourage your team to consider the relevance and validity of current systems (whatever you have identified in the table above). Talking about the need for change will help develop a sense of urgency, but try and ensure that the urgency you create is bouncy and vibrant in nature, not overwhelming and panic-inducing.

Step 2:

Forming a Powerful Guiding Coalition

Our comments:

When you meet with your team, share the need for change that you have identified and ask for their input; when people offer their input, listen carefully and consider their points thoroughly. The team you are leading will be your 'powerful coalition', but you can't fabricate that kind of alliance from offerings of custard creams, an increased printing budget or a colourful action plan; you need to begin by empowering them. Let your team be part of identifying the need for change. Tell them that you will work as a team to plan and implement these changes. Make it clear that you will not be imposing any changes upon them. We believe that it can actually be helpful to point out the things that will not change, whether it's a homework policy, exam boards or an entire curriculum doesn't matter. Just the act of pointing out the non-negotiable, unchanging elements will provide people with a feeling of stability. Highlighting the fact that vision, ethos and your fundamental sense of purpose and day-to-day routine will not change, will remind staff that there are soundness and stability rooted beneath the changes.

Using meeting time, ask your staff to work on change related tasks together or in pairs. Develop shared leadership of these meetings where everyone in the team brings something to the table and goes away with an action to be carried out by the next time you meet. This shared responsibility on a small scale will be an excellent prerequisite to sharing the changes you will make over the coming terms and years.

Step 3:

Creating a Vision

Our comments:

Step 3 is our favourite stage of the model and an excellent opportunity to inject enthusiasm and creative approaches to problem solving and developing changes. We are all well experienced at planning and delivering enjoyable and even exciting problem solving and creative tasks to groups of students. So why do our staff meetings often operate as though they're a public email that everyone must attend? There may be a nod to real discussion – while the person honoured with the task of furiously taking minutes can have no input due to scribbling duties – and a list of jobs might be allocated to whoever doesn't have enough jobs already. Meetings like this occur because of time constraints and limitations and because admin permeates our world, but you cannot bemoan this fact. If your meetings are sluggish with ennui and occur like some kind of recurrent list-reading ritual, you must change them. If, for example, you give an hour of time, as a team, to some blue-sky, green hat, out of the box – call it what you will – thinking, you and your team will benefit hugely in terms of motivation and vision creation. Make sure such a session is well-structured though – an hour of fluffy brainstorming won't produce results. It will produce discussion, debate and possibly some argument. Whatever your chosen approach, you need to adopt one that encourages staff to be creative and innovative without any threat of their ideas being ridiculed or being told their solutions have been tried before. The right environment must be created and ground rules established – plan carefully! After you've involved your team in creating visions for change, take away the ideas and work on your strategy. If you can return to the group with a polished vision and a clearly mapped out pathway for achieving it, your team will love it. Don't always use that approach though, involve and develop others by consulting them in strategic planning stages. Some people find it easy to think creatively and produce a vision, but feel challenged by putting a concrete plan of action together and focusing their attention on detail and logistics. Be aware of your own and others' strengths and use them.

Step 4:
Communicating the Vision

Our comments:
When your team come up with creative ideas and the beginnings of a vision for change, it might look messy to begin with. If you have allowed and empowered them to adopt a genuinely creative approach to idea generation, your staff will not have been hung up on the details and practicalities or worried about time and cost. As we said in Stage 3, you need to go away with their great ideas and start thinking about how they can be put into action. Come back to your team and communicate this vision for change and a strategy – in some detail at least – for implementing it.

Don't just talk to your staff though – start acting out the changes you will make. Lead by example. Create visual and tangible reminders of the vision and the changes. Simple reminders like colourful posters in a meeting area or weekly email bulletins with the vision as a header are great. Don't be shy or modest about displaying a vision and sharing your mission with others. Think about other stakeholders that you will need to share your changes with. Start with your line manager; ask for their support and their input (as long as you think their response will be positive). Ultimately, you may need to share some changes more widely, with students and parents and staff. You could, where possible, consult with students on changes and involve them in creating the vision and planning change.

Step 5:
Empowering Others to Act on the Vision

Our comments:
As we have already ascertained, obstacles and barriers to change are ubiquitous and you will encounter them with irritating regularity. Fortunately, many obstacles appear in the form of an attitude or a mind-set and with the right approach these can be transformed. As you go about the daily toil, talk positively about change and model the behaviours and attitudes to change that you would like to see from your team. Work with individuals and encourage them to be part of

the change process. Support them where they find change a threat or a worry. Ask your team which systems and structures that are currently in place undermine the vision for change that you have created. This will help others see that, in order to make improvements, some things just have to go. An organisation or a department can be like an old wardrobe that is full of unworn clothes: hideously unfashionable clothes, clothes that don't fit, clothes that are totally worn out. If you want to update a wardrobe, you absolutely have to get rid of something to make room for new things. It's the same at work – if systems and structures don't work, discard them. Showing your team that you're not too precious about changing or discarding your own creations will encourage them to do the same.

When you're faced with resistance, you will have to adapt your approaches. Imagine this scenario: as Curriculum Leader, you have plans to develop a creative curriculum at KS3. However, one member of staff is resistant to these changes and prefers to teach units of work she's been using for the last seven years. This member of staff hasn't actually voiced their concerns/thoughts to you, but has moaned and grumbled to the rest of the faculty. How would you deal with this?

- Just tell them that this is what they will be doing.
- Pilot the new curriculum with two of your least resistant teachers and get them to feedback and share results with the rest of the faculty.
- Send the resistant teacher to observe a similar curriculum at another school.
- By using other methods.

Perhaps you would use a combination of approaches, but you will also need to address the moaning and grumbling. Your approach will depend on the nature of the change and the person you are dealing with. The key thing is that you are proactive; you must do something. You may have to try different methods before you are successful, but remember that, ultimately, you are striving to create a team that is positive about change, is willing to try new things and to make improvements. For many people, change is a challenge and part of your role is to make it easier for them.

Other common barriers to change are time and money. As with resistant staff, the prevalence of time and money shaped barriers are common; we suggest you get used to their existence and get creative about dealing with them! One thing we will say is that, as you make small changes and have successes, your team will be perceived as credible and your plans as tenable. Hopefully, you will be viewed as a team worth investing in, a team that produces visible impact through changes made.

Step 6:

Planning for and Creating Short-Term Wins

Our comments:

Constantly provide staff with an opportunity to make small changes. Plan carefully for this though otherwise you'll end up hurling random tasks around the department and impressing nobody. Start by looking at the list of quick fixes you have identified and make some of these changes yourself, thereby modelling the change process. When you've made a small but successful change, make a song and dance about obvious improvements (focus on the success of the change NOT how amazing you are) or better still, let others notice and make positive comments. Next, think carefully about who could carry out another quick fix. It can be something small like the format of meeting agendas or a display or a new certificate. Make sure each change is achievable and will benefit the rest of the team. When the change is implemented, celebrate its impact – we're talking cake and public praise – and celebrate the success of the member of staff. Start by asking the staff who are most eager to be involved and watch a positive change ethos evolve and proliferate. And if, despite all of this, you still have someone in your team who refuses to change, they may leave. This shouldn't be seen as your failure – it will have a positive impact in the long run. *Your team* will change as a result.

Step 7:

Consolidating Improvements and Producing Still More Change

Our comments:

Once you have, with the help of your team, been successful in making some small changes, make some more, much bigger changes. Constantly refer to the vision your team has created for the department so that changes are meaningful. Make developing staff a priority and ensure that everybody in your team has opportunities to develop their skills and knowledge, their mind-sets and attitudes too. All this will, of course take time, and there are some changes that cannot be rushed because if they are, they will fail. Sometimes change must just happen, things will evolve and changes to be made will present themselves – not every change needs to be planned meticulously. As acceptance of change becomes the norm, small changes will occur naturally. Eventually, nobody will be perturbed when meeting formats change, rooms are rearranged or a new column on a tracker is introduced. However, everybody knows someone who freaks out if the milk is placed on the wrong shelf in the fridge; the person who always sits in the same seat in the tea room (they will give you daggers if they find you in it at break time) and the person whose world will implode at timetable changes or students moving between sets. Always have this person in mind when initiating change and consider how you will involve them, reassure them, sell it to them and make them happy about it. It is so easy to be disparaging about people like this, but don't be. If necessary, change your mind-set and approach – we recommend developing *modus operandi* that is patient, sensitive and compassionate. Those new to leadership sometimes avoid showing empathy and kindness because they're worried they will appear weak and wishy-washy. This isn't the case – you can be authoritative *and* nice!

Step 8:
Institutionalising New Approaches

Our comments:
We're not keen on 'institutionalising' and would call this step 'Change and New Approaches Become Part of Our Ethos'. Review changes with your team and make the links between the changes and the successes super clear to everyone. They may be obvious to you, but people are busy and often the successes and the positive impact of small changes go unnoticed or are absorbed by the day-to day stuff. For example, if someone created new attendance certificates and a system for awarding them, and as a result attendance has improved by 2%, the change clearly had some impact. The change that produced the impact could be all but forgotten, perhaps because it happened some time ago or because it

seemed a small and insignificant event. Celebrate the positive impact of change publicly, involving your team, senior leaders and perhaps other teams and departments, too.

More substantial changes can be planned in conjunction with performance management and as part of TLR holders' roles. Develop a proactive approach to involving staff and providing opportunities for your team to develop professionally and as leaders.

Borrowing the basics of Kotter's 8 Step model could provide you with a useful framework for implementing change. However, you should supplement this by observing real models of change within and beyond your organisation. An obvious place to start is with your own line manager and senior leadership team. Approach someone who has implemented change with your set of questions about how they planned and achieved it, the barriers they encountered and how they overcame them. Don't be afraid to do this, senior leaders are there to advise and support not just to instruct and they have a wealth of experience.

A note on planning change

In Step 1, you identified some changes you would like to make in both the short and long term. You will need to plan in more detail how you will implement and embed these changes and measure the impact of them. Using a timeline will provide you and your team with a visual reminder of the on-going nature of change. In this example, using a timeline helps you to stagger initiatives and plan for reviewing changes made earlier in the year. Our example has five changes; a real one will likely have many more. The number of changes you can implement will depend on the size of your team, their willingness, priorities and abilities. Each of the changes can be led by a different person (some staff may well lead numerous changes) so although it looks like a huge amount of work, the leadership of change is distributed. Make sure that monitoring and reviewing become an integral part of your change process. To do this successfully, you need to design monitoring systems that are simple, slick and unobtrusive.

	Homework	*Rewards*
Sept.	Review KS4 homework; Staff lead?	
Oct.		Rewards system Staff lead?
Nov.	Design new homework	
Dec.		
Jan.		Trial new rewards system
Feb.		
Mar.	Share new HW plan	Review trial
Apr.	Trial and review new homework units	New rewards system in place
May.		
Jun.		
Jul.		
Sept.		

Enrichment	*Curriculum*	*Display*
	Current KS2 curriculum reviewed - All staff	New displays Staff lead ?
	New curriculum planning - All staff	
Review current curriculum enrichment	Individual staff planning	
		Impact of displays measured
New Curriculum Enrichment planning - All staff		
	New curriculum teaching starts	
	Review and changes	
New curriculum enrichment plan in place		Displays reviewed

Performance Management and change:

Incorporating changes into performance management targets is an excellent way to ensure changes happen and are reviewed. It's not just about holding staff accountable either; successfully embedding change into performance management targets will reinforce the ethos of change that you are aiming to develop. We suggest that performance indicators are used with each target and that they are linked to changes you have planned.

Our top tips for leading change:

1. As a leader you must lead, rather than manage the change that you would like to see take place. You will probably need to adopt new behaviours to inspire behaviour change in your team.
2. You should talk constantly about the need for change – but remember that the way in which you do this needs to have a positive tone. Avoid inducing stress and panic.
3. Ensure your vision is clear so that the changes you make are planned and directed. However, don't forget that change also emerges and evolves – be flexible and allow this to happen too. Encourage your team to embrace changes that present themselves.
4. Know and understand your team – what do they need from you? What motivates them? What are they afraid of?
5. Consult with the right people at the right time. Plan the methods you will use to share ideas and plans and consider timing.
6. Empower others so they feel they have the freedom to act on the vision and goals, but balance this with firm delegation where necessary.
7. Ensure all your change objectives have planned impact (even if the impact is change itself).
8. Ensure your team sees you tackling all obstacles and resistance to change.

The leadership of change is one of the fundamentals and non-negotiables of your role and a challenge that you should embrace. As we all know, change will happen; it is totally unavoidable and permeates all aspects of our working lives. There are many ways in which people cope with change, approach it and allow it to affect them. Where change is involved, your role is about developing people and changing mind-sets, attitudes and feelings. For change to happen successfully, what they actually are is incidental, but it is a prerequisite that you have a team of happy, willing, confident and well-supported people implementing those changes.

Chapter 5 – November

Innovating in teaching and learning and monitoring the quality of teaching and learning

"The learning process is something you can incite, literally incite, like a riot."

Audre Lorde

We have just looked at change as a powerful tool for the development of your team and the continued improvement of progress and achievement for your students. Change and innovation are inextricably linked and, hopefully, after carrying out the tasks in the previous chapter, you are ready to take a close look at innovating in teaching and learning in your department. By November, you will have developed a good knowledge of your team and have some clear ideas about the quality of teaching and learning taking place on a day-to-day basis. Perhaps your leadership role is a pastoral one – this chapter is of relevance to you too because you will likely have frequent contact with students who benefit from a personalised curriculum and innovative teaching methods.

By innovation we mean, quite simply, trying new approaches; doing things differently; creating new learning resources; testing out theories or experimenting with teaching styles all with the aim of improving progress and achievement. If we were to walk into the classrooms of innovative teachers, we might expect to see that methods of learning, acquiring knowledge, practising existing skills and developing new ones are central to innovation. As we showed in Chapter 4, change for the sake of change can be a good and necessary thing, but when we innovate in teaching and learning, we should always be more than mindful of that central aim – to improve the chances of great progress and achievement for our students. Showing off is not innovation and giddily interactive, ostentatious lessons that resemble a mini-festival might offer the appearance of innovation, but if they don't enable students to learn and make good progress, they are pointless.

If you think back to your own school days, you will no doubt recall a teacher who inspired and motivated you. How did they do this? Perhaps they did things differently, something about their lessons stood them apart from the others. The learning activities engaged you and time passed quickly, you learned a lot and achieved highly – you were successful. We're pretty sure that there was something a little more than the use of innovative tools and techniques by that teacher. There were human relationships in and amongst all the innovative methods. We believe that you can introduce as many new and exciting teaching and learning tools as you like, but if you don't inspire and motivate students as a human being, those tools will be worthless. Before you can innovate as a teacher, you must have in place the basics: good behaviour management; the ability to plan and deliver well-structured lessons which have clear learning outcomes and enable students to make and demonstrate good progress; an ability to differentiate and intervene effectively and offer high quality assessment, marking and feedback. These are a prerequisite to being innovative. Like an avant-garde musician – who needs to know the rules *before* they can break them.

Caroline says…

In the mid-eighties there were two English teachers, teaching Beowulf to Year 8 students in neighbouring classes. The first class did Beowulf with an overhead projector, note making and then produced an essay while the top set next door did Beowulf with mountains of junk and fabric, some costume making and elaborate performances of the text.

Thirty years later, I happily recall spending hours sat on a classroom floor gluing bits of Grendel together while chatting, planning and rehearsing lines. I used to carry Grendel home each day and spend the evening sticking more monstery bits on and learning lines. I remember everything there is to remember about Beowulf, but that doesn't matter. What matters is that creating and being Grendel changed my life, those English lessons changed my life, the teacher and her innovative approach changed my life.

The boxes and bags full of fabric and card and the working on the floor were incidental in making the learning memorable and innovative. What made it great was the thoughtful and structured approach that the teacher took. She allowed us to plan and organise our learning; she ensured that we discovered and understood themes, ideas and language; she helped us develop our confidence and creativity; she insisted that we demonstrated our learning and progress and solved problems along the way.

Letting students cobble together a costume is not a hugely innovative achievement by any means but that approach of doing something differently to engage, inspire and promote learning is at the heart of what good innovation should be. What about the guy teaching in the classroom next door? The teaching methods may have been tried, tested and effective, but the students were not inspired or motivated. Surely one of the reasons we become teachers is because of a desire to inspire and motivate young people? It stands to reason then that innovation is an important factor in what we do – we try out new things and we do it to inspire, engage and foster a love of learning, and of the subject we teach. Nobody is going to say, "You know what? I love volcanology, but I'm going to teach it in the most straightforward, time-efficient way I can because I don't care whether it bores others or not". If we love our subject, we naturally want to share our passion for it and inspire others in doing so. If this all sounds quite simple and somewhat idealistic, it's probably because you know, as well as we do, that we are often so overwhelmed by data, targets, exams, deadlines, report writing and assessments that it feels like there is little time left for creativity, inspiration and innovation. Well, there has to be – it's as simple as that. And part of your role is to ensure your team has the time and the motivation to innovate in teaching and learning.

This chapter is not about us disseminating a catalogue of innovative techniques that you can take away and use in your classrooms. We have probably all seen those lessons that are brimming with interactivity, gadgets and student-led mini-plenaries. They look innovative and well they might be, but we implore you to adopt a meaningful approach across your department with regards to innovation in teaching and learning. Always focus on the learning, the progress and the achievement of students.

We will look at the ways in which you can foster an innovative approach in your team and encourage staff to adopt innovative approaches in their classrooms. Sharing good practice is integral to discovering new ideas and approaches so we'll consider effective methods of doing this.

Let's begin with your departmental meeting time which is an ideal place to generate and share innovative ideas. Use this time to promote a learning environment amongst your team rather than an environment dedicated to disseminating information and allocating tasks. Encourage staff to engage in a dialogue about learning and teaching and ensure this happens at every one of your team meetings. This dialogue may cover more than teaching and learning ideas for the classroom and can cover ways in which you can enhance students' engagement through extra-curricular learning too. Sharing good practice through your team meetings can also offer your staff opportunities to develop professionally, both through delivering and sharing their ideas, strategies and innovations and through learning about what others are doing.

We recommend calendaring the sharing of good practice so that each of your staff know when and what they will be delivering or sharing with the rest of the team. For example, in your February meeting, Mr Jones (an experienced teacher) will have a 15-minute slot to share the new unit of work on bread making that he's planned and taught. He will talk about the practical work that inspired the students and his new approach to peer-assessment using Frogsnap. He'll share his resources with the team and show them examples of students' work and assessment. In your June meeting, Ms Jones (an NQT) will share her learning from a course on outstanding teaching and learning that she went on in May and discuss the impact it's had on her teaching practice, sharing resources and examples of students' work. In July, Ms Evans (departmental ETA) will share the learning highlights of the year and tell the team about examples of great learning and progress as well as lessons where she has seen deep engagement with the tasks in your department throughout the year. She will bring examples of students' work, photos of displays and students working. If you plan these sessions (even if it's quite loosely) in advance, staff will know what they are doing and when, but more importantly, if you plan for the sharing of good practice it's much more likely to happen. However, it doesn't always have to be planned and, of course, the very nature of inspiration and innovation means that it will likely happen on a more random basis.

You have to create a climate where day-to-day discussion is about teaching, learning and innovation and you have to deliberately provide platforms for your staff to do this. Consider your informal meeting times. Perhaps it's tea breaks or lunchtimes in a windowless departmental office that's full of paperwork, old textbooks and a dodgy microwave. What do people chat about when they converge around the kettle and the custard creams? It's great if they enthuse over a new pair of shoes or a holiday booked or if they laugh over an anecdote from the weekend. However, we don't think it's great if they lament the behaviour of Year 3 or grumble about the demise of the pencil case. It's not at all great if they spend their entire break or lunchtime bemoaning the amount of marking they have to do or being noisily underwhelmed by school dinners these days. Basically, this kind of negativity is not ok and you should see it as an important part of your role to banish it if you want to foster an innovative and creative environment. So, how do you do this? You model the behaviours you expect to see within your team. Turn up in the tea room and wax lyrical about the achievement of your Year 10s when you encouraged them to write without scaffolding, enthuse about the way you used iPads with Year 8, be excited about an article on growth mindset that you read online last night. They may look at you strangely for a week or so if this kind of discussion has not been the norm in the past, but we guarantee that if you persist, everyone will be doing it within a few weeks!

Meeting time – both formal and informal – will be limited so you need to use other ways to share good teaching and learning practice. Most of the time you are busy teaching so use the time to share the great things that you and your team are doing. As a Leader or an NQT you will have had planned, mandatory opportunities to see good teaching and learning in practice and to learn from this. It's important that you offer and provide these opportunities for everyone in your team. Again, this might not be something your staff are used to. If so, begin by inviting them all to see you in action. Encourage your team to observe each other and provide time for them to do so. Whether this is a routine activity or not within your organisation, make it a routine in your department. You may need to enlist the support of your line manager as providing staff with cover to observe others will have cost implications. If you have a plan for sharing good practice through lesson observations and clear expected outcomes, nobody can say that it won't be time or money well spent. Some organisations have this kind of practice well embedded, in which case it will be simpler for you to develop within your department and to extend to other departments. In fact, we think it's helpful to look beyond your own team and share good practice more widely. You could partner with another department within your organisation to observe lessons and share good practice. When you plan for these kinds of activities, make sure you factor in time for discussion after the observations have taken place.

Another helpful practice you can adopt is that of an "open door policy". Lots of teams and departments teach with their classroom doors open which promotes a receptive and sharing ethos. Other staff, from your own department, can wander in and have a look at the learning that's taking place. It's important that staff know that while they're very welcome to call and informally observe the lesson, they must be careful not to disrupt learning. Most people find that as you embed this practice within a department, students pay very little attention to staff who may wander in and out, perhaps looking at their books or asking the odd question. This policy works if it's adopted whole-heartedly. There is no point teaching with your door open if you're going to glare in annoyance at anyone who walks into the room!

We so often work in our departmental areas without having many opportunities to venture out into the rest of the school, let alone beyond it. You need to physically get out of your area as often as possible and see as much as you can of teaching and learning across the organisation. There may be formal opportunities provided for you to do this, but to be honest, you have to do the running here. Talk to other teachers, ask them about teaching and learning in their subjects, ask if you can come and see what they're doing and encourage your staff to do the same. Then, expand on this. Make links with local schools and organise visits or exchange visits. People do this a lot less than they should or could. Part of this is down to time, but we think a lot of it is down to fear and avoidance. We are safe with what we know. We feel confident and comfortable in our own working environment. What if we go to another school and they do things unrecognisably differently or brilliantly? We won't feel so confident and comfortable then, will we? If you make the effort to develop links beyond your school, what you're actually likely to discover are fresh ideas and approaches, colleagues who are facing the same challenges as you – alone! Just working with someone doing the same role as you can be of huge value in as much as they can become part of your support network. We know that when we run middle leaders' courses, participants love meeting people who are in their position to share creative ideas and innovations. We always encourage participants to exchange email addresses and they often contact each other afterwards, sharing plans and resources. The bottom line is that it's much less hassle to *not* make lots of contacts up and down the country, it takes time and commitment, but if you want to lead an innovative and well-supported department, you should make the effort. And of course, you will have ideas and support that you can offer to others, too.

Technology is a useful tool when it comes sharing good practice and many of you will know the benefits of using a system like Iris to objectively carry out shared lesson observations. It can save huge amounts of time and money in terms of timetabling and cover implications. A recorded lesson can be used as a valuable resource for improving teaching and learning across your department. Most schools don't have Iris so we'll focus on some of its qualities and consider how you can adopt a makeshift approach within your organisation. If we begin with filming and recording – you don't need Iris to do that. Using a tripod and camera to record lessons might produce a somewhat 'home-made' result, but can still be used effectively when reflecting on teaching and learning, particularly if two teachers watch a video and strike up a reflective dialogue. Lesson observation can, unfortunately, be fairly subjective and are often one person's perception of the teaching and learning that takes place. For this reason, a combination of video and shared observation can be helpful. Consider setting up teaching and learning triads in your department. A & B observe C followed by feedback, reflection and dialogue between A, B & C and so on.

Let's consider the value of the whole lesson observation thing. Lesson observations are great. Observing, reflecting and learning is great. Being observed, reflecting and learning is great. Why is it then that lesson observations are frequently so dreaded and reviled? We think it's down to ethos. If your ethos is one of openness, welcoming, trusting and above all, learning – lesson observation won't be so feared. Developing this ethos is something you will have to build slowly and steadily towards if your team's experience to date has been of periodical and very formal observations followed by feedback with little opportunity for reflection and dialogue. However, there are many arguments you could throw at our sweeping generalisation that lesson observations are great. Sometimes, of course, they are not great. They are absolutely dire if they are something that is *done to* teachers without thoughtful agreement and planning. If you just rock up to a lesson of your choosing with notice via email, observe, make notes and tick boxes, and then feedback without any meaningful dialogue, the experience will be awful for the teacher. If you make judgements based on a single lesson and label a teacher, very little will be gained. If your lesson observations are all about performance management and quality assurance (important yes, the only reason for observing, no) that is all that will be achieved – performance management and some form of quality assurance. Ofsted don't judge and grade lessons – what does your school do? You may have to work in line with your school's policies and protocols, but you are in a leadership role and therefore in a position to work to drive change within your organisation. Hopefully, you're working in an organisation that doesn't judge and label teachers based on an individual lesson, but makes judgements about teaching and learning based on achievement and progress over time. Ofsted don't base their judgements of the quality of teaching and learning on individual lessons and they don't grade the lessons that they observe. What they do want to to see is that the school's judgement of teaching and learning is accurate. You will play a key role here and have to be confident in your judgements about the quality of the teaching and learning that is taking place in your department. You also need to be able to identify areas for development and be able to say how you are addressing these.

We've come up with a list of what we think is important practice before and after a lesson observation.

- You should agree the time and length of the lesson observation with the teacher. This should be done in consultation. It's possibly a time when email is not the preferred method. Go and see them, ask which class they'd like to be observed with. If, for example it was a Key Stage 3 class last time, perhaps it would be good to see them teaching KS4 this time. Discuss what (if there is one) the focus will be. Ask them if there is anything they would like you to focus on. Perhaps they had an area for development after their last observation and they'd like you to look closely at that area.
- Make sure the teacher is clear about information that they need to provide you with. Do you require a full lesson plan, data or resources? Let them know exactly what you require of them and when. Clarity is key and people detest the type of uncertainty that stems from any lack of it.
- Plan when the feedback will be given at this stage. Agree a time and a place, preferably on neutral territory, making sure you allow

plenty of time and that the feedback is as soon as possible after the lesson has been observed.

- When you give feedback, it's important that you won't be disturbed and that you allow adequate time for reflection and discussion. You will want to discuss the strengths of teaching and learning and support the teacher in areas for improvement or development. Anything you identify as an area for development should be coupled with tangible suggestions of support that you can offer the teacher in order that they can develop. You should encourage the teacher to be as self-reflective as possible and explore strategies for improvement together. Again, clarity is key. There is nothing worse than receiving feedback and coming away from that meeting feeling as though you have only a vague – or indeed *no* idea – of what you need to do to improve teaching and learning.
- We recommend that you carry out some paired observations with your line manager or other members of SLT, particularly if you're inexperienced at doing so. This could involve paired feedback as well. Paired observations provide you with a benchmark, as well as a clear understanding of expectations and protocols in your organisation.
- Above all, good manners and kindness are important!

James says…

Some of my top tips for carrying out lesson observations aren't very Ofsteddy, but more to do with just being a good person:

- ***Be courteous and arrive on time, stay for as long as you pre-agreed, and ensure your presence is unobtrusive;***
- ***Never cancel or postpone or, worse, forget to go;***
- ***Don't say anything negative about the lesson unless you can fully explain how this might be rectified in the future, offering a range of suggestions not just "what I would've done is…";***
- ***Do your homework on the class so you're not noisily rustling through paperwork provided by the host teacher while they're trying to teach;***

- ***Act as their support assistant when pupils are engaged in longer tasks or discussion, and ask the teacher where you could be best deployed – you're in the room, why not?***
- ***Return the favour and let the teacher come and observe you;***
- ***Arrange to feedback very soon after the lesson, that same day if possible;***
- ***Don't demand anything special, unusual or gimmicky, just let them do what they do (unless this actually is special, unusual or gimmicky!).***

Sharing good practice through the observation of teaching and learning is vital if you and your team are to have a clear and thorough understanding of the quality of teaching and learning in your department. We observe lessons because we are committed to continually improving, developing and innovating so that we give young people the best chances of learning and achieving well. It's our job, it's what we do and we genuinely care about this. There is, however, always an Ofsted shaped shadow looming somewhere on the horizon and schools, senior leaders and teachers don't ignore what Ofsted are saying at any given time. Why would you? Therefore, as we take a closer look at the process of observation and how you arrive at your judgements on teaching and learning, we make no apology for referring in this chapter to the School Inspection Handbook because it is genuinely useful (we are using the one from August 2015 which will undoubtedly have been replaced by the time you read this). Whatever the year in which you are reading this, we suggest that you have a copy of this document – or the one that has superseded it – to hand.

When you observe lessons, you will see a range of teaching styles. Individuals will use a huge range of methods and styles to suit the class, subject and abilities or planned learning outcomes at any given time. Sometimes teaching style might depend on past experience or training. Ofsted '*does not favour any particular teaching style*' which is great news because as a school, a department and as a teacher, you can decide how best to teach your students in order to ensure they learn and make good progress. You don't have to adopt a one-size fits all approach to planning and teaching because inspectors will be '*looking at*' the effectiveness of what you are doing rather than '*looking for*' you doing specific things. This means that you should be doing just this when you observe a lesson. There is no need to be ticking boxes that ensure there has been an interactive starter activity, three mini-plenaries, an extended period of writing, use of technology, group work, paired work, peer-assessment opportunities and a student led plenary. You just need to look at the actual teaching and learning that takes place and make conclusions about the effectiveness of it. You *do* need to look at how well students are learning and how they engage with the lessons you observe. You *don't* need to expect to or insist on seeing certain elements that, in the past, you may have been told must be present in order for a lesson to be outstanding.

You will certainly want to see evidence that a teacher knows their students well and is using differentiation and personalised learning to ensure that all students can make good progress in their learning. In the past, lesson observers could – and have been – handed a different worksheet to match the abilities of every student in a class. Here is the 'working towards 4a' worksheet, here is the 'working towards 5c' worksheet and here is the 'working towards 5b' worksheet. Oh, and here we have a list of key words for students on the blue table and an extension activity for the students on the yellow table and last but not least an extended but optional homework project for the students on the green table. This isn't – hopefully – what teachers do on a day-to-day basis; it's what teachers do when they are forced into providing evidence that the learning needs of all students are being met. Of course, this kind of planning and preparation is not fundamental in ensuring every student learns and makes progress. It says, in the handbook: '*it is unrealistic, too, for inspectors to expect that all work in lessons will be matched to the specific needs of each individual pupil*'. So, as far as differentiation is concerned, what are you looking for? In a word – nothing! You are not looking for any particular methods of differentiation. You are looking at the learning and progress of all students and groups of students over time. What you do need a teacher to provide when being observed is accurate and up to date data that provides clear information about the progress each student is making. You will look at the data; you will look at the books of students of different abilities and educational needs and of students belonging to 'groups' of students (identified either nationally or by your school as at risk of underachieving) and you will make a judgement about whether students are engaged and learning and progressing. If all the students are making great progress, it's highly likely that the teacher is differentiating and personalising the teaching and learning activities on a regular basis. But, guess what, for the purpose of a PM observation, it doesn't matter too much how they are doing this and most importantly it doesn't matter whether you see specific evidence of it in a specific lesson.

Ofsted have provided some helpful clarification about the inspection process complete with emboldening of key words and frequent repetition of 'does not' in reference to itself. Further change is afoot though if Educational Excellence Everywhere is to be read as gospel:

'So Ofsted will consult on removing the separate graded judgements on the quality of teaching, learning and assessment. Inspectors will still report on the impact of teaching, learning and assessment through the other graded judgements, but will no longer separately grade the quality of teaching.

Ofsted will also consider how best to further streamline the handbook so that inspection is focused closely on what matters most – outcomes not processes.'

Ofsted – School Inspection Handbook – for inspecting schools in England under section 5 of the Education Act 2005 – Handbook August 2015 – Reference no: 150066

We have picked some key quotes from the 'Clarification' section of the handbook that will be of relevance to you and your team. Under each quote there is space for you to make some notes. Consider, where appropriate, what this means for you and your team, approaches you take throughout the year and the evidence you gather. If the quotes are dated, extract the new ones from the latest handbook. Consider any changes you might want to make to your methods of observing and/or carrying out quality assurance.

'Inspectors must not advocate a particular method of planning, teaching or assessment.'

'Ofsted does not require schools to provide individual lesson plans to inspectors.'

'Ofsted does not specify how planning should be set out, the length of time it should take or the amount of detail it should contain. Inspectors are interested in the effectiveness of planning rather than the form it takes.'

'Ofsted does not award a grade for the quality of teaching or outcomes in the individual lessons visited. It does not grade individual lessons. It does not expect schools to use the Ofsted evaluation schedule to grade teaching or individual lessons.'

'Ofsted does not expect to see a particular frequency or quantity of work in pupils' books or folders.'

'Ofsted does not expect to see any specific frequency, type or volume of marking and feedback.'

'Ofsted will take a range of evidence into account when making judgements, including published performance data, the school's in-year performance information and work in pupils' books and folders, including that held in electronic form.'

'Ofsted does not expect performance and pupil-tracking information to be presented in a particular format.'

'Ofsted will usually expect to see evidence of the monitoring of teaching and learning'

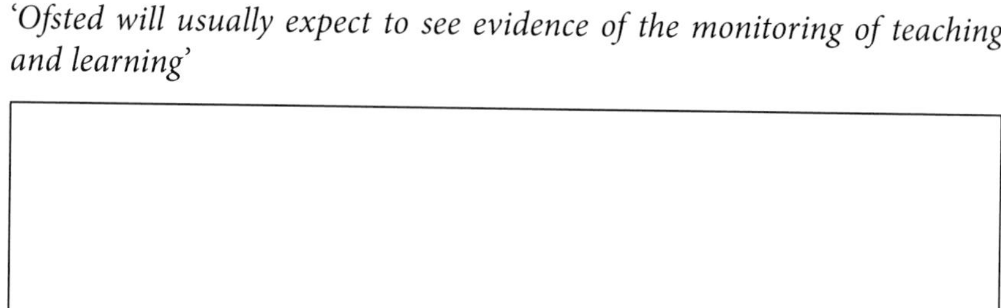

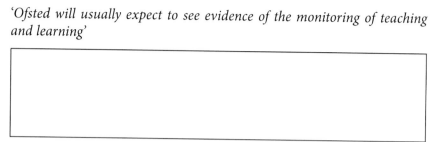

Gone are the days – thankfully – where a lesson is expected to have four or eight parts or chunks and move seamlessly between these chunks – with alarms, hand signals and flashing lights signalling the transition between chunks. Those days where the teacher had to ensure students were working from the correct one of the 12 worksheets; engaging in debate with a well-chosen group of similarly able students; kinaesthetically recording their learning on a specially designed, ICT-based, interactive self-assessment facility and singing a mini-plenary. You could, in theory, observe a lesson where a teacher talks for 60% of the time, students talk for 20% and write for 20% and it could deemed to be outstanding because the quality and challenge of the work set has a profound impact on learning and progress. Students might, in this particular lesson, learn a lot while they are listening to a teacher talk and they might be able to then articulate their learning through talking and practice or develop their understanding through writing. There is no right or wrong way and as teachers we have at our disposal an infinite number of teaching methods that we use at different times for different purposes. What matters is impact.

Inspectors do gather evidence about how well pupils acquire knowledge and learn and engage with lessons. Therefore, the questions you are asking when you observe are: are these students acquiring knowledge – right now and over time? Are these students learning – right now and over time? Are these students engaged – right now and over time? These are fairly big questions but we think that the answers are a simple 'yes' or 'no'. A person is either acquiring knowledge or they are not, they are learning or they are not and they are engaged or they are not. However, the methods employed to ensure that the answers are 'yes' are multifarious. Also, you are not looking at one student – you are looking at a group of students so you need to look carefully to see whether all, most, some, few or none are learning and engaged.

Let's take a look at the criteria that Ofsted say constitute outstanding teaching, learning and assessment. We have added our thoughts – do the same with your team. These are the very same criteria you should be taking into consideration when you make judgements about teaching and learning. It's pointless being all curmudgeonly, cross and opinionated about Ofsted; accept Ofsted for what it is and use their guidance and resources. You are fortunate because you work with your staff every day and have the opportunity to notice and consider these elements in casual observation and by popping into classrooms. For a leader to really know and understand what is happening in teaching and learning and then to improve it through innovation, that leader must be astutely observant.

'Teachers demonstrate deep knowledge and understanding of the subjects they teach. They use questioning highly effectively and demonstrate understanding of the ways pupils think about subject content. They identify pupils' common misconceptions and act to ensure they are corrected.'

Our thoughts:

In your role, you will have access to the bigger picture. Your observation of a member of staff isn't a one off, it's contextual and an on-going process and therefore you will know whether they are reflective and seek to assess their effectiveness to adapt or improve it. During an observation, you might find evidence of this through plenaries or through student responses and feedback to marked work in books. You might hear questions from a teacher, such as: "Has doing X task helped you understand this concept or did you find it easier to understand when we did Y?" A great teacher asks these kinds of questions frequently, sometimes formally or perhaps informally, as students leave a classroom or while they circulate and facilitate a learning activity.

Is the teaching and learning (in the lesson you observe and over time) fully inclusive and differentiated? Here you will look at the planning, resources, the lesson's activities (including tasks set, support, questioning, dialogue and expectations) and students' books. When you're observing, it's unrealistic to expect to look at every book, but you should use the data the teacher provides you to ensure that you are looking at the books of different abilities and groups of students. Are they all showing evidence of progress and learning?

'Teachers plan lessons very effectively, making maximum use of lesson time and coordinating lesson resources well. They manage pupils' behaviour highly effectively with clear rules that are consistently enforced'

Our thoughts:

We recommend encouraging teachers to adopt their own methods of planning. Planning is a very personal process and what suits one teacher will not suit another. This doesn't mean that team attitudes to planning become an 'anything goes' approach with the odd bulleted list and spider diagram. It just means that autonomy, albeit within a strong framework, is important.

Wasted time is common and you should make a point of noticing it – just imagine how those squandered minutes add up over days and weeks and years!

As far as rules and behaviour are concerned, always check that the teacher is managing any behaviour issues in line with your organisation's policies, protocols and systems. Secondly, look at the start and end of lessons – we always think these are quite telling and a good indicator of day-to-day practice in a classroom. Finally, observing teachers who command respect is interesting. In our experience, that complete command of respect is an almost intangible quality that some teachers seem to have and some don't. For some it comes naturally and it can be difficult to describe, in concrete terms, how they achieve it. For others, systems and strategies are employed by the teacher in order to command respect. Sometimes it's a combination of both. Whatever it is, it's something you can easily get a sense or feeling of.

'Teachers provide adequate time for practice to embed the pupils' knowledge, understanding and skills securely. They introduce subject content progressively and constantly demand more of pupils. Teachers identify and support any pupil who is falling behind, and enable almost all to catch up.'

Our thoughts:

There are two points within this point and the first is that students need time to practise new skills. Reading between the lines, we think they are saying, "Please, teachers, stop bouncing from one showy activity to the next and give the students a bloody chance to try it out in peace for a few minutes". The second point is the focus on progression (and demanding MORE). What you should be seeing is that students, for example, learn how to do something then practise doing it, and then learn the next step, practise that and so on. You will see evidence of this in books as well as during lessons.

'Teachers check pupils' understanding systematically and effectively in lessons, offering clearly directed and timely support.'

Our thoughts:

We think that the best teachers are great listeners. They listen really carefully to responses from students during lessons and then are able to adapt their approach. Unfortunately, lots of teachers (due, perhaps in part, to the pressure of being observed) are so busy mentally preparing and planning the thing that they are going to say or do next that they can't listen effectively. Look out for this as you observe.

In books, you should find evidence of checking understanding and adapting planning. Perhaps a topic or skill is revisited or practised again. Feedback or homework set might show that a teacher has adapted planning. You might see resources or entire lessons that are not in the departmental unit of work – these are great evidence that the teacher is adapting their approach to the students' needs.

'Teachers provide pupils with incisive feedback, in line with the school's assessment policy, about what pupils can do to improve their knowledge, understanding and skills. The pupils use this feedback effectively.'

Our thoughts: (doesn't seem to be completely about the above point?)

In observing the responses of students, you should be looking at all their communications. They may respond verbally, through writing, through note taking, through planning or perhaps through drawing or performing. There are myriad ways of responding. The key is, do these responses show 'gains' or progress? A student can put together a highly articulate and hugely eloquent response to a question and actually have made no progress in terms of gaining knowledge, skills or understanding. Conversely, another student could stumble through a poorly articulated answer to a question, but actually be going through a process of beginning to understand a new concept. Learning isn't neat and tidy and always well-articulated. It's often a messy and haphazard process. Looking at students' books and their assessments will help you to understand whether 'gains' are being made, but be wary of making judgements based solely on responses made in a lesson.

Although the majority of evidence of assessment will be found in students' books, do look as well at the informal assessment of learning that takes place throughout a lesson. We think it's important to pay attention to peer- and self-assessment. Where there is evidence of this taking place, clarify that it has been checked by the teacher for accuracy and whether they are using it to inform planning. Peer- and self-assessment for the sake of it (or for the sake of making a teacher's life easier) is not a good sign! It should always be used by the teacher to inform planning and differentiation.

Hopefully, the students you teach and observe are not totally fixated on grades or levels and hopefully they don't read from a highlighted list of skills if you ask them what they need to do or learn next. The best way to look at whether students understand how to improve is probably to talk to a few of them about the work they are currently doing. Engage in a dialogue with students about their work and ask them how they think they can improve. Don't mention levels or grades. Listen to how well they can explain the skills or knowledge they need to develop. Don't worry too much about the language they use or how articulate they are (it can be hard to describe what you don't yet know!), but look at whether they have a sense of direction and understanding of what they have to do next and how they might achieve it. The second best way to look at whether students understand how to improve is analysis of some of their books and the quality of not just the marking and feedback, but of the dialogue between the teacher and student, something we will discuss in much greater detail in the second half of this chapter. There should be frequent evidence of the kind of marking that offers clear and precise targets for improvement as well as opportunities for students to reflect meaningfully on their work and the marking of it. Of course, the most obvious way to evidence whether students understand how to improve is the dialogue that takes place in the lesson. This might be comprised of: a teacher feeding back verbally to a whole class and setting targets for the next sequence of learning based on learning and progress made by students in previous lessons; one to one dialogue between teacher and student as the teacher circulates the class while students are working; perhaps a task or activity is paused while a teacher checks for learning and progress and sets a new target or explains what the group needs to do to improve; or students' understanding of how to improve could be as a result of self- or peer-assessment during the lesson. You should expect to find evidence of these different approaches both in the lesson and through looking at students' books.

'Teachers set challenging homework, in line with the school's policy and as appropriate for the age and stage of pupils, that consolidates learning, deepens understanding and prepares pupils very well for work to come.'

Our thoughts:

Whether homework is set in line with school policy is easy to judge, but look at the levels of challenge.

'Teachers embed reading, writing and communication and, where appropriate, mathematics exceptionally well across the curriculum, equipping all pupils with the necessary skills to make progress. For younger children in particular, phonics teaching is highly effective in enabling them to tackle unfamiliar words.'

Our thoughts:

In this area, a cohesive approach from your team is the best way to go. It could be that you have a collection of homework tasks or well-produced resources to aid written or spoken communication. Whatever you do, do it consistently and make it clear (in student work) that you have a well-thought out approach. What you do will, of course, be in line with school policy.

'Teachers are determined that pupils achieve well. They encourage pupils to try hard, recognise their efforts and ensure that pupils take pride in

all aspects of their work. Teachers have consistently high expectations of all pupils' attitudes to learning.'

Our thoughts:

If you have ever heard a teacher say something along the lines of "Well, nobody in that group will get a C, they just can't do it. They all came in on a Level 3" and felt annoyed by the low expectations on the teacher's part, you already know how important high expectations are. As with ethos, high expectations should permeate learning, work completed, displays, homework, human interaction and behaviour.

It can be helpful to look closely at the support in lessons you observe. As a department and as a leader, you have hopefully implemented clear plans for support within the lessons in your department. In individual lessons, you should expect to see support from teaching assistants that is targeted to students' needs and support that has been well planned for. There should be evidence that professional dialogue takes place between teacher and support staff and above all the support staff should be having an impact on the learning and progress of the students they work with.

In a lesson observation, pupil pride and 'trying hard' are easy to assess – are all the students involved, as directed by the teacher, in the learning activities? Look for signs that students are not engaged and are doing something else, but don't assume that thinking or gazing or doodling are necessarily signs of disengagement. If you think students might not be engaged in the learning, look for concrete evidence that this is the case over time. Perhaps their books show unfinished work or the data shows lack of progress. It's not uncommon that, on occasion, teaching and learning during a lesson observation lacks challenge. This can happen because teachers are afraid to challenge students while they're being observed in case the whole lesson falls apart when the students 'don't get it'. It's tempting, as a teacher, to teach a lesson in which you can be sure students will 'perform' well and therefore demonstrate learning/ progress. What you need to look at are the levels of challenge in a lesson. Are all the students being challenged? Does the level of challenge match the ability of the students? You should see differentiation, but it doesn't need to be as explicit and ridiculous as five different worksheets for students working at different levels!

'Pupils love the challenge of learning and are resilient to failure. They are curious, interested learners who seek out and use new information to develop, consolidate and deepen their knowledge, understanding and skills. They thrive in lessons and also regularly take up opportunities to learn through extra-curricular activities.'

Our thoughts:

There isn't much need to comment here. We love that the word "love" is in an Ofsted criteria and, in its entirety, this point perhaps best sums up why we all do the job that we do. We want to develop and foster love of challenge and resilience and we want learners to be interested and to thrive. This is where you should see the results of any work your team has put in to creating a great ethos and evidence that everyone is working towards the vision that you created. You're looking at the atmosphere and at how students feel about their learning.

'Pupils are eager to know how to improve their learning. They capitalise on opportunities to use feedback, written or oral, to improve.'

Our thoughts:

Ideally, you have worked hard with your team to devise excellent systems and procedures for giving feedback and students will know and understand these well. Evidence that students know how to improve learning comes from what they say and from the progression seen in their books. You also might expect to see displays that foster improvement and activities where students are encouraged and given time to draft, edit and proofread written work or have another attempt at something more practical. Whether you see students 'capitalise on opportunities' to improve their work will be very much dependent on the ethos you and your team have developed. Planning for this and ensuring staff do the same is important – it's about developing and embedding practices and mind-sets over time.

'Parents are provided with clear and timely information on how well their child is progressing and how well their child is doing in relation to the standards expected. Parents are given guidance about how to support their child to improve.'

Our thoughts:

This is very much down to the policies your organisation has in place and the approach it takes. Make sure your team make an excellent contribution to this process. You might consider whether you have a quality assurance system in place for report writing. We mentioned approaches to this in Chapter 2.

'Teachers are quick to challenge stereotypes and the use of derogatory language in lessons and around the school. Resources and teaching strategies reflect and value the diversity of pupils' experiences and provide pupils with a comprehensive understanding of people and communities beyond their immediate experience.'

Our thoughts:

The bottom line is that you must make sure your staff don't let behaviours that need challenging go unnoticed and unchallenged. Every teacher has a responsibility to plan resources and strategies that value diversity. This should be something you discuss as a team and are conscious of in planning. For many students, their breadth of experience is narrow and their fields of reference might be limited. How do your curriculum and other learning activities help '*provide pupils with a comprehensive understanding of people and communities beyond their immediate experience*'?

An observer who goes into a lesson with a tick list, expecting to see each and every feature of 'outstanding' teaching and learning is going to be disappointed. Worse than that though, they will make a poor judgement. Maybe a couple of students didn't demonstrate full concentration for the entire duration of a lesson and perhaps there was very little independent learning taking place in this particular lesson, but, as an observer, you are looking at the learning gains over time. If teachers are trying to perform to a checklist of features deemed to be 'outstanding', they are likely to be doing little more than just that – performing. A final word about the grade descriptors used by Ofsted when making judgements about the quality of teaching. They state that:

'These descriptors should not be used as a checklist. They must be applied adopting a 'best fit' approach that relies on the professional judgement of the inspection team.'

So, don't use a checklist and remember that you are looking 'at' teaching and learning rather than 'for' specific features or strategies.

Quality Assurance

> *"Take nothing on its looks; take everything on evidence. There's no better rule."*
>
> Charles Dickens, Great Expectations

In driving to improve the quality of teaching and learning that takes place in your department, it is equally important to consider how you will ensure the high quality is sustained, and how you will monitor those standards, too – essentially your quality assurance, often called QA in schools. The start of your second half term in charge is an ideal place to begin your formal, structured monitoring of the teaching and learning taking place in your department. Up to now, as a new middle leader, you will have been busy immersing yourself in the school, dropping in to classrooms (learning the names of the really naughty students along the way!) and acquiring a *feel* for the daily diet being offered to students by your team. In Chapter 2, we talked briefly about effective performance management, setting targets to be achieved by the end of the coming year linked to your development plan. Now, you'll want to start looking for how those targets are being fulfilled by your staff and, perhaps more crucially, where they are not. Meticulously following a calendar of QA will allow you to build up the fullest picture of the performance of both your students and your team. You may not realise it now, but you or the senior team might potentially require this evidence later on in the year if it becomes necessary to carry out more formal processes to ensure improvements in teaching and learning, or perhaps the performance of a member of your team. Unfortunately, there are times when staff are either unable or unwilling to meet the standards set by you or the school. While this isn't the sole purpose of QA, you need to approach it with the mind-set that you may need detailed, accurate evidence at some point in the future and you, in your role as a middle leader, are key from both an evidence-collecting and supportive point of view.

The first stage of this is to carefully formulate a QA calendar for the year ahead. This will need to include all of the following:

- Exercise book and marking scrutiny.
- Learning walks.

- Moderation and standardisation.
- Academic Progress Checks (see Chapter 6 for a full run down on these).
- Gathering student feedback.
- Gathering the views of other stakeholders.
- Monitoring behaviour for learning.

Formal lesson observations as part of your school's performance management or appraisal process should be kept kind of separate from QA which is why we have focused specifically on these in the first part of this chapter. They can still form part of your evidence base, but for much more reliable substantiation of your judgements the frequent use of our list above is recommended. Organise these into your calendar month-by-month rather than half term-by-half term. The school year rarely divides itself neatly into equal chunks so work out which activities can be placed in which month, remembering to allow for holidays and key moments in the academic calendar such as parents' evenings or exam periods. For each activity, consider:

- Who will be involved – the responsibility does not need to rest solely with you. You must enlist the assistance of your SLT line manager, your TLR holders and, indeed, all members of your team. Why not? For most, it will be excellent professional development, extending your policy of distributing leadership.
- How it will help to improve teaching and learning – you have to be explicit here, clear with yourself about why you are monitoring a particular aspect so that, in turn, you can be clear with your team. It will help when you encounter resistance (which you will) and will help when it comes to the final analysis – what is effective, what isn't and what do you need to change?

Start pencilling in when you will do each of these, how often and who will assist you on the following calendar. At the same time, consider your school's policy on observations, and what exactly is classed as an 'observation', so as not to contravene any agreed limit, policy or procedure. This calendar doesn't need to be your final version, you can move things around later, but it's at least a chance to start thinking about the logistics of QA:

QA Calendar

	Behaviour for Learning	*Academic Progress Checks*	*Gathering the views of other stakeholders*
Nov.			
Dec.			
Jan.			
Feb.			
Mar.			
Apr.			
May.			
Jun.			
Jul.			

Student Voice Activities	*Standardisation and Moderation*	*Learning Walks*	*Exercise book and marking scrutiny*

Exercise book and marking scrutiny

Caroline says...

Attention to detail, absolutely unswaying objectivity and a constant focus on the purpose of marking are the three key ingredients I suggest you need in order to carry out a successful work scrutiny. You may also need an assistant because a large team will produce a lot of marking and completing the job properly will take time. I have a real bugbear when it comes to work and marking scrutinies. I cannot tolerate the approach taken by some, the approach where staff are allowed to choose for themselves which books or folders are scrutinised! You can't just invite members of your team to rock up with a few books chosen by themselves and expect to obtain an accurate picture of the quality of work being produced and marking being undertaken across your team. Always, always choose the books you want to scrutinise using your departmental trackers and I recommend letting progress be your guiding force. Pick students who are making average progress, great progress, and awful progress in each Year Group or Key Stage. Don't try to look at too many books and folders to begin with, BUT if you see evidence of any problems, ask for more books immediately so that you can get a better picture. Carry out a work and marking scrutiny with attention to detail, objectivity, and focus on progress and achievement of students. If the marking you scrutinise is not contributing to progress and achievement, you must do something about it.

Quite often, an Ofsted inspection nowadays begins with a book scrutiny since the appearance, standard and contents of the books can tell the inspectors so much about the school they are about to judge. And, on this point at least, they've got this right, because a set of student exercise books can tell the story of a school.

Complete the diagram below by filling in the circles with all the information you think you can get just from looking at a set of books. This will help you to set clearly in your mind what you would like to achieve from your rounds of book monitoring:

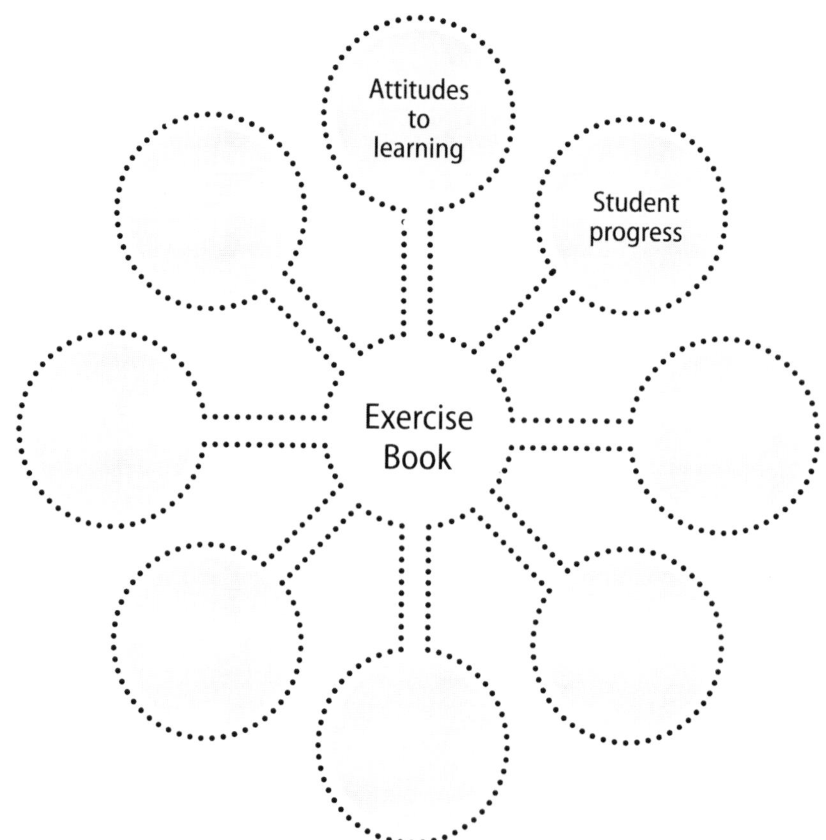

Your first book scrutiny (and when we use the word 'books', you can always substitute it for another word like 'folders' if that's what you use) will be one of the most important you carry out all year. It will provide you with bags of valuable information that you can use in all sorts of contexts. The front of the book is the obvious place to start, so think about what you want this to tell someone who picks it up: look that all vital information is completed neatly and accurately by the student; it's a good idea to have student target data on the front of the book as well as ongoing assessment data – check whether this has been kept up to date; and you need books to be graffiti and doodle free – any of this nonsense speaks volumes about student attitudes towards learning, in-class behaviour and teacher expectations.

Next, venture inside the book and look at presentation. We recommend you be fastidious in your insistence in all students maintaining high standards of presentation in their books. As a team, you could even decide upon and design a house style that all students could follow, as we once heard Geoff Barton, the education writer and headteacher of King Edward VI School in Bury St Edmonds, say at a conference. Mock this up, copy and laminate it, display one in every classroom or glue to the inside front cover of all exercise books. You could insist upon: the labelling of classwork or homework; the underlining of titles (with a ruler!); your preferred format for a written date (important this since it shows how a student's work progresses over a number of days and weeks – and will highlight if there are periods of inactivity); the need for neat handwriting; the drawing of any diagrams in pencil; any worksheets are glued in and labelled, not just folded and shoved in the back; a double line to mark the end of a piece of work and the start of a new one; and anything else that fits into the requirements of your subject. But please, please don't insist on all students writing out the learning objectives, which amazingly still goes on. What they were learning about that lesson should be implicitly obvious from the work they completed in the hour or so they were in the classroom. Additionally, stress the need with your team that their *own* presentation, handwriting, use of language and grammar in student books needs to be legible and neat, and that they are effectively modelling the standards they expect from the pupils.

Your attention should next turn to the substance of the students' work. Think carefully about the evidence you are gathering. Some questions to pose as you read through:

1. Are they doing enough? Are they doing too much?
2. Is work mostly complete or are there too many incomplete pieces? Does this tell you anything about behaviour in the class?
3. What is being taught? Is it correct? Is it as you directed? Has the teacher gone 'off piste'? Is this divergence justified? Does the teacher have good subject and curriculum knowledge?
4. Are they at the point in a unit of work that you'd expect, or are they going too slowly or too quickly?

5. Are topics being skirted over or is there sufficient depth?
6. Are there a variety of different tasks and activities? Do activities lack value or substance?
7. Do students appear to enjoy what they are doing?
8. Is there evidence of originality and individuality in their work? Compare books – robotically similar work could indicate a pedagogical problem and would need tackling.
9. Is progress being made (don't look at any grades yet, look at the standard of the work, the quality of the writing, the knowledge and skills being demonstrated)?
10. How does the teacher promote high expectations? Are students being challenged?

Finally, consider the teacher's marking. In August, you formulated an effective feedback policy, a substantial part of which was how and how often you expect students' work to be marked and assessed, all agreed with your team. Now you need to formally check that this is being implemented as fully as you imagined and that it is having the desired impact upon student progress and achievement. In Chapter 2, the two questions we said you would need to ask of the marking were, 'Have the books been marked in the way you all agreed they would be' and 'Is it having an impact upon progress and achievement?' Resist any element of box-ticking and try to stick to writing freely and in detail in answering these questions about the quality of the marking you are seeing – in your own words, as far as possible resisting the temptation to attach an Ofsted phrase to your commentary, an action that would only depersonalise the process. You can always look at how your observations tally against the Ofsted inspection handbook later when someone, inevitably, asks you to do so. For your purposes, your intuitive responses are going to be more than adequate here. Take photos of marking or scan and save them as PDFs that you can use in your feedback later. We recommend giving yourself a 24-hour window in which to feedback to the teacher; a short email is perfect since it's a time-stamped, written record for both your evidence files and their own, but make sure you keep the paper copies of anything you wrote down during the scrutiny (scanning and saving these, too, if you can) to be kept safely in an evidence file. Give them your observations, your targets for improvement and also when you expect these to occur, with an indication of when you will be returning to check that changes have been made. Don't forget to include yourself in this process, opening up your own classes' exercise books to scrutiny by another member of your team and having them provide you with their feedback in the same format.

Learning Walks

Of all the QA strategies we've suggested, learning walks are possibly the most problematic since they come with something of a bad reputation. In the wrong hands, the humble stroll around a school dropping in to classrooms can become a weapon of mass destruction, used by the unscrupulous to hound 'failing' teachers. They can breed resentment and paranoia. With improper management, they increase workload and stress. Without standardisation, they can be next to useless. In short, you have to get these right from the outset to avoid ruining the good work you've done in the opening months in the job.

In this next activity, consider the possible barriers that could stand in the way to you successfully implementing a system of learning walks in your school and the possible ways in which they could be overcome. We've suggested some potential barriers to get you going:

Barrier	*How it could be overcome*
Staff are reluctant to consent to an 'open door' policy and view learning walks as 'spying'.	
A sheet provided to you for learning walks is just lots of boxes to tick, or only allows you to write yes or no against a series of set statements.	
Staff carrying out learning walks are unsure what they are looking for and make generalised statements with no evidence.	

Your first tasks with introducing a system of learning walks are to dispel any myths surrounding them, allay any fears, attempt to overcome any barriers you have identified and agree, with your team, upon the key principles to which you will all adhere. Here are the four principles we believe you should stick to so that your learning walks are successful, four principles that are very much in the same vein as the process we recommended for your book scrutinies:

1. Shared responsibility

   Just how much of a shared responsibility you make this is going to be something of a judgement call on your part as you assess both the ability and readiness of your team to take part in learning walks. We recommend your schedule should accommodate two types of learning walks: those carried out by you and those carried out by the rest of your team. If you aren't a regular visitor to your classrooms by now, you certainly should be. For your own learning walks, you can do these with higher frequency than those of your team, on your own or in tandem with a trusted deputy or SLT line manager, to gather the depth of day-to-day evidence you'll need when it comes to talking confidently about aspects of teaching and learning in meetings or writing about the team in any review process. Try to use all staff at your disposal to carry out the second type of learning walk, attaching themes and foci to them that may or may not be directly linked to their own fields of interest or their experiences, and, in this instance, instructing them to seek out good practice for reporting back to you. For example, an NQT could carry out a learning walk in the second half-term on student engagement – you get lots of enthusiastic observations about how positively students are working (hopefully!) while she/he gets to spend time seeing how other teachers engage and motivate their students. This will generate a broader range of evidence than if you monopolised this task yourself. Additionally, this process is a two-way street, since the member of staff carrying out the learning walk will inevitably pick up strategies, techniques, ideas and tips they would not normally have acquired, like our NQT in the example above. Don't expect your team to make judgements on each other or give gradings for what they have observed; besides being an unreliable indicator, it is unlikely that they would feel in any way comfortable with deciding the standard of a lesson, nor would the teacher being observed in the classroom want that judgement to be made. Anyway, learning walks might only be five minutes in each classroom, nowhere near long enough to make a decision against Ofsted criteria, something that not even Ofsted do now over a full hour as we stated earlier.

2. Calendared

   Decide on the dates for these learning walks in advance – not the exact dates, just the week in which you'd like them to happen – and stick to them. Don't move them for anything or they'll get forgotten, half-heartedly squeezed in elsewhere or probably never happen at all. To that end, you need to make sure that the weeks you choose are the right weeks – that you are avoiding big events or high pressure moments that would make the carrying out of a learning walk an inconvenience or nuisance. Remember, we said these *could* be a hard sell, so anything to show your consideration of workload in their administration is a bonus. Similarly, you will have to judge carefully the amount of learning walks you do so as to avoid saturation since there will likely be others in school, such as senior leaders or those with a responsibility for an aspect of whole-school teaching and learning, simultaneously following their own calendar of learning walks. To attempt to coordinate these would most likely be hellish so you and your team will have to accept some overlap here. However, you should subsequently seek out any evidence these staff collect for your own files.

3. Open door policy

   As we stated earlier, in order to successfully implement a full complement of learning walks, you will need to work towards a mutually agreed open door policy. Start with your own door, physically throwing it open to anyone who wants to come in and see you teach and then gradually reciprocate, returning the compliment, visiting those who've been to see you and spending some time in classrooms, pre-arranging at first if necessary. What you do there is up to you, but there's room for creativity here – mysteriously hovering around at the back of the room for ten minutes, stern-faced and with folded arms isn't going to foster the trust you're looking for. Sit and work with some students, plan to team-teach a section of a lesson, do a bit of marking or moderation, and then look for other staff to start doing the same. What you're looking for here is the engendering of a natural sense of curiosity and inquiry in your team balanced with an equally natural sense of pride in their own practice and the bravery to show it off. If this is established, and it can be established quickly, then rolling out your two tiers of learning walks should be no problem.

4. Shared outcomes

   The results of any learning walks need to be shared, but you should carefully choose the format for this based on the nature of the findings. Personalised feedback is a priority; your first post-learning walk action should be to send quick messages of appreciation and praise to the staff you went to see. Publicly share your findings in meetings with your team, extracting key observations to reinforce any messages you might be aiming to deliver. Where the learning walk revealed elements of concern, then you should choose to meet with the teachers involved individually, unless the issues were common and widespread in which case you may need to do something more as a collective.

Moderation and standardisation

These two are closely linked, but each process is markedly different. With moderation, the aim is to make sure the marks, levels or grades awarded to pieces of student work are accurate. This usually takes the form of a meeting in which you look at samples of each teacher's books or a particular piece of work, swap them amongst yourselves and check the accuracy of the marking, especially pertinent for staff teaching the numerous new specifications currently coming live. Moderation is especially useful, and we might suggest mandatory, after an assessment such as a mock exam. Some schools even employ an external moderator to run the rule over their teachers' marking since the results of tests and assessments feed into forecasting of final grades. The accuracy of this data, therefore, is essential. Without established moderation procedures, you cannot ever say that assessment data provided by your team is 100% accurate; inaccurate data will impact on your intervention planning, students will slip through gaps, your headline figures will be miles out, and you'll end up looking like you haven't got a handle on progress and achievement. Don't let this happen, plan for regular moderation opportunities now.

When it comes to standardisation, the idea is for teachers to have the chance to assess the same pieces of work and then to compare the marks awarded. At GCSE level, exam boards have always provided standardisation materials to schools so that teachers can see what students are expected to do to achieve each grade. It's easy enough, however, to produce your own materials, copying pieces of work of differing standards to use with your team, giving them time to mark them and then talking through their ideas. There's bound to be some disagreement, but as long as you are all generally in the same area there should be no trouble. Watch out for any outliers, though, as those who are either way too generous or way too harsh will require extra training and possibly a full audit of their pupils' current work so you can, in the same way as moderation, ensure the quality of your data. Standardisation will occur less frequently than moderation, but it's ideally placed near the beginning of the year to allow for the training of new staff, maybe even by an expert you bring in to train your team, and for the sharing of new or updated grade criteria.

Academic Progress Checks

For a full description of Academic Progress Checks, our idea for fully reviewing the state of an entire year group, flick forward to Chapter 6 where you will find them discussed in detail.

Gathering student feedback and gathering the views of other stakeholders

Hopefully, you are working in a school that doesn't just pay lip service to the idea of pupil voice, often the fourth or fifth priority of a put-upon Assistant Head who occasionally remembers to bombard students with a series of questionnaires, the results of which are compiled but ultimately have no impact or bring about no change; another box ticked, a pile of papers filed neatly in the bin. Too much of what people term pupil voice is utter rubbish: pretending to care what the students think about aspects of their school or staging sham consultations that lead pupils to believe their opinions are having an impact on a decision that was made weeks ago by SLT. That's maybe a little cynical. If this sounds like your school, then be the driver of change here, setting an example of excellent practice within your own area. Pupil voice is extremely important (so important that it needs to be someone's job in your team) since children are more shrewd and discerning than many give them credit for. They know decent teaching when they see it, they're braver and more intuitive with new technology, they are open to new ideas and experiences, they'll ask questions and challenge when they're given the chance. They are a great source of understanding for you as a middle leader and, in short, should not be ignored when it comes to QA.

Here's the ideal process, as we see it:

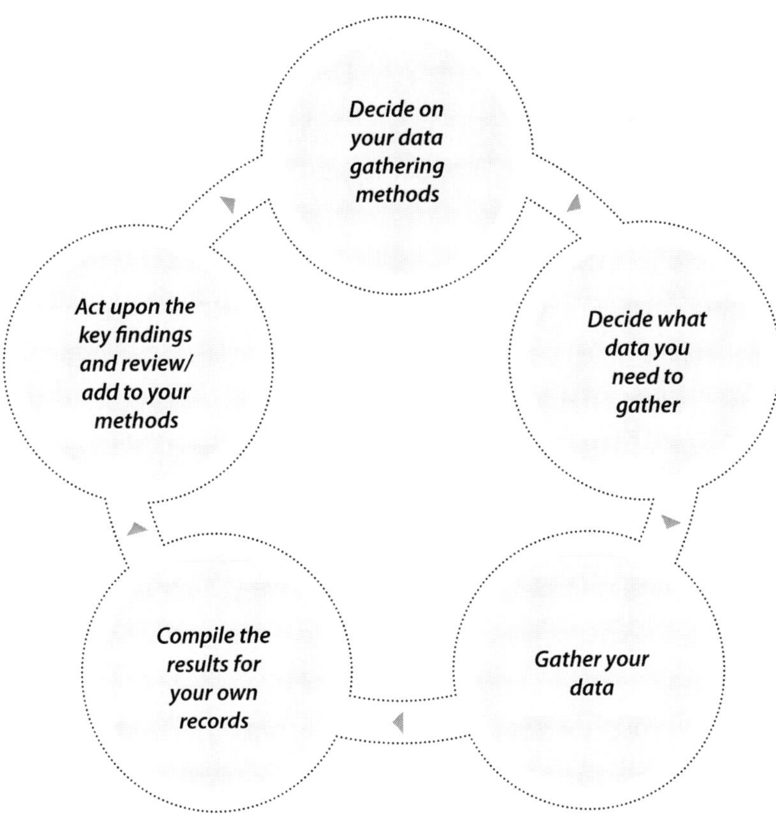

This is a simple starting point, but it provides the fundamentals to any attempt to encourage a culture of pupil voice and demands that you review and then renew your chosen methods regularly instead of just rolling out the aforementioned questionnaire. Which isn't to say don't do a questionnaire. No, along with all the other methods we will discuss in this section, it is certainly a useful tool for gathering data, if you write, structure and pitch it correctly, and if it's used as part of a suite of data-gathering techniques. We recommend doing the following:

1. Keep it short – five questions should suffice with only one or two of these inviting students to freely write an answer.
2. Keep it accessible – think about your wording and your mode of address. It should strike the right balance between formal and friendly.

3. Keep it focused – ask questions on a particular area of your work such as marking and feedback or curriculum enrichment.
4. Keep refreshing it – don't just print off another fifty copies in six months' time, unless you're interested in measuring how much something has changed or progressed, in which case you'll need to rephrase your questions anyway.
5. Keep records – detail who you gave them to, how many were returned and what kind of responses you've got...but don't do this yourself. A member of the support staff can handle the logistics of a task like this quite easily, leaving you to take responsibility for acting upon the results. Ensure these results then get fed back to your team, too.

Additionally, many schools now have subscriptions to web-based survey tools. Creating and running a questionnaire on here is simplicity in itself and could potentially improve your number of returned responses since a link can be quickly emailed to whole groups of pupils or home to parents. VLEs also have their own in-built survey machines. Try both web- and paper-based methods to see which works best for you, your pupils or your school. If these are already a feature of pupil voice at whole-school level, then insist that any results or findings are fed back into your own work to save duplication which, as well as being obviously twice the work, is irritating for pupils who end up with a kind of survey fatigue; under the law of diminishing returns, if your questionnaire is a pupil's fifth one in a week then chances are their responses might reflect their building ambivalence, invalidating the results.

You could also implement a suggestion/comments box, positioned somewhere centrally. Be clear about how you expect this to be used, and be equally clear about how you will feel about any abuse of the system; for every budding Oscar Wilde there will be a wannabe Keith Lemon to provide the immature, the inane or the impertinent, so pre-empt these with clear instructions and expectations. Check the comments box regularly and share anything genuinely pertinent, useful or creative with your team. Similarly, you could implement exit polls, asking students to feedback on post-it notes on the way out of the classroom for instant, brief feedback. Kids are astute; you might find that much of what is written simply confirms your feelings or impressions, raises issues of which you were already aware or tells you something you suspected all along.

If you'd like to go down the student leadership route, you might start by looking for class reps. Each class could nominate or elect a representative who collects feedback from their classmates to pass on to you. You, one of your team or even someone external to the school could gather them together every so often for fifteen minutes sharing collective experiences. Take their suggestions seriously. Give them a different focus every half-term if necessary (homework, behaviour, curriculum content), but be very, very clear about what kind of feedback you are looking for – no personal comments, no criticism without suggestions on what could be better. Periodically, you could use your meetings to survey the pupils, too, since they are a ready-made cross-section of the student body. Combine your meeting with your questionnaire from earlier to kill two birds with one stone. Use your class reps to interview other students as well since that may give you markedly different answers than if you asked the questions yourself.

Monitoring behaviour for learning

It's crucial that someone amongst your support staff team has the task of compiling and collating data on behaviour. You can't be the person sifting the figures on this – it would consume you. Your role is to respond to those numbers with decisive action, so someone needs to regularly provide them for you. You will need to know: which pupils are causing problems and who are your star pupils; how many on-calls there have been (broken down by teacher and by time of day); data on detentions, internal seclusions and external exclusions; information on parental/home contact and its impact; information on the use of any behaviour or rewards system particular to your school; and which teachers are having issues with behaviour that need resolving. If your team use your school's information management system consistently and correctly, this can all be easily extracted from there for you.

Once you have your numbers, you can get to work. Establish routines for your monitoring, creating grids or tables if necessary that you can then easily update with the latest figures when they become available. In your analysis you need to beware of two things: spiking figures which may have been caused by NQTs, supply teachers or weaker members of the team; and no data where you know there should be some. There shouldn't really be any surprises in this analysis, however, rather it should be confirmation of what you already know. But there should also be confirmation, hopefully, of your policies and your philosophies about behaviour in action.

Now, a slight diversion. Think about what you want to achieve in terms of behaviour. We are great believers in the power of positive behaviour strategies so an emphasis on the positive seems to be a natural starting point. Aim for a ratio of ten to one in favour of the positive in all measures – ten positive phone calls home for every negative, ten positive behaviour points for every negative, ten letters of praise for every letter about a student causing concern, ten referrals to you for excellent work for every on-call. This doesn't need to be a pipe dream and, while you may be sat reading this picturing an especially difficult Year 10 girl or a spectacularly naughty boy in Year 3 and thinking, "Yeah, right", there's nothing wrong with aiming high here. Good behaviour in lessons, making a positive contribution, should be normal. Make it your normal. Leaving aside the obvious pre-requisites for good behaviour addressed elsewhere in this book, such as excellent teaching, engaging lessons, a creative, stimulating curriculum, properly-deployed support staff, strong parental involvement and so forth, here are some quick, additional ideas to get you going:

- Letters home. Postcards will do as well, but there's still nothing like receiving a well-written, formal letter on headed note paper in an envelope from your teacher. To save time, write ten or so letters that can be used for a variety of reasons and occasions – excellent work, fantastic contributions, great behaviour on a trip, helpfulness, selflessness, courtesy and kindness – and send them at the end of every half term with each member of your team nominating at least one person from each class. Ensure records are kept of who receives your letters, too, especially so you don't end up sending the same letter to the same pupil twice.
- Star pupil. Every lesson can have a star pupil. Buy some of those cheap, pre-printed pads of paper that say 'Star Pupil' or something

for each member of your team and get people to start dishing them out.

- Stickers. All kids love stickers. Even too-cool-for-school Year 11 boys will say yes to a sticker. Cheap, quick and effective.
- Credit stamps. Great for instantaneous rewards and saves your teachers time, too. Have the pupils keep running totals and have awards and prizes for reaching significant milestones (50, 100, 150…).
- Displays. Ensure everyone keeps their display boards up to date with examples of excellent student work. Additionally, have a display board for a star of the week in each year group with a reason why. Create a rota for your team to share-out responsibility.
- Phone calls. There's nothing better than phoning a parent and telling them their child is ace. Do it on a Friday just before you leave school, too – a great way to end the week.

You'll have your own ideas and there'll be policies and procedures being operated by the school as a whole which you'll need to adopt. But when you begin your monitoring, it will be far more satisfying to see how your positive behaviour strategies are impacting on all areas of work as evidenced in each aspect of your QA: a higher standard of work in books, positive feedback in pupil voice activities, high quality learning in lessons. Yes, consequences for poor behaviour need to be consistently and rigorously enforced – in your role as a middle leader, you should follow *everything* up, being terrier-like in your pursuit of serial offenders or detention non-attenders – but a relentless focus on the positive will bring dividends. Ok, not all pupils will be won over, it won't come totally naturally to all your staff, you know this. It isn't a great leap, though, to see how you can affect real change through the implementation of some of our ideas above, because it's about creating an ethos within your team (more on ethos in Chapter 7), a way of working that they will all need to at least try to buy into. Your role in this is key, selling your team this vision and then monitoring it through your QA.

Chapter 6 – December

Dealing with data

"Everybody gets so much information all day long that they lose their common sense."

– Gertrude Stein

In this chapter, we are going to focus on the wealth of data that is available to a middle leader and guide you through what can often seem a confusing maelstrom of numbers, statistics, groups, sub-groups, graphs, tables, matrices and spreadsheets. Indeed, it may be that you are among those teachers who identify the effective handling of data to be a personal weakness (there is a curious modern tendency for people to claim they "Can't do maths" as though this is acceptable! It isn't. They wouldn't proudly declare the same thing about reading, so why maths? As a middle leader, you will have to "do maths" and exude confidence when handling data – it will be one of your most powerful attributes). But when you place this task alongside the multitude of roles and responsibilities we adopt on a daily basis, many of which require great nuance, sensitivity and skill, the analysis of data is an easily learnt and incredibly valuable tool. It really isn't a big deal to do it well and get it right.

So, look at this list from Eric Hoyle, written in 1969 in his book, 'The Role of the Teacher':

- Representative of society (inculcates moral precepts)
- Judge (gives marks and ratings)
- Resource (possesses knowledge and skill)
- Helper (provides guidance for pupil difficulties)
- Referee (settles disputes amongst pupils)
- Detective (discovers rule-breakers)
- Object of identification (possesses traits which children imitate)
- Ego-supporter (helps pupils to have confidence in themselves)
- Parent surrogate (acts as object of bids for attention from younger children)
- Target for hostilities (acts as object of aggression arising from frustration created by adults)
- Friend and confidante (establishes warm relationship with children and shares confidences)
- Object of affection (meets the psychological needs of children)

Do a lot, don't we? Let's add one more (times have changed a bit, Eric):

- Statistician (monitors the progress of students and intervenes when they are falling behind)

And now, in your role as Middle Leader (and already explored in Chapter 1), let's add another couple while we're on the subject:

- Leader and Manager (leads a team of professionals, manages their work, problems, needs and development)
- Conduit (between the Senior Team and the department, and vice versa)
- Buffer (sheltering the team from the pressures and demands that are put on you)
- Visionary (creates the vision and communicates it clearly)
- Enabler (delegates and distributes leadership, promotes belonging and loyalty)
- Corporate Representative (positively promotes the school)

- Master of Data (sees the bigger picture; monitors, tracks and measures the data)

Maybe 'Master of Data' overstates things a little bit, but why not aim high? Learning about data is *not* beyond a teacher and there should be no embarrassment about asking for help developing this skill if you feel fazed by this aspect of the role. That's what this chapter is here for, after all. In fact, you should *expect* help from your senior team and you should seek it as a priority on beginning your role. Even if you think this aspect of your work is a strength, there's bound to be new stuff particular to this school for you to learn about.

Firstly, let's look at some key principles for use of data in school. If you adhere to these, each of which we feel are equally as important as the other, then you will have a strong foundation upon which to base all your data analysis and the actions you take as a result.

1. Data should be **accurate**

It will be your job to ensure the accuracy of the data generated by you and your team, triangulating between trackers, books and what you see in classrooms. You must be certain of the accuracy of marking and assessment, and therefore have a rigorous system of regular standardisation and moderation of student work. This should go some way to guaranteeing that assessment data provided by teachers is accurate.

2. Data should be **timely**

Schools operate an assessment and reporting calendar so establishing your own routines around the monitoring and analysis of data will be somewhat tied to that schedule – have a copy in front of you when you plan out your tracking activity for the year. This calendar, however, is hopeless if it isn't timely and available to inform decision-making at the relevant moment. Make sure yours is. For example, when Year 9 reports to parents are due, ensure you and your team have bang up-to-date assessment data on the system; matching this to your long-term curriculum planning is also recommended.

3. Data should be **relevant**

There is a recurring grumble among teachers that they are swamped by data, so pre-empt this by being particularly selective about the data *you* provide (to your team, to your students, to parents, to your line manager on the senior team). This data should support a professional judgement in reaching an informed decision. It does not need to distract or muddy the waters. Choose carefully the story you want your data to tell. Your team probably don't need to know every students' Year 6 Writing Paper score even if it's available or all the different component scores from their CATs tests. So don't give it to them. In fact, you should decide as a team what data is relevant and what is required.

4. Data should be **manageable**

Similarly, data should be selected from the full range of potentially available data. Ask yourself, "What is the minimum necessary that meets all requirements?", and stick to that. Think carefully also about the efficiency of data collection; avoid doubling and duplication, it sends everyone mad.

5. Data should be **accessible**

While you are learning about data, remember that your staff also need this knowledge. Again, ask: "Do staff understand the data? Can staff access it at the right time and in an easy-to-use format?" We'll discuss the issue of access in more detail later in this chapter.

6. Data should be **used**

Data must sit within a wider set of school systems, e.g. assessment for learning, curriculum planning, self-evaluation and whole-school planning, so that its implications inform the action you take. It is a terrible waste for teachers to spend so much of their day recording information that is not then handled or manipulated either by them or the leadership teams within the school.

This is your data mantra, six key tenets for handling data that need to be borne in mind as you work your way through this chapter and indeed your first year in charge. And if you are someone who thinks the data-handling element of the job will be a challenge, then use the space at the end of this chapter to create your own Data Glossary, a handy list for easy reference, that you can refer back to again and again.

Tracking

A good place to start when it comes to data is how you will organise your tracking procedures. For each year group, subject or course, we recommend a separate tracker, certainly electronic in basis and one that uses your school's information management system (like SIMS), MS Excel or both. Some schools have decided to invest in extra systems to support the analysis of data such as SISRA, 4Matrix or Insight, all of which provide a wealth of statistics, or they have designed their own innovative data management systems. If your school has chosen to use one of these, you will find it provides a level playing field for the analysis of data within the school's middle leadership team – as long as you receive the proper training – and certainly streamlines this aspect of your role. If they haven't, not to worry as you will soon find your own way of keeping up to date with the key headline figures relevant to you as well as establishing your own procedures for 'drilling down' into the data you are presented with. This section will show you how.

Your trackers are going to be important when it comes to accountability. By this we mean how you can be held to account by your senior team line manager or how you can hold your staff to account for their own performance. Therefore, they need to be created with your data mantra in mind (our six principles from earlier) and they need to be personal to you and your team to reflect your curriculum and course content. You should ensure they are centralised, too. Making full use of the school's information management system works best for data input because you can have multiple users working on one marksheet at once and these systems represent the most up-to-date list of students on roll. For practicality, however, most people choose to export from here to Excel and keep these documents on a shared school drive where everyone can access them. This then enables you to colour code assessments against targets (we recommend red for below target, green for on target and a lovely lilac colour for above – it means that kids who hit their target grade look like they've achieved as you expected them to rather than having an amber warning light hanging over the grade) or filter the information so that you can see performance by: class, set or teacher; gender; ethnicity; prior attainment (low, middle and high attainers); assessment foci or objectives; or any other parameter you choose to set. Additionally, you can then easily access these trackers during team or line management meetings to allow for more informed discussion.

Once you have exported your information from your school's central database, you will need to decide which information to keep in your trackers and share with your team. Export as much as you can and then delete or hide the superfluous details. You'll work out which information is not immediately required when you look at the list of data you can choose from, but it will depend on your role and the context of your school. A good basis to begin with would be the list we first encountered in your results analysis in Chapter 2:

- Gender
- Ethnicity
- EAL
- SEND status
- More Able
- Form/Tutor/Year group
- Free School Meals status
- Pupil Premium
- Prior attainment (KS1, KS2, KS3, KS4, or previous year's end of year result)
- Summer born children (particularly at KS1/2)
- Looked after children
- Target Grade

It should be noted that some of this information will require updating by you on a regular basis, particularly for any school with low stability (i.e. lots of children arriving/leaving). Remember to add an autofilter on your top row so that you can sort the data easily and look for patterns and trends. Once stored on your school's shared drive or VLE, all your staff can begin to access the information contained within and begin to input assessment data as and when you instruct them. It's worth considering that anyone who has access to these trackers should be also instructed not to begin messing about with any of your formatting, adding new students who arrive or deleting those who leave, or choosing to use their own colour coding system (a particularly heinous crime, this one). Furthermore, ensure you always keep your own central copies and consider regular backups. If you really, really think you can't trust your team to do this right, either because the data they enter will be inaccurate or because they just won't do it, use your judgement when deciding on the procedures you want to put in place. The reason we have placed this task in December is so that you have had time to judge their skills and competence. But if you establish the standards and procedures for using these trackers from the outset, you will find them to be a useful, informative and indispensable tool.

Next, consider whether you want the members of your team to also use a standardised electronic markbook for them to be able to monitor homework and assessment completion and results. In terms of accountability, this can be a good idea for ensuring that homework is being set and marked regularly and that assessments are being completed and assessed by your designated dates. There may be some complaints that this is leading to the duplication of data entry, that data entered into a teacher's own class markbook is then being transferred to a faculty or school tracker. On the contrary: data entered in a teacher's class markbook should only serve to *validate* any data that is then entered into a faculty tracker. It is the evidence trail, proof of how individual teachers have arrived at their judgements of a student's current or predicted grade, or the effort they are putting in to class and homework. There may be a tendency for weaker teachers to enter the result of a student's latest test rather than taking a holistic approach to making a judgement. You will need to clamp down on this quickly otherwise you will end up with wildly fluctuating monitoring data, completely useless to you and your school. Additionally, a class markbook that is religiously completed, kept up-to-date and *used* (data tenet number 6!) by a teacher is an excellent tool for using when reporting to parents, either in a written report sent home to parents or for discussion during parents evening (N.B. if a class markbook is used during parents evening, then teachers should be wary of accidentally revealing any sensitive information about other students when discussing another child's performance; insist on this information being 'hidden' on the tracker so that this does not occur. Similarly, we have found displaying and discussing your class markbook to the students it concerns during lessons can be an extremely powerful, motivational tool – but you have to ensure it is the 'lite' version of your markbook, minus anything that should not be revealed e.g. SEND status).

Let's finish this section with a couple of activities that focus on the issue of practicality. We think a department calendar that you match to the school's assessment and reporting calendar is a useful tool for helping your staff map out where and when they will be required to input, handle and measure data about the students they teach. Use the grid below to fill in the key dates and activities you will undertake in the year ahead:

Date / Term / Half Term	*Year Group*	*School Reporting or Assessment Activity*	*Department / Faculty Data Activity*
		e.g. report to parents, parents evening, monitoring cycle	e.g. tracker input, SLT line management meeting
Sept.			
Oct.			
Nov.			
Dec.			
Jan.			
Feb.			

Date / Term / Half Term	*Year Group*	*School Reporting or Assessment Activity*	*Department / Faculty Data Activity*
		e.g. report to parents, parents evening, monitoring cycle	e.g. tracker input, SLT line management meeting
Mar.			
Apr.			
May.			
Jun.			
Jul.			
Aug.			

Academic Progress Checks

As we said in Chapter 2, it is vital that you pre-plan the main agenda items for your department meetings for the whole of the academic year ahead. Within those plans should be a number of meetings left for what we have termed Academic Progress Checks. These APCs will be a chance to fully review and audit a whole year group. They can take any form you like – indeed, we would positively encourage you and your team to be creative and experimental with the format and content – but should certainly try to cover some or all of the following:

- Data analysis – this could be analysis of data done in advance of the meeting and shared with others or, perhaps more powerfully, this could be data analysis carried out within the meetings. Look for trends and patterns by searching out underperformance within teaching groups or groups of students (use your tracker groupings from earlier in this chapter). Use your filters to look for where there are discrepancies between the achievement of, say, boys and girls in Year 4 or how White British students fare against target grade in Year 10 Spanish or how Pupil Premium students compare to non-Pupil Premium students in Year 6…and then go further. Look at who teaches the under-performers, whether behaviour is preventing progress being made, if a class is being taught by a non-specialist or long-term supply teacher, if a class is split between two or more members of staff…and so on. You will have the benefit of having your whole team in attendance so ask them what they think – they will have a view and a perspective that you may not, although this is not the arena for airing excuses or grievances. Keep the meeting positive. Whatever you find out needs to be acted upon – ensure there are actions to be taken because of the findings of the APC. This might mean intervention by the class teacher or intervention by yourself. Make sure you plan, track and measure any intervention you determine necessary.
- Curriculum review – an audit of the curriculum and/or course content is also a good idea. Look at what you currently teach – are there any gaps? Is it fit for purpose? Does it meet the requirements of the current National Curriculum? Do students enjoy the work?

Does anyone in your team have any fresh ideas? Again, come away from the APC with some decisions about curriculum, a time-scale for change (if any) and an idea about who will take responsibility for engineering these improvements.

- Student voice – in advance of the APC, survey the students in that year group to discover their views. Ask them about: the curriculum; their experience in the classroom; the range of enrichment available; their perceptions of the progress they are making; their feelings towards your marking and assessment policies and anything else that you would like to find out from students in that year group.

If you work in the primary school sector, you may already be used to this kind of procedure, obviously on a much smaller scale as, even in larger schools, departments are smaller than in secondary schools. The focus will usually be given to Literacy, Numeracy and Science across all year groups since it is in these subjects that primary schools are judged on their effectiveness via external testing, and not a single year group as in secondary. There will, inevitably, be heavy SLT involvement in these meetings, too. If you're in charge of a non-core subject, you might even find that there is no time available to you to lead on an APC in your area, but you will have to feedback to your SLT on your individual tracking and assessment, so these meetings could follow the format that we're suggesting. If you are a subject coordinator or SLT member with responsibility for a key area, be all-encompassing and don't just stick to the data analysis – APCs need to be seen as opportunities to audit and review all aspects of student progress and achievement. Have lots to say, but ask lots of open questions, too – who are the most vulnerable students, do we do enough formal assessment, are pupils excited by our (insert subject) lessons? The views of your team or your colleagues on your focus area will undoubtedly produce some surprises and provide you with that depth of understanding you're looking for.

Similarly, you may find that curriculum review is already a fully embedded and separate process within your school. Primaries, like secondaries, have had to weather a near constant storm of changes – to the National Curriculum, to assessment procedure and to the rising expectations of achievement within primary schools – so it's bound to be. However, we recommend your own review process, led by you and focused on your area, is initiated straight away. Think about posing the following to your team:

- What needs to change (if anything)?
- What gaps have we got?
- Have you got any ideas for new schemes?
- How are we going to monitor their implementation?
- Do staff need any professional development in order to introduce a new initiative?

All of your APCs need to finish with a "What next?", an action plan that outlines all of your changes, the time scales you are working to, resources you require and how you will review their success.

If you work in the secondary school sector, first of all distribute the responsibility for leading these meetings among your team, but ensure you take the lead on the first one to show what you expect to be covered. We recommend six meetings in the year be designated as APCs (hopefully your school is generous with department meeting time – one every four weeks or so is ideal) – two for Year 11 and one each for Years 7-10. Begin with Year 11, finish with Year 10 (so that your first APC the following year leads on directly from your last) and intersperse the other year groups in and amongst, possibly positioning your remaining Year 11 APC in the run-up to their final exams.

Just a note for Heads of English or Maths: if this is you, why not consider holding joint departmental APCs, especially for GCSE? We have found this to be a very valuable and informative experience leading to many positive changes in areas like behaviour management, setting and intervention planning. Staff see their students in a different light ("She's going to get an A in English!") and are able to see how it is their joint responsibility to help the school maximise the proportion of students achieving both English and Maths. Back in the classroom, teachers will be able to hold more informed discussions with students about their performance in both subjects while, as a middle leader, you will be able to assemble an intervention cohort made up of students forecast to miss the mark in your subject.

You might be tempted to make the content of your APCs pure data analysis where staff are expected to delve into the departmental trackers to look for groups of underperforming students. What's missing here, but what could easily be added, is a review of the curriculum and the inclusion of a survey of pupil opinion – after all, none of us will have ever met a single child not desperate to share what he/she thinks! – plus anything else you think would generate fresh insight into the year group in focus.

Intervention

As a consequence of your meticulous tracking and the results of your APCs, you will next need to think about an intervention strategy. Here, intervention is defined as any activities or undertakings you deem necessary over and above your normal working practices to help pupils perform as expected, behave as expected or attend as expected. In class, you will fully expect your teachers to make telling and effective interventions already: when a pupil doesn't quite get a concept so the teacher spends time on a one-to-one basis explaining in more detail; when, during pair work, two pupils fail to work effectively together and have (loud and emotional) differences of opinion requiring the teacher to mediate or when a group of students need close support and a teaching assistant is directed to work with them. Intervening in a timely manner like this happens on a daily basis and is driven, not necessarily by data, but by the instant needs of the students in the class, particularly for stronger teachers.

In your role as a leader, however, your interventions do not only need to be driven by the data, they must also be carefully monitored and their impact closely measured using a range of data you collect. You need to maintain a careful balance of overview mixed with a keen eye for the fine detail; you need the headline figures, but you also need the individual faces behind those numbers. (In fact, it's a really good idea to do just that – print off the photos of students who are causing concern or falling behind and use them to familiarise yourself with your key cohorts. We have certainly seen some clever examples of display boards being used to create intervention walls where both staff and pupils can see the state of play, and can also see the effect their efforts have on progress and achievement as pupils make improvements – to grades, to attendance, to behaviour and so on.) It will also be necessary to establish your own intervention tracking systems, subsidiaries to your year group trackers, so that you can closely monitor and assess the impact of your interventions. Quite often, intervention activities have a cost attached to them and, therefore, an added layer of accountability – someone somewhere will want to know that it was money well spent. The insistence on accountability matched with an open-minded approach to creative intervention will have real, measurable results. You must ensure you adopt a similar approach.

Intervention ideas

Being as creative as you possibly can with your intervention ideas is pretty essential if you are to generate enthusiasm and, ultimately, results. We've put together a list of ideas for intervention here, but would suggest each one needs your own special spin putting on it if it is to work effectively in your school setting.

- After-school boosters: these are the first thing anyone thinks of when someone brings up intervention, and their inclusion on this list, therefore, at first appears to fly in the face of our missive on the need for creativity. However, done right, after-school boosters can become powerful tools for raising attainment. Plan the content carefully so that it complements and extends classwork rather than simply repeating what students have already covered. Group your students by target grade/tier of entry/area of need so that the content is always appropriate and relevant with question-level analysis. Invite particular students to particular sessions based on need. Log attendance carefully, too, and ensure that you create a praise and rewards system for regular, positive attendance (as in, students don't just turn up, they turn up and contribute positively). A good, whole-school one we've seen in a Secondary School was 'Passport to the Prom' where Year 11 students collected stamps for attending booster classes and then cashed-in their completed card for a discounted prom ticket. Or why not order in pizza or buy a tray of doughnuts as a reward for work well done? Pens, pencils and all sorts of other exam equipment make for good prizes, too, and remember our belief in the power of the sticker!

- If you are a Head of secondary English or Maths, you could create an intervention form group made up of target Year 11 students for you to take, potentially increasing curriculum contact time by up to 90 minutes a week. This could also work for Year 6 students as they work towards their SATs. Fix the number of weeks you will take them for (say, six) and then change the groups to reflect the progress students are making, bringing in others who have been identified through your data analysis or APCs as falling behind. A good group size would probably be about 15. If that's going a bit too far for your school, then request responsibility for a form group that is removed from you so that you can carry out tutor time intervention, 20 minutes(ish) daily sessions on focused tasks eg a Year 8 SPaG group, a Year 10 maths group on vectors. Again, the request to give up being a tutor may be balked at, but set out your careful plans, your outcomes and your reasoning and you will have a good chance. Such changes require a flexibility among your SLT for them to come to full fruition. You could also rope in a TA or two to help out, sharing the responsibility for the group or breaking off a small group of students for him/her to focus on.
- A few years ago, someone at Ofsted decided Learning Outside the Classroom was a thing now so we should all do it… as if we hadn't been! Visits and excursions are a great way to get creative with intervention and should be seen as opportunities to break out of the often rigid nature of the school day. Take students to work in a museum or art gallery or an away day in a hotel or conference centre. The change of environment to somewhere stimulating, exciting and patently different can reinvigorate learners. Take lots of photos, too, and make a big display on your return to school so that the experience is always visible and raises the profile of your work. And don't be frightened of the paperwork. A decent school will support you in completing risk assessments and guide you on rules and responsibilities. If your school has a minibus, ask to be put in for the test so you can make full use of it with your many planned outings.
- Visiting speakers and experts, such as GCSE examiners, poets, writers, scientists, MPs or sports people, are great for reinforcing

the messages and teaching received by students on a day-to-day basis while also extending and enriching their understanding of whatever topic they come to discuss.

- Breakfast clubs – study time for students run by teachers. Invite parents, too, for a crumpet, a cup of tea and the opportunity to sit with their child and their child's teacher reading for pleasure, revising key topics or learning revision skills that they can use at home.
- You may be in a department or a school where you have overstaffing. More likely, you won't be, but we have come across these situations in the past and the most effective use of this is to double up teachers to focus on key groups of students across the timetable. For example, you could look at Year 9 high ability students and use your double staffing to target those students who will be aiming for the highest grades at GCSE. Once again, finance will be an issue here and double staffing will be the most expensive thing you could ever do in terms of intervention, and therefore the level of accountability will be very high. There will be a high level of scrutiny, too. You will have to make clear to your team what the stakes are and that you will expect results. But it's obvious that this is preferable to seeing your overstaffing being used to staff seclusion or be asked to teach subjects outside of their specialism.
- A summer school and/or Easter class are very popular among students who, amazingly, are often not prepared to spend their holidays lounging around watching Spongebob Squarepants (or whatever it is the kids watch these days!) and are very eager to continue and extend their school work during this time. In a similar vein to the booster classes, you should aim to make these distinctly different to your daily curriculum offer. Indeed, a good idea would be to team up with a couple of other middle leaders in your school to offer a mini-timetable of events and activities, possibly even thematically linked – English/Literacy, music, science and PE, for example, deliver a week of activities on climate change. Think about the impact again and how you measure it, but maybe don't think in terms of grades or scores – the increase in the level of engagement among a group of students or an improvement in their attitude towards school and learning are also

perfectly viable and entirely admirable performance indicators. Survey your students afterwards, take photos, make your display, follow them up with assemblies to different year groups...anything to raise the profile of their work and your endeavours so that the next one is even better.

- Setting up a mentoring programme, if your school doesn't already have one, can also have a powerful effect on the performance of particularly disengaged students, but there are a couple of cardinal rules to follow if you are to get it right. First, choosing your students is critical – you have to explain to them very clearly the expectations you have and you have to be sure yourself about the success criteria for each student, which should certainly be different (remember that personalisation). What is more, it is crucial to have the full support of the staff you are using. It's possibly even a good idea to ask for volunteers to become mentors rather than making it mandatory. Look beyond school, too, to local businesses or religious and community leaders. You then need to match the right member of staff with student; for example, look at where you have a strong male member of staff who could mentor a young lad who needs that kind of role model. Engage with parents, too, and invite them in to launch your scheme, giving them a chance to meet their child's mentor face to face. Insist on regular meetings between mentor and mentee, and also ask that your mentor establish good routines with regards to home contact to keep parents up to speed. Lastly, design a method of monitoring your mentoring programme to keep track of attendance and cross-reference with your performance trackers to measure the impact on attainment.
- An even more powerful mentoring programme can be when you use peer mentoring. You could have Year 6 students mentor Year 3 students as they transition to Junior school or Year 10 high ability English students work with Year 7 disengaged readers. This sort of scheme needs very careful monitoring, however, and a real investment in the training of your mentors.
- There is a huge market for revision materials so why not guide your students to the most appropriate and useful ones and give

them £10 towards revision guides while you're at it?

- The most sensible route with intervention may be to invest in something that, in the long term, leads to the eradication of intervention altogether. Endless research (see the work of John Hattie for full verification of this) says that learning and teaching strategies focused on AfL and the quality of feedback students receive are the most effective strategies for improving student performance. Make this a priority for your team, giving them access to the training they need, showing them best practice and ensuring they have the time to properly fulfil all you're asking them to do. There are also real opportunities to get creative here, too, so think of ways to make marking fun!

James says...

Don't think of any of these intervention ideas as necessarily needing to be exclusive to 'groups' of students. My most effective use of catch-up premium money, £500 per Year 7 student who entered the school below Level 4 in Reading and/or Maths, was to take the entire year group on a succession of trips to 'The Children's Bookshop' in Lindley, Huddersfield and give them £15 each to spend on anything they liked. The aim of the funding was to improve standards of literacy in students, surely a nationwide whole-school target, but it would have been in turn both mad and cruel to have only taken those who qualified for the funding. I wanted to engender a love of reading in ALL students, take them somewhere special and give them the opportunity to own books of their choosing. The buzz among students these trips created was fantastic and I would unreservedly recommend any school organising similar trips.

Considering the views of other people

When you embark on this aspect of your role, it may come as a surprise to you to find that not everyone is totally enamoured with the idea of intervention. In the next activity, you will get the chance to consider the views of five separate groups of people who may hold negative views about your plans. Think carefully about their perceptions of intervention and then consider how you would go about countering any negative views. Pre-empting any concept of negativity towards your activities is the first step to establishing an ethos of intervention.

How do these groups of people often perceive intervention? In and around each box, putting yourself in their shoes, write as many ideas that you have about their perceptions of intervention, with a focus on the negative.

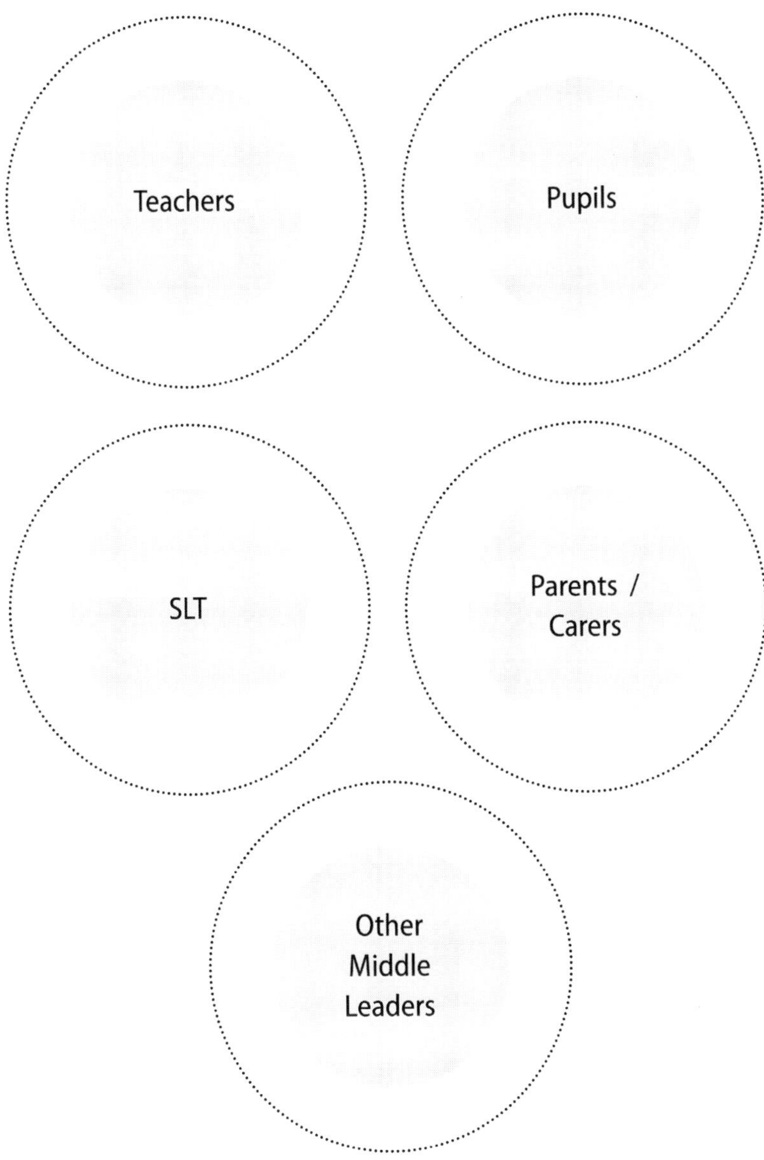

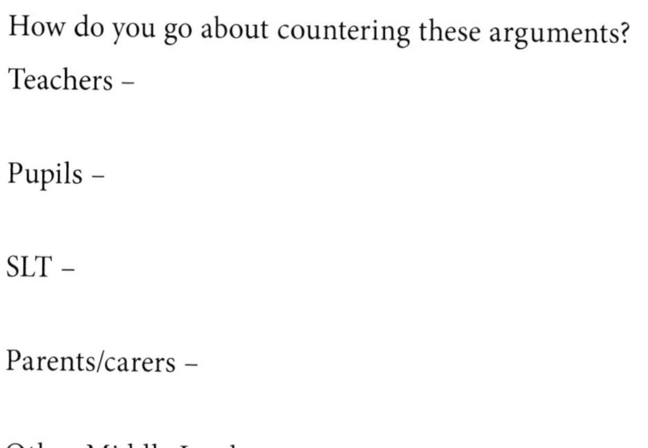

How do you go about countering these arguments?

Teachers –

Pupils –

SLT –

Parents/carers –

Other Middle Leaders –

There will of course be a great deal of positivity from each of the groups above about action you take to intervene with students. However, some of the negative things you may have considered in that last activity are worth just going over now as it will only be once you have surmounted any negativity that you can begin to have real impact in any intervention activities you organise.

Firstly, teachers within your department, area or faculty have to be on board, especially if you are asking them to undertake commitments beyond their allotted timetable. After school boosters, pre-exam boosters, a mentoring scheme – all can only have the desired effect if the teachers delivering them are willing to put in the hours. You have to lead from the front on this – don't expect them to do things you're not also prepared to do. You may be lucky to have a team who gladly go the extra mile. You may have staff so recalcitrant that they make you wonder if they even like children. Either way, intervention needs to be seen as a team effort, a fully integrated part of your working practices and not a back-end emergency add-on. Talk about it in these terms from September in any forum or arena you can so that, certainly in a school where the idea is alien, you can begin to normalise intervention. Any intervention activities instigated by you should, therefore, be ready to go after Christmas (or earlier if you have identified a more pressing need in your August results analysis – see Chapter 2). Ultimately, the ideal would be to eliminate intervention by eradicating the need for it altogether. We'll talk about how you might begin to do this a little later.

In our experience, one of the most difficult groups to engage in intervention from the five above is pupils, but this depends on your school's context. Quite often, their reluctance is justifiable; maybe they need to repeat work because of previous inadequate or totally absent teaching and they feel this is a punishment; maybe they've been instructed to attend Science boosters every Thursday after school, but that's when netball practice is; maybe this is their third primary school in as many years and they have struggled to settle in or maybe they are so in demand from all their teachers that they can't prioritise or organise...and so give up. Consider these factors when you are forming your plans and, wherever possible, personalise your intervention to take individual situations into account. You may need to market what you are offering, too, clearly outlining the ultimate benefits to taking part while also rewarding and acknowledging the efforts of pupils who take full advantage of your interventions: think about a rewards scheme and build in the cost to any original bids for money you may make; write effusive letters home to parents or have rewards postcards printed and sent to those who take part. Think carefully about how you market your initiatives: showcase your work in the school magazine; make a short, funny video for the school website or ask previous and successful Year 11 students to return and talk about their experiences in assembly. Finally, help them to attend or join in by being flexible with your scheduling and timing.

When it comes to engaging the support of a Senior Leadership Team, this (in theory) should be no problem. After all, why wouldn't the school's management want you to maximise student learning experience? Well, it could be the cost implications, in which case you have to be pretty certain your efforts and ideas will pay off – prudence is not just a word being bandied around by the Chancellor of the Exchequer, it should be your watchword too, if you want to garner goodwill from your SLT and maintain it. Don't be frightened to ask for the cash – just make sure you've done your homework. An evidence-based bid for funding is not only more likely to be approved, but will also likely be more successful.

Additionally, the considerations your SLT will give to the impact of your intervention on the headline figures will be a contributing factor in granting you funding. At Secondary schools, they may even prioritise core or EBacc subjects, and may readjust where their priorities lie as successive governmental changes impact upon the way your school will be judged and measured. If your subject is outside of this list, you may have to be much more creative with your ideas for engaging students in intervention activities as they find themselves making choices based on which subjects have more 'value' to them or which are 'needed' more. There are only so many hours in a week and your SLT may deem your allotted curriculum time sufficient for getting the grades they're expected (and who could blame them?). Finally, SLT may enforce their own agenda on your intervention in terms of *who* they want you to intervene with; the groups of students who are causing particular concern may be imposed to address the needs of the school. If you are a pastoral leader, this could be more to do with improving behaviour, attendance and punctuality, and reducing the number of exclusions.

Engaging the support of parents in all aspects of your work is naturally very, very important, but especially when it comes to intervention. The concerns of your students discussed above may be echoed by their parents. The first stage is to ensure you keep them informed – write letters that require a tear-off reply slip is returned or invite them in to launch your plans with a professional looking presentation or text/email them details of how their child is involved...but don't overdo it or they could find themselves bombarded with school communications. Coordinate any parental contact with other middle leaders to avoid duplication or clashes. Once more, you should think about marketing your plans to parents, possibly using booklets or flyers that you hand out at parents evening, with a focus on challenging any preconceptions they may have about their child being involved in activities they may view as 'remedial', a stigmatised word synonymous with those unruly kids in Willy Russell's play, 'Our Day Out'. When intervention is working, word gets around – in such situations, we have certainly found parents phoning up to request their child's involvement and, while they may be outside your targeted group of students, the goodwill generated with parents and pupils in acceding to these requests is priceless. Remember, the aim of your intervention is to make it as personalised as possible so find a way to fulfil any requests to join an intervention cohort.

The coordination of intervention plans with the rest of the middle leadership team is paramount. Indeed, it is quite likely that a member of SLT is tasked with coordinating the intervention offer to all students, a big job by anyone's standards, particularly in secondary schools. There may even be an agreement brokered between middle leaders as to which days each faculty or department can use for intervention and at which points in the year; as a team of middle leaders, you should be strategically planning when in the academic year different groups of students need to be given priority. Calendar as much as you can and stick to it. Any deviation on your part won't go down well and unnecessarily standing on the toes of middle leaders, your natural allies, is a no-no. In primary schools, teachers keep the same children all day everyday so will have much more ownership and control over their intervention planning. They will probably have more access to support staff, too, and access to a much greater amount of money since funding is, quite rightly, considered best allocated to the earlier stages of children's schooling. There is less of a logistical issue with intervention planning – staff are all working towards the same goals and are not in competition with other departments for students

An Intervention Cycle

We have devised a cycle of intervention to allow you to uniformly structure the way you go about your intervention work. Its five stages should be considered each as important as the others if your intervention work is to be designed and delivered effectively. Start at 'Identification of need' and work your way around...

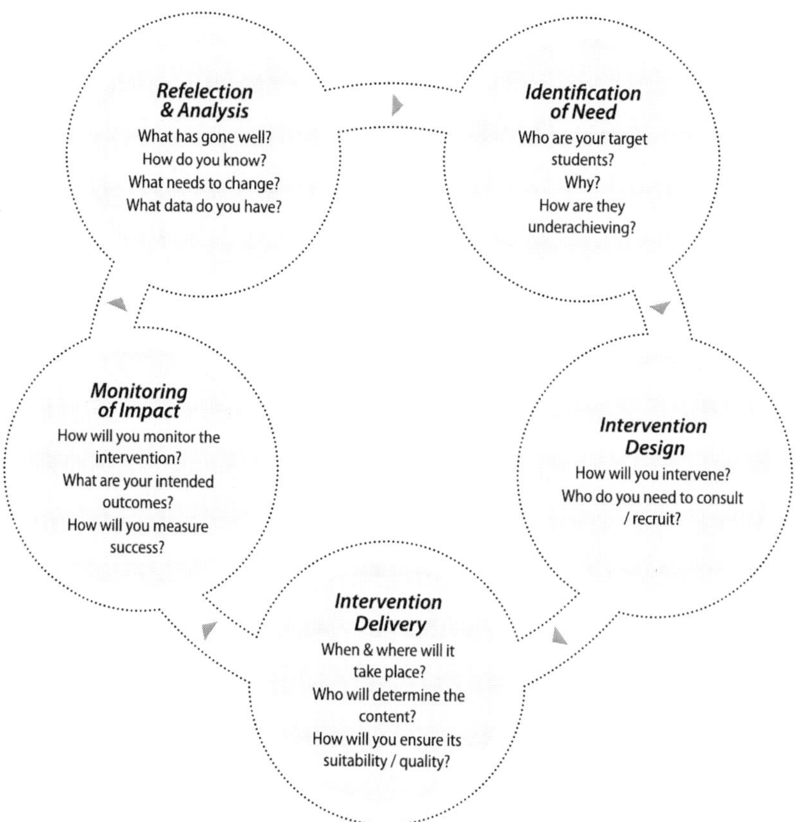

1. Identification of need

Although this feels like the most natural place to start, and indeed the place at which we just told you to start in the last paragraph, there may actually be the need to carry out some reflection on, and analysis of, any previous intervention work that has taken place in this department, subject or area in the past. Consult with those who delivered it as well as the students who experienced it. Work closely with your team and ask them what they thought worked well and, crucially, how they know; their views will have to be borne out by the data, ultimately. If you can, find out the names of students who received any intervention before your arrival/promotion and track their progress. How exactly did these students perform as a result of this intervention? Was this above or below expectations? Can this performance be directly attributed to this work, or even blamed on it if it was deemed a failure?

Once you have ascertained these details, then you should begin to identify who your target students are from your current cohorts and why. How, specifically, are they underperforming? Examine your trackers closely, but also talk to their teachers to gather details about attitude, personality and personal history, all vital indicators of potentially successful intervention (of course, the focus of your intervention may actually be addressing a student's attitude, personality or personal history, as much barriers to learning as a lack of knowledge or skills in a subject). Prioritise your intervention work, too. It could be that the most pressing need for intervention is in Year 6 if you are a primary teacher or Year 11 if you are a subject or pastoral leader in a secondary school, both high pressure year groups that may need your immediate attention. If this is where you have to start, then fine, but keep one eye on other cohorts of students and don't wait for the post-exam period in July to start thinking about your strategies for them. It will already be too late. Distribute the leadership for this intervention work to other members of your team as necessary, but brief them on the process of the intervention cycle so that their planning and preparation is as rigorous as your own.

2. Intervention design

This is where you need to get creative. Refer back to the extensive list we have collated for you earlier in this chapter by all means, but also bear in mind the context of your own school, students and staff when choosing which strategies will be most appropriate and effective. Don't just do something because "That's the way we always do it here" or even because "That's the way I did it in my old school". Think about who you involve, too. This is your opportunity to initiate something powerful and original, and a chance for you to stamp your identity and ideas on the school.

3. Intervention delivery

Consider the where and the when and the how at this point. Thinking about the logistics of your work early on is critical here – it would be depressing to reach a point where you are about to begin an initiative only to find that the ICT facilities you were relying on are unavailable or that the minibus is in for its MOT, all your blue-sky, green-hat thinking undone by the mundane or the trivial in one stroke. Remember when you were an NQT and everyone told you to make friends with the caretaker and the lady who does the photocopying? Think about who you need to make friends with for this task: who can send out a load of letters for you and collect in the replies; who has control of booking rooms, ICT equipment or making sure that the minibus is full of diesel and who might need to give permission for any of this to go ahead? Write a list and tick them off as you get to know them.

Next, consider who will physically deliver your chosen activities. Will they be fully entrusted with determining the content and focus or will you need to take a more hands-on approach? Do they have the right training, qualifications and credentials? If not, how will you help them to address this shortfall? How will you ensure the content's suitability and quality?

4. Monitoring of impact

From the outset, you will need to be clear with all involved what your outcomes are for this intervention work. How will you be measuring its success and at what points in the process will you be checking that the work is having an impact? Build in your own quality assurance procedures for your intervention work, maybe using learning walks, if appropriate, to establish that all is well, and drafting in your SLT line manager to help if you're engaged elsewhere at the time. Use student voice strategies to gather their views on the activity, through questionnaires, interviews or a suggestion box. Be clear on the data, too – this is where all your work on how to handle the figures pays off.

5. Reflection and analysis

This is your chance to pause and reflect upon the work you've carried out, and to determine what is working and what clearly isn't. There's no point plodding on with an initiative if all involved are miserable and forlorn or you simply aren't seeing the results. It's also the point where you need to be most confident at handling the data available to you.

Gather your facts and figures and then physically present your findings – even if this is to yourself – in a Powerpoint so that you have a clear record of student progress and achievement as a result of your intervention. Keep it simple, stick to around five slides only, but ensure you highlight what your targets were, your attendance figures, who were your success stories, who weren't (and why) and an overall judgement. Then think, what needs to happen next? Are these students done? Do you need to move on to a new cohort or are some still in need of further intervention? And, if so, do you need to do something completely different, in which case you return to the 'Identification of need' and the cycle begins again.

In this next task, we would like you to practise designing intervention plans for a range of different scenarios. Choose the one most appropriate to your own role or school context and use the Intervention Cycle to assist you in planning the steps you would take:

1. You are a Secondary Head of English and have identified 25 Year 7 students who are weak readers, disengaged with books and cannot see the importance of having strong literacy skills. How would you intervene to improve their attitude towards reading and their literacy skills?

2. You are a Primary Coordinator of Maths and work in a school where literacy intervention has been prioritised for a number of years. You would like numeracy intervention to have a similarly high profile. How would you go about making sure this happens?

3. As the Head of Year 8, you have 15 boys who are disengaged, have poor behaviour records and poor attendance. How would you intervene to re-engage these students?

4. You are a Year 6 teacher and have an unusually small number of girls in your class (8 girls to 22 boisterous boys), and all are high ability. How would you go about ensuring you get the best out of these bright girls?

5. You are a Secondary Head of Science and have identified a group of high ability Year 9 girls who are below target in Science, but on or above target in English and Maths. How would you bridge the gap between their attainment in Science with that of English and Maths?

6. You are a Primary Assistant Head with 2 students in Year 4 who have increasingly demanding behaviour issues and appear to be spending an awful lot of time withdrawn from classes to work with a teaching assistant. How would you begin to re-engage them in mainstream teaching?

Choose your scenario, or one of your own if none of them apply, and then use the simplified version of our Intervention Cycle below and surround it with your ideas for each stage.

Scenario No.: _________

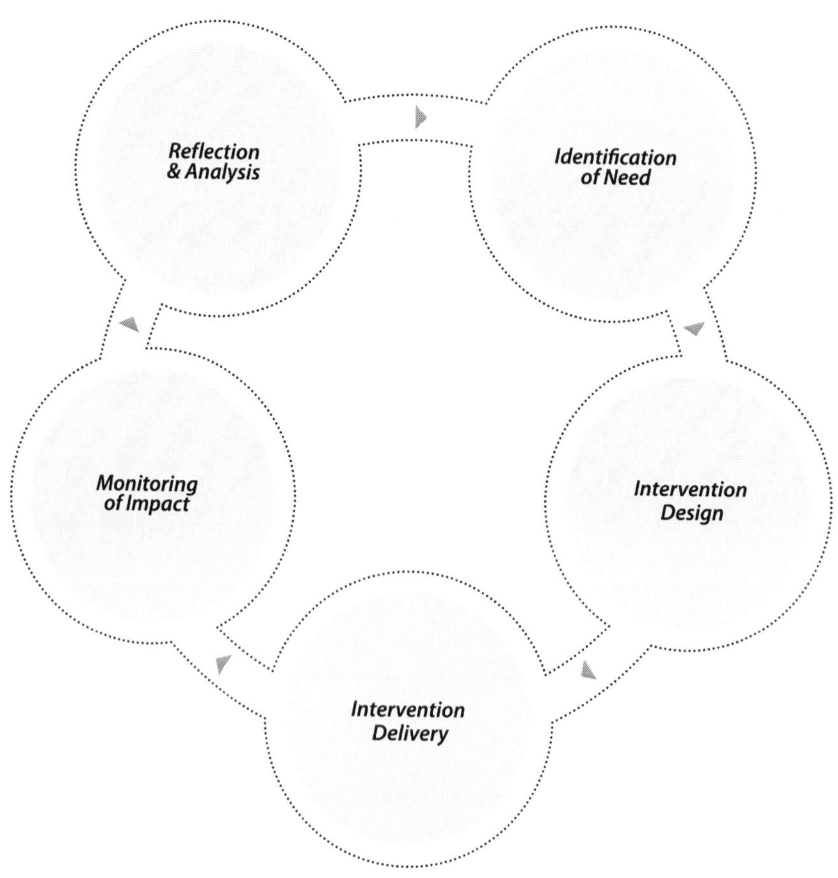

Ethos of intervention

Establishing the right conditions for intervention is fundamental if your work in this area is to be a success. For more on creating a powerful ethos in general, see the next chapter. As a prelude to that, let's think of the behaviours and characteristics you would like to engender in your team, your pupils and your school to make intervention a success.

A common complaint about intervention that comes from some quarters is that it's seen as last-minute, that its use is inevitable, that it becomes so expected that it devalues the work that is actually being completed in curriculum time. Some may consider creating an ethos of intervention is in itself counter-productive, that you are essentially saying to pupils, "You haven't tried your hardest, you didn't plan your time well, you've messed about for a year – not to worry, it'll be us picking up the pieces in the end."

We don't hold much truck with these views. They ignore that there are real, young people's life chances hanging in the balance. Of course you have to pick up the pieces! If you discover that this sort of thing is being parroted by members of your team, it would seem to indicate a more deep-rooted problem, one that suggests they maybe don't support the ethos of the school. Students who have fallen behind or are in need of crucial extra knowledge or skills, for whatever reason, whether their fault or not, must be given every opportunity to succeed or make right in the end and not left to fail. That success, or at the very least vindication of their efforts, will look and feel different for every student, reflecting their own level of ability or personal story, but it will be hard-earned and appreciated by all those groups whose views you considered earlier. And while we're in this area, this idea that teachers are cheating on a massive scale to help their students achieve grades far above their abilities is insulting and absurd – *maybe* you will come across some instance of malpractice among your staff, but the accusation that this is widespread is plain daft. Finally, we have given you enough of a variety of intervention ideas, we believe, to counter any grumblings about work/life balance as well, but your approach must bear this in mind (as if you wouldn't – you want a life, too!).

If you have arrived at a school where intervention is viewed negatively or perceived as extra work for staff and students, you will have to challenge these perceptions head on, certainly by considering ways in which you can be creative with your intervention, but mainly by thinking about these issues early enough to do something about them. Rewind to the August chapter where you were thinking about your vision for the department; how did you build in to your plan ideas about creating a team, about communicating your values and about maximising the potential of the students? You will need to rely on these now.

To begin building an ethos of intervention, you could ask yourself some of the following questions:

- What do we want to achieve in the short term?
- What will this short term success look like? Put some numbers on this.
- What about over a longer period?
- In the long term, what behaviours and beliefs are we aiming to instil in our school community – the value of reading for pleasure, the importance of breakfast, the significance of full attendance?
- Who do I need to bring on board?
- Who might I need to persuade to my way of thinking or recruit to realise my plans?

Ultimately, all your plans and schemes have to feed in to the completion of a much bigger picture. You're intervening to plug gaps, but your work becomes increasingly futile if those gaps repeat year on year, and even more futile if those gaps continue to increase in size. People talk about thinking strategically, acting strategically – so this is it, right here. You must have a strategy for eradicating the issue on which you find yourself intervening; this has to be the eventual aim of any intervention activities you undertake. In doing so, you will inevitably reveal additional avenues to explore, additional gaps you need to plug. Not to worry, these will become increasingly smaller and increasingly less challenging.

Take the example of reading for pleasure from above. Say you're responsible for whole school literacy and succeed in fostering a love of books in your school community through a range of intervention activities: you've got parents reading with their children at breakfast in the canteen; your librarian organises monthly events that cause a sensation in the school; all staff talk about the books they're reading daily; even Michael Morpurgo came and did a reading in assembly… so what next? Well, you have another year group coming up so you'll have to bring them up to speed, but that's ok because your systems are in place, your staff have been trained and you've got a school full of students who want to share their love of reading. However, your data analysis identifies a group of high flying girls in this cohort who need stretching, who need challenge – and there's your new gap. Smaller, achievable, a short term project for someone in the school to get their teeth into, with clear outcomes, and that contributes further to that bigger picture, that vision of yours.

We don't think this is a fantastical scenario. If you have decided that you need an intervention strategy, then you also need to decide that there is a definite endgame, one that resolves to intervene early and intervene effectively, moving to eradicate last-minute, sticking-plaster intervention. This is a long term aim, obviously. Upon arrival in your new school, you know you'll have to get in there and address your most pressing needs. More importantly, though, is getting down to formulating your vision and your ethos.

Your Data Glossary

Here you can note down some of the key terms you encounter again and again, and add your own notes to explain their meaning and the contexts in which you find them.

Term:	*Meaning*

Term:	*Meaning*

Chapter 7 – January

Culture and Ethos

> *"Don't let your special character and values, the secret that you know and no one else does, the truth – don't let that get swallowed up by the great chewing complacency."*
> – Aesop

In Chapter 7, we explore the importance of ethos in your department and examine different methods of developing and embedding a strong and positive ethos within your team.

January can be a tough month and the post-Christmas clichés of desolate, dark days, of wretched battles with vile weather and the seeming eternity that exists between now and the next time you will see actual rays of sunshine is your reality. However, as a midway point in the year, this is an excellent time to reflect on how your team is functioning. It's a good time to stand back and look at everything that you do (and the ways in which you do it all) from an objective viewpoint. To assist you in objectivity, you can enlist the help of another middle leader – ask for their views on your department and offer the same in return.

We think a team's reputation can be quite closely linked to its ethos. Have you come across the team who always seat themselves in the same place (as though they actually own that area) in the staff room? It's the team that NEVER supports you by allowing a student to miss their detention to finish a group rehearsal. The team that teach with their doors closed and scowl if you trespass into their teaching area. Perhaps the same team are renowned for failing to actively participate in staff meetings/discussions. It could be that team is well known for writing very short reports and famed for having never organised an enrichment activity. You don't want to be that team or one with a similar reputation or ethos.

There are other teams, and you'll recognise the kind: the team that is communicative and engages with staff across the organisation. Visitors are always welcome on their corridor (which incidentally has stunning displays) and their classroom doors are always open. The team are frequently in the limelight because of events and competitions they have held and trips they have run. Senior leaders praise this team publicly for successes, sometimes relating to progress and achievement, but often for things like engaging the community, making links with businesses or managing to wangle a visit from a sporting hero. These are the characteristics you should be aiming for.

We have dealt with the nitty-gritty of data and worked on the teaching and learning that is the core of your role, probably the reason we are all here. Culture and ethos are somewhat more ephemeral than data and intervention and can be harder to define than outstanding teaching, but they underpin the work that we do.

Unlike leadership (with which culture and ethos are inextricably linked), the skills are harder to define, learn and practise. What we aim to do in this chapter is to break down the concept of culture and ethos into tangible and manageable pieces that you can work with. You will decide what great culture and ethos do/would look like in your department/role and plan ways of developing and embedding a successful ethos.

So what do we mean by culture and ethos? We are talking about the fundamental values that are central to the work of your organisation and we are talking about its characteristics, almost as if your school/organisation is a living being, the personality of the place. An ethos often supports the vision of an organisation. The characteristics and features, the values and behaviours are all present to support the movement of the organisation on its journey towards its vision. We like the idea of character though and believe that you can work to develop your team/department/subject area so that it has a unique character – it becomes the person everyone wants to hang out with.

When you first visited your school, you got a feel for it. If you have visited – or worked at – a few schools, then you will be able to describe the feel, the climate or the vibe of the place. You will get a sense of a school's values by walking around and interacting with students and staff. We can get a sense of the ethos of an organisation from its physical appearance and the interactions that take place within it. Some schools feel very corporate, others are very relaxed, some feel results driven, some feel creative. A fee-paying school popular with the super-rich, aristocrats and politicians will have a very different ethos or vibe to a rural primary school. Your school will already have an ethos. The school ethos may be strong, in which case every corridor, classroom, meeting and activity will be permeated by that ethos. The school ethos may be developing. There may be reference to it on the website and it may be referred to frequently. The work that people do across the school may at times, and to varying degrees, reflect the ethos. Staff will be able to articulate the ethos and subscribe to it on a day-to-day basis.

Think about your school. Your first task is to reflect upon the ethos of the whole school.

Areas in which the ethos of the school may be evident	*Your comments and observations*
	Imagine you describing the ethos of the school to someone who has never been there. You're not trying to sell the school to them though - describe it honestly and objectively as possible.
School's official ethos	
How the ethos supports or is linked to the school's vision	
The school's key values	
Ethos of praise and rewards	
Ethos of attitudes, behaviour and relationships	
Ethos of hopes, dreams, aspiration and achievement	
Ethos of creativity, innovation and risk taking	

Areas in which the ethos of the school may be evident	*Your comments and observations*
	Imagine you describing the ethos of the school to someone who has never been there. You're not trying to sell the school to them though - describe it honestly and objectively as possible.
Ethos of decision making, collaboration and participation	
Ethos of enrichment and extra-curricular activities	
Ethos of student voice and leadership	
Ethos of the physical environment	

The process of reflecting and making notes on your whole school ethos should enable you to consider the areas in which the ethos is strong and the areas in which it needs developing. For instance, student voice may have a very strong ethos in your school and the ethos of praise and rewards may be weaker. Ask yourself why. What makes ethos strong or weak? There may be a number of factors and you may not be in a position to identify why an area has a weaker ethos. Don't worry about that – how you perceive it to be is fine for this exercise. Ethos may be about the feelings and the reasons that permeate everything we do, but it is also very much about others' perceptions of our organisation. What do they see and feel in our school?

You may be able to ascertain some of the reasons for weaker or stronger ethos in different areas. Think about leadership and how leadership may affect the strength of ethos within your school, different areas or within departments. How important to a school's ethos is leadership?

Let's repeat the exercise but this time zoom in on your area or department within the organisation.

The ethos of your area or department	*Your comments and observations - these could be your own reflections or you could involve your team.*
School's official ethos	
How the ethos supports or is linked to the school's vision	
The school's key values	
Ethos of praise and rewards	
Ethos of attitudes, behaviour and relationships	
Ethos of hopes, dreams, aspiration and achievement	
Ethos of creativity, innovation and risk taking	

The ethos of your area or department	*Your comments and observations - these could be your own reflections or you could involve your team.*
Ethos of decision making, collaboration and participation	
Ethos of enrichment and extra-curricular activities	
Ethos of student voice and leadership	
Ethos of the physical environment	

How do the different areas compare to your notes on the ethos of the organisation as a whole? If there are areas in your department where ethos is weaker, consider why this might be.

Up to now, we've reflected on the current state of ethos. We have looked at and dissected the character of the school and the department (which is an excellent place to start) and we have probably identified areas where character is strong and shines out, and where character is weaker and more vague. Next, we need to be clear about what our ethos will be. How will those in it describe the character of our department? What will it feel like and how will it appear to others?

Your task now is to describe the ethos you would like your department to have. If you want to, use the list of characteristics below to help you construct a paragraph describing the ethos of your department. Remember that we are describing what we are aiming for rather than the current ethos. It will be helpful to have your organisation's or department's vision in front of you while you do this. It may also help to describe the ethos in terms of environment, behaviours, expectations and aspirations.

Characteristics and Personality

Vibrant	Traditional	Innovative	Secure	Caring
Efficient	Supportive	Encouraging	Stable	Rewarding
Sharing	Driven	Aspirational	Resistant	Independent
Disciplined	Academic	Enthusiastic	Challenging	Committed
Proud	Positive	Trusting	Organised	Nurturing
Successful	High-tech	Effective	Collaborative	Colourful
Friendly	Unique	Rewarding	Forward-thinking	Inspirational
Considerate	High-profile	Decisive	Open	Creative
Relaxed	Exciting	Structured		

Description of the departmental ethos that I would like to foster and develop

We are going to work on developing ethos within your department by breaking the task down into four key elements that together contribute to a strong positive ethos:

1. Environment
2. Behaviours
3. Attitudes to learning and aspirations
4. Creating a high-profile department

Let's begin with looking at the ways we can develop a strong departmental ethos through environment. We start here because the environment is the most tangible of areas and, for that reason, perhaps the easiest to focus our attentions on initially. We can also work with our environment to make statements and sound out messages that will help us develop a sense of ethos quite quickly.

As well as the obvious, like walls, displays and the layout of rooms, other elements like resources, students' books and even the curriculum and its design could come under the 'ethos of environment' umbrella. If you need to, refer back to Chapter 2 where we asked you to assess the environment.

If ethos is about the character of your department and you want a strong sense of character, then it seems obvious to us that consistency is key. To a visitor, a strong sense of character and departmental/team values will be evident if it can be seen everywhere. If your physical space is, for example, five classrooms and a corridor and they all look fantastic, vibrant and focused on learning and progress, that is, of course, great, but if each area reflects the individuality of the member of staff who inhabits it, a coherent ethos will be difficult to see. We don't suggest for a minute that you adopt a full-blown corporate approach to display, but it's important that you develop some coherence through your physical working space that demonstrates your ethos. It may be that your leadership responsibility takes your work across the whole school. In which case, consider how the elements on which you lead are visible across (and even beyond) your organisation.

Again, it's worthwhile taking some time to plan the look of your department. You could do this yourself and then slowly get your team to adopt your approaches or you could get creative together.

Have a look at these examples and then plan your own environment with your ethos in mind. Constantly ask, how will this demonstrate our character and values to the people who work and learn here as well as to visitors from across and outside the school?

Environmental factor	*What it says about our ethos*
Tables in classrooms are all grouped	We value teamwork and student-led learning
Classroom doors all have "I am currently reading..." posters on them	We value reading for pleasure
Teacher, peer- and self-assessment sheets use the same departmental design with space for feedback and reflection	We believe that assessment and progress are important and that everybody is involved in the process
The entrances to the departmental area / s all have "welcome to..." signs	We are proud of the work that we do and happy to have you here
Posters with AFs and progress measures are the same in each classroom	We believe that consistency is important. We want you to know that it doesn't matter which class you are in - you will be able to achieve and make progress anywhere in our department
Reward certificates or postcards have a consistent design / colour scheme across the department	We are aspirational and like to celebrate achievement
Students' books all have the same sticker on the front of them	We value pride in our work

Some of the examples might seem a bit trite, but don't be put off. There can be a real power in physically mapping out ideas and seeing your thoughts and values take shape on paper. You may find you come up with a wealth of ideas that can be easily implemented and make a real difference to the way your ethos is perceived. A helpful activity could be to consider how your department might look if money and time were no object. This allows people to be creative and ideas can be suggested that may otherwise have lain dormant. Of course, you are unlikely to be able to afford tablets for all, water fountains and healthy snacks in every room or redecoration of an entire area in a chosen colour theme. However, an exercise like this can help your team get a feel for the department's ethos and, with that in mind, you can work with what you have. Often this kind of planning exercise will reveal creativity in your team and if you're lucky, you'll discover that someone has hidden talents and can produce great displays and resources.

The way the people, staff and students, in your team or department behave plays a significant role in the ethos you develop. For some of you, behaviour itself will be your area of leadership, perhaps across a year group, key stage or whole school. In considering behaviour in terms of developing a strong ethos or character, we are focusing on the behaviours of your team (and that includes the students) rather than the actual behaviour policies that are fundamental to your role. It's helpful to think of your team as a character or personality. Does that character shout or talk calmly? Is that character optimistic or pessimistic? Imagine your team is actually a person. What are the key characteristics that person has and how are those characteristics evident in the way in which they behave? Below, we've suggested some example behaviours for a welcoming department. List your own characteristics and explore the behaviours with which they could be associated.

Characteristic	*Behaviours that demonstrate this characteristic*
Welcoming	• Staff are always at their classroom door greeting students as they arrive. • Lessons take place with classroom doors open. • If a visitor arrives at a classroom, a student leader welcomes the visitor and offers to explain what they are learning / working on that lesson. • Student leaders show visitors around the department during open events. • Supply staff are welcomed with offers of tea and coffee and somewhere to put their belongings. • Support staff who work with your team are always copied in to emails, included in bulletins and involved in planning (as far as is practical within the parameters of their role).

Some of the examples of behaviours that demonstrate your desired characteristics appear so trivial and basic that they don't need stating. Unsurprisingly though, demands of time and the everyday hustle and bustle of getting jobs done, simply getting through a day, mean that these small things are easily overlooked. Over time, you can find yourself part of a department that actually isn't that welcoming at all. Imagine that we visit your school and department: a middle leader greets us with "Do you mind carrying my folders for me?" and dumps them in our arms. During the entire journey to their department area, they talk to another member of staff about the behaviour of a Year 9 class and their concerns about their car getting through its MOT, ignoring us struggling with folders and navigating crowds. We arrive in the departmental area and the classroom doors are all closed. We come in to a class and nobody acknowledges us because they are too busy. At break time somebody tuts loudly because we have clearly sat in the wrong seats in the staff room. Nobody offers us a tea or coffee or one of the chocolate biscuits and we overhear a member of the team saying, "Who are those two? I can't be arsed with bloody visitors today". Ok, so a visit couldn't really be that bad but you get the picture? All of the small behaviours matter a great deal when you're talking about ethos.

Attitudes to learning and aspirations are another key element of your developing ethos. It goes without saying that we want our students to have great attitudes to learning and to be aspirational, but how do we go about fostering and developing that as part of our ethos? A few motivational posters will not cut it here. In developing your departmental ethos, behaviours that demonstrate your ethos of aspiration and learning must be visible as well as firmly embedded in every day behaviours and attitudes.

Our 'aspirations and attitudes to learning' ethos
(summarised in a sentence or two)

Those characteristics that are fundamental to that ethos

The behaviours and appearances that demonstrate and are inextricably linked to the characteristics and the ethos (what people see and hear and feel)

Again, it will be helpful – and we make no apologies for asking you to repeat this task – to map out, to get down on paper, what it will actually look like in your department when aspirations are high and attitudes to learning are amazing. What we suggest this time, however, is that you involve a group of students in the task. For this reason, we've made it a little more structured and prescriptive, but you can, of course, adapt this to suit your needs. The aim of involving all stakeholders in developing the ethos of your department is, in the main, to move away from any superficiality. Anybody can create an ethos for their department on paper and announce it on their website, but for it to become real, tangible, visible and effective requires the involvement of all and a lot of persistent hard work. You cannot create an ethos and then forget about it. It's a bit like having a dog – you need to take it out and walk it every day! More than once!

So, let's start by involving student voice or leaders. We recommend getting a group of students – mixed ages and abilities – together and leading a 'workshop' on aspirations and attitudes to learning. Use the planning tool below to help you structure the session and record outcomes. This is an ideal task for you to delegate to a second in department or a TLR holder.

Areas to address	*Possible approaches*	*Outcomes & further actions required*
What do we mean by attitudes to learning?	This could be a question posed to the whole group. Answers could be recorded on post-its (or electronic equivalent) and displayed for discussion.	
What would really positive attitudes to learning look like: • In the classroom? • On corridors? • In the canteen? • Outside school?	These could be answered by groups working in a carousel. Use giant paper and get groups to feedback.	
What do we mean by aspiration?	As before, a question posed to the whole group. Answers could be recorded on post-its (or electronic equivalent) and displayed for discussion.	

Areas to address	*Possible approaches*	*Outcomes & further actions required*
How can we support each other in being aspirational in (insert dept / organisation here). How can staff and students share their aspirations?	Paired activity and feedback.	
How can we ensure that our attitudes to aspiration are inclusive?	This could be a question posed to the whole group. Answers could be recorded on post-its (or electronic equivalent) and displayed for discussion.	
Agreeing an ethos	This might happen at a second meeting, all the initial ideas could be brought along in a clear format and discussed - are we going with this or not?	
How can we share this ethos?	Creative approaches to sharing and embedding an ethos	

Finally, we will look at developing a high profile department and team. As far as ethos is concerned, raising the profile of your department is important in that a high profile is intrinsically linked with being aspirational as a department. You don't want to merely exist in a silo, doing your job day in day out – perhaps you want to become a beacon of excellence and share the amazing work that you do with others in order that their teams and students can benefit. The impact of your work could be wider reaching than the end of your corridor. We believe that it is possible to raise the profile of the work that you do and of your team without becoming a relentlessly self-promoting irritant to others. There is, as we all know, nothing appealing about someone who hogs morning briefing time to share news of their every achievement, spends the day plastering the corridors in posters promoting their events and the evening copying the whole world into their emails about their latest initiatives if, in reality, their impact on learning and progress is unimpressive. We don't mind, however, hearing from an individual or team who is successful in terms of students' progress and achievement and the quality of teaching and learning in their area.

Your profile could be mapped in these terms:

Where are you now and where would you like to be?

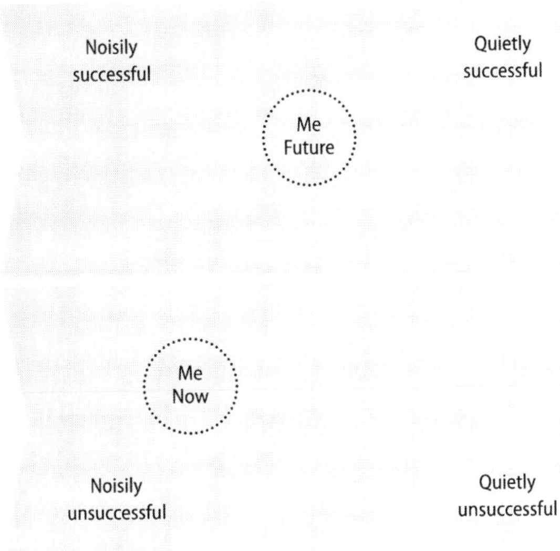

Place your own two dots on the chart – where are you now and where would you like to be? Think about teams or departments that, in your opinion, would fall under each of the four headings. What characteristics do those teams have that make you place them here? What behaviours do they exhibit? Are there teams that you aspire to be more like?

Ultimately, in order to raise the profile of your team, you want to be noisily (but not annoyingly so) successful. For this reason, we suggest you have some successes before you start strategically raising your profile. It's January so by now you are likely to be at a stage where you can do this, or at least plan to raise your profile, and it does require some planning. You could liken the process to a carefully executed marketing strategy. Timing, methods and audience are all vital considerations when you're creating your profile-raising plan.

Let's begin by looking at your audiences and the methods you might use to raise your profile. Use the table below to plan some profile-raising initiatives. We've put some ideas of our own in, but add to this and delete where necessary.

Audience	*Methods you might use to engage these stakeholders with your teams' work and achievements*
Students	• Posters • A weekly electronic team bulletin • Photo galleries of best work on the VLE • Videos of speeches / performances on the VLE • Regular rewards of badges for achievement and effort • A blog • Great looking classrooms and corridors • Staff always greet students at class doors • Trips and enrichment • Worthwhile homework • Positive calls and letters to parents
Staff	
SLT	
Parents	
Junior schools	
Colleges	

You may not feel you're ready or able yet to have a national or global profile as a middle leader in a school and indeed it may not be something you aspire to. What about your team, though, particularly the students? Their aspirations should be high and students connecting with schools from across the world (perhaps in a joint learning project) is not such a ridiculous aspiration to have in the 21st Century. The sensible approach will, of course, be to start small – raise your profile within your school first and as your success grows, share it more widely. If you have successfully planned to and raised the profile of your team within school, expanding on this will be easier in the future.

Creating a positive ethos and raising your profile is something that will happen over time. If key strands and elements are in place and leadership is strong, the ethos will evolve naturally. However, this evolution can always be supported with planned strategies and actions. These could be anything from a corridor conversation with a colleague to holding a summer festival of talent complete with a celebrity compere, student-made snacks on offer and a beautifully produced book of student writing for sale. You can be quite creative with your approaches and ideas.

Chapter 8 – February

Leading Professional Development – Developing A Coaching Model

> *"The role of a creative leader is not to have all the ideas; it's to create a culture where everyone can have ideas and feel that they're valued."*
> – Ken Robinson

> *"Change is one thing. Acceptance is another."*
> – Arundhati Roy, *The God of Small Things*

If you have a well-developed coaching model in your organisation, this chapter will help you consider how your team engage with the model in order to develop themselves and the team as a whole. If your organisation doesn't have a coaching programme established, this chapter may serve as a starting point for you if you decide you would like to develop a coaching ethos within your department.

One of your roles should be to support every member of your team in their continued professional development and there are, of course, a variety of ways of doing this. Your organisation will likely have a structured programme of CPD and processes for identifying training needs. Coaching may or may not be an integral part of this programme but we will explore ways in which you might use coaching or develop a coaching style to benefit your team's professional development.

During an inspection, Ofsted (2015 School Inspection Handbook) will look at: '*The quality of continuing professional development for teachers at the start and middle of their careers and later, including to develop leadership capacity and how leaders and governors use performance management to promote effective practice across the school*'. Coaching comes under the CPD umbrella, but Ofsted does not specify it explicitly as something that inspectors will look at or expect to see. Interestingly, one of the criteria for outstanding leadership and management states: '*Staff reflect on and debate the way they teach. They feel deeply involved in their own professional development. Leaders have created a climate in which teachers are motivated and trusted to take risks and innovate in ways that are right for their pupils*'. Although the word 'coaching' is not used explicitly, we think this describes perfectly a coaching style of professional development where reflection, debate, feeling deeply involved and being encouraged to take risks and innovate are what constitutes outstanding CPD.

Coaching has, for years, been ubiquitous in the world of business and we are all aware of the role of a sports coach. These days you can hire a coach for pretty much any area of your life: health and wellbeing coach, diet coach, relationship coach, executive coach, management coach or indeed a life coach to address it all! You can be coached in parenting or use a coach to help you make a career change. A coach can help you de-clutter your wardrobe or your whole house. You can have a virtual coach with coaching sessions taking place online and via Skype. We are not, however, at all cynical about coaching – it is a powerful tool for reflection and development – but we think it's important to be aware that coaching is big business. Where there are easy opportunities to make a lot of money in an unregulated industry, there will be people offering a poor or costly coaching service, bad advice or expensive and ineffective training. Our advice, if you are looking for an individual or organisation to train you or your team in coaching, is to take care and follow trusted recommendations.

What is Coaching in an Educational Context?

It is a structured process involving two or more people (most commonly a coach and a coachee) in which, through dialogue, questioning and reflection, participants find ways to develop their skills and professional practice. A key feature of coaching is that it encourages staff to take ownership of their development and thus creates a sense of independence rather than reliance on a trainer or mentor.

A coach doesn't have to be an expert in any particular area and their role is not to to give advice on anything. The coach's role is to support the coachee in reflecting on their situation and developing their own strategies and plans for improving and developing their skills and practice. The coachee usually selects their own focus for learning and development and this doesn't have to have any link to performance management targets.

Coaching and mentoring are very different. Coaching is a dialogue that is part of an on-going process of development whereas mentoring more often takes place at points of career change. An NQT or a new senior leader, for example, may be assigned a mentor. A mentor is generally someone more senior and experienced who will set the agenda and direct the learning and support given. A coach, however, can coach anyone – there should be no hierarchy in a coaching programme and for this reason alone, the process is often a more appealing one than mentoring. Coaching shouldn't be a part of performance management, although a good performance management review may well adopt an effective coaching style.

Sometimes people view coaching as a rather abstruse and a somewhat easy or soft approach with a common concern being that it is a bit vague and new age and might not have real impact. We think that a great coaching programme is nothing of the sort. A good coach can ask challenging questions (without being at all threatening) and enable coachees to reflect deeply while taking ownership of their development. There is and will always be a place for formal and informal mentoring and there are times when mentoring will be much more appropriate and effective, but we believe that developing a coaching ethos in your team can have great impact on the mind-set and development of your staff.

What are the benefits of coaching?

There has surely been plenty of research carried out on the effectiveness of coaching in different industries and its benefits for individuals, leaders and organisations and for coaches and coachees. In this short chapter though, we're just going to give you our thoughts on the possible benefits of coaching. If you want hard data, you'll have to hunt it out elsewhere!

Benefits for coachees:

- Performance in a certain identified area might improve
- Feel supported and perhaps motivated or inspired by the coaching process
- Become more skilled at reflecting on their progress or performance and develop self-awareness
- Take ownership of learning and development and problem solving

Benefits for coaches:

- Develop coaching skills
- Enjoy the opportunity to support others and make a difference
- Opportunities to meet and work with new people and strengthen relationships
- Can be a rewarding process

Benefits for a whole school or organisation:

- A cost-effective approach to developing knowledge and skills
- Improvements in performance of staff and students
- A supportive ethos
- Improved and strengthened relationships between staff and departments
- Motivated, happy staff
- A culture that fosters reflection and self-awareness and self-improvement
- Being seen to be committed to the development of staff

What does a coach do? What does a coachee do? Who organises all this?

Let's start with the organisation and coordination of coaching. Many schools will have a whole school coaching programme with procedures and protocols, monitoring and quality assurance plus a designated Coaching Coordinator. This role may be filled by a member of the senior leadership team as one of their strands of leadership or perhaps by an aspiring leader as an additional responsibly. We think that a whole school coaching programme should not be viewed as an accountability tool or method of driving up results, but as a tool for developing people and ideas and for creating, experimenting and for sharing good practice. An organisation should establish a vision for coaching, be clear about why they are doing it and what they expect the impact to be. Our thoughts are that coaching can have a positive impact on the confidence of staff and their approaches to self-reflection and professional and personal development. Coaching can help foster a supportive and creative working environment and give staff opportunities to approach problem solving in a creative and experimental manner without fearing failure. It's probably not a great idea to introduce coaching with the intention that it will result in a 10% increase in your number of 'outstanding' teachers or a 20% improvement in results or progress. A great coaching programme might contribute to such improvements but shouldn't be a school's sole or primary reason for having a coaching programme or it quickly becomes target-driven with an undercurrent of accountability. You will need to measure the impact of coaching, of course, but we think that what you measure requires some careful consideration and there will need to be some measurement of qualitative impact involved.

A school might have a person responsible for coordination of the coaching programme and a number of coaches. These coaches may offer coaching in certain areas of expertise such as leadership or teaching practice. Our concern is that a model like this identifies experts and therefore becomes mentoring rather than coaching. A preferable approach and model would be to have a group of staff who have undertaken some training in coaching, are committed to developing their skills and to giving time (don't worry, we will soon look at the issue of time!) to the programme.

A coach would typically work with a coachee through a structured coaching cycle, and within this, support the coachee in identifying a focus. If, for example, the focus is centred on teaching practice, a cycle might include:

- A meeting to calendar the sessions.
- A coaching session to plan the focus and perhaps discuss elements of lesson planning hopes and concerns. ***A coachee identifies AfL as an area for development. The coach supports the coachee in identifying some actions that could be taken to develop knowledge and skills in this area. The actions might include some research, some CPD, some shared planning and some observations – to be followed by a taught lesson where learning could be put into practice and reflected upon.***
- A lesson is taught – this could be observed by the coach or the coachee may film the lesson or perhaps just produce their own commentary and reflective notes. ***The focus for an observation would be purely the AfL as identified and the purpose of a coach observing would be purely to enable them to support the coachee in their own reflection.***
- A coaching session to reflect, problem solve and identify the actions that need to be taken next (at this point you may decide to run another cycle of planning, carrying out and reviewing). ***The coachee might decide that the cycle was effective and that they have formulated an action plan for continued development but that they don't need a further coaching cycle. Or they may decide that another cycle on AfL will be useful or that they would like to start a new cycle with a focus on questioning.***

A coaching cycle centred on an aspect of leadership might include:

- A meeting to calendar the sessions.
- A coaching session to identify issues or leadership skills that could be improved or developed. Identify the actions to be carried out. ***A coachee identifies their organisation and leadership of team meetings as an area for focus. Their team meetings are dull and laden with resistance and negativity. Through questioning, the***

coach encourages the coachee to consider ways of solving the problems and improving the situation.

- The action/s gets carried out (and possibly observed or recorded where practical or appropriate). ***The coachee runs one or more meetings, trying to embed the actions identified.***
- A coaching session to reflect, problem solve and identify the actions that need to be taken next. ***The coach supports the coachee in reflecting on the leadership of the meeting/s and the impact of the improvement actions that they implemented. Perhaps they tried a new approach to agenda setting, developed some ideas for ensuring that all attendees participate in discussion and planned some possible approaches to dealing with negativity***

A coach leads these cycles and supports the coachee in their learning, development and problem solving, but they don't *tell* them what to do. They listen and they ask questions, which sounds easier than it is. We naturally tend to give advice and instructions quite easily and it can be a challenge to develop the patience required to listen and help a coachee find their own answers. This is why training is important. Coaching is not ridiculously difficult or time-consuming to learn, but it is important to know the principles and skills involved. The training of coaches may well be led and organised by a coaching coordinator and ideally a coaching programme and ethos is part of whole school development. Where you don't have an established programme in your school, it's perfectly feasible that you could organise some training and develop a simple programme for your team – it is not impossible to develop your own successful coaching ethos. It may end up being very successful and could end up being a key factor in raising the profile of your team and it becoming a beacon of good practice!

A coachee commits to taking part in the coaching cycle and has a desire to learn, improve and develop skills. In some organisations, a coach and coachee are matched by the coordinator based on practical or logistical factors or sometimes on what the coordinator perceives will be a successful partnership. While suggestions from a senior leader (who may have a better overview of staff skill sets and personalities) can be helpful, another approach is to simply have a list of coaches and leave coachees to approach a coach of their choice. Most likely an organisation will have a combination of approaches, but it is important that protocols are clear and that all participants know and understand the process and find it accessible. If it's a programme filled with complex paperwork, record keeping and deadlines, it runs the risk of becoming impractical, unpopular and therefore ineffective. When a coaching programme is being planned, it really needs to be constructed with accessibility and clarity as core values. If the process is complex, clunky and overly time-consuming, participants just won't engage with it and it will become another task imposed upon them and resented for being so. Coaching should be a fun, sociable and enjoyable way to develop and learn, and it is really important that those organising programmes are mindful of this.

Performance Management and its Relationship with Coaching

Our preference is for coaching programmes that exist independently and are unrelated to performance management, but many organisations will use performance management reviews as a means of identifying perceived coaching requirements. This is not fundamentally in the spirit of coaching and might create problems in the ways in which it is received by staff.

Performance management reviews should certainly identify training needs and mentoring needs, but we think coaching is best kept as a separate entity and its primary reasons for existing shouldn't be about improving performance. This will not be the opinion shared by everyone and perhaps organisations link performance management and coaching because they believe support will be better targeted and have greater impact using a linked approach. We think that any initiative linked to performance management is likely to feel more threatening and could ignore the principle that coaching should be about identifying your own needs and taking ownership of your own development and learning. Where staff need support and mentoring in order to meet targets, give that support and intervene appropriately, but don't attempt to use coaching as another tool to make staff accountable. It could be that a coaching program has an integral set of aims that help ensure that coaching sessions are underpinned by a key focus of the organisation. Perhaps along the lines of 'all coaching activities should support the improvement of teaching and learning'. Whatever an organisation decides, a vision and clear aims will be vital to the success of a coaching programme.

The Thorny Issue of Time!

We cannot ignore the fact that a coaching programme requires time if it is to be successful; time to meet and time to observe and time dedicated to uninterrupted coaching sessions. We'd like to share with you our imagined, perhaps utopian, scenario for the smooth running of a coaching programme:

School leaders have invested time and money in developing a coaching programme, recruiting a coordinator and training coaches. Most importantly though, they have dedicated space and time to coaching. Space and time both come at a cost, but our imaginary school leaders see this as an excellent investment.

There is a dedicated room or two in which coaching sessions can take place. The rooms are pleasantly furnished and equipped with a meeting table, paper, pens and copies of any coaching paperwork. Someone has responsibility for the upkeep of the coaching rooms and they are never littered or dusty dumping grounds. They have windows and water fountains and do not in any way resemble a storage cupboard. These rooms are resources that are bookable via the VLE and used for the purpose of conducting coaching sessions and nothing else.

All coaches have taken part in a good quality training programme which they have attended voluntarily. On completion of the training, coaches practise coaching each other and carry out an agreed number of hours of coaching practice to consolidate their learning. As a team, coaches meet half termly to discuss ideas, issues and successes. Trained coaches have timetabled allocation for delivering coaching sessions.

Coachees complete a VERY SIMPLE coaching request form and the coordinator and/or coaches match the coachee with an available coach. A coachee can request as much or as little coaching as they like. Everybody requests some coaching because they know it has value and is valued. Coachees can request cover for coaching sessions to fit in with their coach's scheduled times for coaching. Their requests don't get turned down. Sometimes there may be a short waiting list, but that's a positive thing. When they have completed a coaching cycle, coaches and coachees complete A SHORT ONLINE SURVEY where they log the focus of the cycle, aims, actions and outcomes. Any paper-based recording is done purely for the convenience of the coach and coachee and they can choose whether to keep their notes and records (most people do because they see them as useful references and valuable evidence).

Everybody within the organisation is involved in the coaching programme and COACHING IS NOT JUST FOR TEACHING STAFF.

The reality of a coaching programme in a school may bear little resemblance to our little coaching wonderland, but there are some – in our opinion – non-negotiables in there. The non-negotiables are time and space. If you don't give people time to engage in coaching or somewhere to do it, your programme is likely to struggle or fail. If you're a middle leader working is a school without a coaching programme, you can still adopt these basic principles and ensure that you dedicate some of your meeting time to coaching sessions, supporting your team in requesting cover for coaching observations. If there is a coaching programme in place, but it isn't well led and it hasn't been resourced with training or given time and space, meet with the appropriate senior leader and make some suggestions.

Create your own coaching vision for your team. What would it look like and how would it work? How does it compare to the coaching reality where you work?

Barriers and resistance – again!

As well as the issue of time, space and poor planning or leadership of coaching, there are other barriers you might encounter as a coach or as a middle leader, and they come predominantly in the form of resistance or negativity. We might be at risk of repeating what we said in Chapter 4, but our repetition is a worthwhile one, we think. In our experience, negative attitudes to initiatives and reluctance (or even refusal) to engage in activities stem from feeling fearful or under threat in some way. When you encounter resistance and negativity it may well irritate or anger you that you have to deal with it. Our tip is to consider the fact that the badly behaved, obstinate person in front of you who is oozing negativity from every pore – is just scared. They are frightened of being rubbish, of failing, of trying new things, of looking stupid, of wasting people's time, of getting it wrong…the list could go on. If you view negative people in this way, they will annoy you less and you may well feel some empathy. At some point in our careers, we have all been scared. Most of us are understandably scared or anxious about certain events or situations, but some people operate with low-level fear as their default setting. These are possibly people who will benefit hugely from participating in a coaching programme so try and see past the folded arms and the glare and coax them into taking part in coaching.

People will often say that they don't have any problems so they don't need any coaching. You don't need to be struggling with anything or have a problem to solve in order to benefit from coaching. Coaching can help you reflect on your current practice and role and consider your strengths and areas in which you would like to develop skills. A great coach will be skilled at asking questions that will enable you to do this. You could turn up to your first session with no idea what you want the focus of your cycle to be and your coach could help you decide.

Obviously, if you tell an individual or a number of individuals that they have been identified as requiring coaching and must take part in a programme, they are more likely to feel fearful and under threat than they would if they were to participate in coaching of their own accord.

Other staff may say that they are already very skilled at reflective practice, but coaching can always help people reflect differently and support them in exploring different perspectives. Some schools develop a coaching model that works exclusively with teachers and make teaching and learning the focus. Other organisations will offer coaching to leaders, support staff and administrative staff as well as teachers. An inclusive approach to coaching helps develop a stronger coaching ethos and coaching is perceived as something that EVERYONE does. Occasionally people will be resistant to being coached by someone who has a less senior role or less experience than them. This is understandable – it could be a new approach for many people who have worked in a traditional organisation with very rigid structures of hierarchy – so help them out here.

Where a coaching programme is well planned, the vision and aims are shared with staff and senior leaders visibly drive and support the programme, the resistance is likely to be less. If a programme lacks vision and clarity and purpose, people will feel confused and anxious and this will cause them to resist.

What happens in a coaching session and what does the coach actually do?

The first thing a coach does is build a rapport with their coachee – they will have learned methods of rapport building in their coach training. Building rapport may come naturally to some, but it is a skill that can be learned and developed. It's vital that rapport building happens and the coachee feels comfortable. During coaching sessions, a coach should help build confidence and create an atmosphere that is relaxed and easy while also being challenging.

The coach will also have been trained to use a variety of listening and observation techniques. They will be skilled at asking challenging and probing questions, and also at providing clarity and structure to the process of reflection – they can help the coachee clarify their aims or area of focus.

A coach is impartial and doesn't offer opinions or advice – this doesn't mean that they aren't warm and supportive, but their role is to provide guidance and facilitate reflection rather than providing answers or offering solutions.

A skilled coach will be able to challenge the coachee's current thinking deeply and support the coach in trying out new ideas or approaches.

The best coaches don't make judgements, but they might offer some feedback and they certainly ensure that the coachee is accountable for their planned actions and that they invest the required time and effort in the coaching cycle.

A coach should leave their ego at the door and the partnership between the coach and coachee should be an equal one. There is no place for power or authority within coaching.

Yes, but what actually happens?

Perhaps the best way we can begin to answer this is by describing a couple of coaching scenarios. Later in the chapter we will look at the types of questions coaches can ask, adopting a coaching model and the inevitable paperwork that SHOULD serve to make the coaching process simple to carry out and we'll provide a structure that is easy to follow. Let's look at some coaching scenarios.

Scenario 1

J is a Year 3 teacher and is having difficulties with his planning. He is excellent in the classroom and his students are making fabulous progress. He is enthusiastic and motivated, but he spends between five and seven hours planning every evening. He has identified this as an issue and would like to be coached so that he can find a way of solving this problem and regain some work/life balance.

J is coached by C, a very experienced Year 5 teacher who is similarly motivated and successful. She also spends a lot of time planning and would benefit from achieving a greater work/life balance.

The coach doesn't have to be successful in the area that the coachee has requested as the focus for their coaching. The coach just has to be a good coach. In fact, the coach might also develop insight and solve problems as a result of the coaching process.

C approaches J and they agree a time and venue for their first meeting. At this meeting J talks about his focus and what he wants to achieve. He doesn't have a negative or resistant attitude but he is fairly downbeat about the situation and desperate for some help to make his life easier. J already knows that C will not be offering him any answers or solutions. C encourages him to explain the current situation and the ideal situation. Through skilful questioning, she helps him identify clear aims. They were to:

- Reduce the amount of time spent planning
- Improve time management skills

At the first coaching session, it is agreed that because of the focus of this coaching, a lesson observation didn't need to be part of the cycle. Some time is spent establishing the nature of the problem and J is encouraged to think about why he spends so much time planning. He discovers that the main reason is because he becomes absorbed in attention to detail, illustrating slides and worksheets; producing resources that are beautifully crafted and are creative and original. He has become obsessed with the appearance of his resources. C guides J to consider the purpose of planning and its impact on learning and progress. J and C engage in a dialogue that touches on (amongst other things) Bloom's Taxonomy, school policy on planning and how he feels about his resources. The discussion is thought-provoking and guided by C, but it's fluid and natural at the same time. C – again through skilful questioning – has to support the coachee in choosing appropriate actions and making decisions about what will happen next. This process leads to J deciding that he will:

- Use some pre-planned lessons that had been produced by other members of staff and adapt them as necessary
- Put a cap on the time he allowed himself to work for in the evening
- Shadow someone doing their planning and ask them to model their planning process for him

The next coaching session takes place a week later and J arrives armed with notes he has made having carried out all three of his planned actions. C asks him lots of questions about what he had learned, what had happened that week, why it had happened and how he felt about the changes he had made. J is also encouraged to reflect on his successes and accomplishments since the last session and to explore how a different approach to planning might benefit others and have positive impact. C encourages him to consider his next steps and plan further actions that will help him reach the desired outcome. J decides the desired outcome is to halve the time he spends planning and to dedicate the time saved to activities that are unrelated to work. Between them they establish some future actions and the coach ensures that the coachee's successes are identified as such and celebrated. J decides he will spend some time researching further approaches to planning and continue with the self-imposed cap on working hours. Both C and J complete a simple summary and evaluation of the coaching that has taken place.

Scenario 2

N is a Maths teacher in his second year of teaching. He struggles with managing behaviour for learning and feels embarrassed about this. He would like to use coaching to help him identify issues and improve his practice. N is coached by B who is Head of the English department and an excellent teacher. She is also an experienced coach, but she feels she would benefit from some refresher-style training to ensure her coaching practice is top quality.

They meet initially and discuss the focus for the coaching cycle. N is uncomfortable and embarrassed about the problems he has with behaviour. He has observed other teachers and received some advice and support from his line manager, but nothing has improved. Because of this, he's a little pessimistic about the possible success that coaching will have. When the focus has been identified, B asks N if he would be happy for the coaching sessions to be observed so that she can receive some feedback on her coaching from a colleague. N is happy for this to happen and they decide that the first step will be B observing N teaching a Year 9 class that he finds difficult.

N emails B his lesson planning and resources and the observation takes place. During the observation, B makes no judgements whatsoever but notes what she observes in relation to behaviour and attitude of students and the approaches taken by N to promote behaviour for learning. B can see that there are a number of problems to address and that N needs to change his style and approach in order to resolve these problems. As she observes, she doesn't formulate a list of tips and advice, she formulates a list of questions she will ask.

The coaching session takes place immediately after the lesson. They planned for this to be the case so that N doesn't go home and worry and so that the lesson is fresh in their minds. B takes five minutes to plan and structure the coaching session and consider her approach. The coaching session lasts an hour and a half. B begins with questions that are designed to help N identify the problems and the possible reasons for their existence. She then asks questions which challenge his current approach and pushes him to reflect deeply on where he might be 'going wrong' as he puts it. They engage in an in-depth dialogue in which they identify alternative pedagogic approaches and the coaching conversation becomes a more collaborative, two-way dialogue. B's input means that N and B collaboratively produce ideas for solving the problems. At the end of the coaching session, N decides on a plan of action and distils the session's ideas and explorations into a list of specific actions. During the next two weeks, he will:

- Read a book about 'behaviour management' that B recommends
- Make three changes to his planning practice
- Make five changes to the methods he uses to engage learners
- Make one change to the way he uses his voice
- Keep a reflective journal each day.

S has observed the coaching session and offers some feedback based on her observations:

- N was very guarded and uncomfortable at the beginning of the session, but relaxed as the session went on and responded thoughtfully to questions
- B used brilliant questions
- B was kind and supportive, but she made N work really hard
- B listened really carefully and when she responded to N, it was clear that she was genuinely interested
- When N and B started to collaborate and create ideas together, the coaching session became almost a two-way learning experience

and they were both totally engaged and enthusiastic

- At times, the session appeared to lack structure and direction
- It was really obvious, at the end of the session, that N felt much more positive and motivated than he had at the beginning.

At the next coaching session, N arrives having completed every task on his list of actions. He has been committed to the process and allocated time to make the changes and carry out reflections. B facilitates N's reflection on the changes, the impact they had and how he feels now. As part of the coaching process, B challenges N's views on his planning. She can see that improved planning would have an impact on the engagement of learners. N can't see this so she challenges him and presents different scenarios and options that he must consider. Because they have established a good coaching relationship, B can really push N to make difficult reflections without him feeling threatened or uncomfortable. N is open to the process of having his thinking and habits challenged. The coaching session is successful and further actions are planned. The pair decide that the cycle should not end here and that another coaching session will take place in two weeks' time.

Again, S observes and offers feedback:

- This session is more clearly structured and seemed to be better planned. B is prepared with a set of notes and she also made a few notes during the session.
- B is really patient with N while he was resistant to considering changes to planning. She also shows herself to be really knowledgeable about this area. Has she done some extra research in preparation for the session?
- Despite being patient, B is really tough with N and makes him answer difficult questions and forces him to look at different options and approaches to planning
- At first, N seems visibly annoyed by some of B's questions but as she persists, he becomes more engaged and opens up. By the end of the session, he appears to relish the challenges and seems more open to making changes.

After the third coaching session, B and N complete a simple summary and evaluation of the coaching that has taken place and agree to carry out a follow up coaching cycle in three months' time.

Coaching Models

There are an infinite number of coaching models that are used, adapted, or amalgamated to suit different organisations, individuals or coaching purposes. If as a department or a school you buy in some coaching training, you will most likely learn two or three key models and it will be decided – probably by the coaching coordinator and the coaches – which model you will adopt for your programme. As an organisation, it is helpful to adopt a model initially as this will provide clarity and structure for both coaches and coachees. Where coaching is successfully embedded within an organisation and the coaches are skilled and experienced, it is likely that coaches will use a variety of models in coaching sessions. This could be because they have a personal preference or it could be that they use different models at different times. We think that using a simple coaching model is a good idea as a coaching programme is initially established, but coaches should become more autonomous as they become more experienced and skilled. In order to develop and improve their skills, coaches need continued training. We don't think a one-off coach training session is enough!

We're just going to look at one popular model (we have both used it) here in this chapter (the GROW model) and consider its effectiveness and, as ever, offer our thoughts and opinions. Coaching is a lot more than the model it uses. A model provides a framework for the process of coaching, but work done by the coach and the coach's skills and approaches within that framework are the essential ingredients of great coaching. The importance of providing good quality coach training should not be ignored; it's not something that we suggest scrimping on. Paying to ensure that coaches receive quality training (it doesn't have to be hugely expensive though it will need some time investing) will be money well spent.

The GROW model (it's an acronym for Goal, Reality, Options/Obstacles and Will/Way Forward) can be used to structure a coaching session, providing a process of four clear steps to the session.

Goal/s

A coach helps the coachee identify or establish what their goal is. The coach might ask questions like:

- What is it that you would like to achieve?
- What would achieving this goal be like? How would it look/feel?
- What do you want the outcome to look like/be?
- How will you know when you have achieved this goal?

We think knowing one's goals is not always where we start when we are being coached. Sometimes we can't see the goal or the solution, we might be unaware of its existence or just bogged down by a current situation. Knowing your goal is not always easy, we often begin by knowing that we don't like the current situation and we might be totally committed to improving that BUT we can't see what it would look like if it did improve. Sometimes a coach's questions can help us with this, but it might be that looking at the current situation needs to come before goal-setting. For coachees who are not beginning with a problem or an unsatisfactory situation, beginning with a goal might be easier and a coach could encourage them to be creative and ambitious in their goal-setting. It will be helpful at this stage to establish goals that are specific, measurable and achievable.

Reality

During this stage, the coachee describes their current situation and how they feel about it. It requires them to be reflective and honest. A good coach will ask questions that prompt the coachee to explore the nature of the situation or problem without getting too lost in process by sharing anecdotes, dwelling on perceived failures or blaming others for the situation.

- The coach might ask questions like:
- What is your current situation?
- What is the main issue?
- How do you feel about this situation?
- What actions have you taken to change this situation?
- What is the cause of the problems you are experiencing?

Options or Obstacles

Coaches might encourage coachees to explore options or obstacles or perhaps both. During this stage of the process, the coach will support the coachee in exploring the different things they could do or the approaches they could take. It's possible that (without the session evolving into mentoring or advising) the coach can suggest ideas, alternatives or solutions for the coachee to explore. The 'options' stage is where collaborative dialogue is likely. A coach might also encourage the coachee to identify and explore the obstacles stopping them from achieving their goal or looking at the barriers that need to be overcome.

The coach might ask questions like:

- What could you do?
- How could you improve this?
- What are the possible ways forward?
- What could you try out?
- If you were coaching me, what would you suggest I try?
- What are the obstacles in your way?
- What is stopping you from achieving your goal?
- What will make it difficult to achieve your goal?
- What are your key challenges and how might you overcome these challenges?

Will or Way Forward, or What Now?

During this stage of the session a plan of action is created. The coachee is supported in making decisions about their next steps. They will consider the options discussed in the third stage and produce a concrete plan of action that, if followed, will support the coachee in achieving their goal/s and improving their situation.

The coach might ask questions like:

- What will you do now?
- What will your next step be?
- When will you do this?
- How will you do this?

- When will you start?
- Will you need resources or support in order to do this?
- How motivated/committed to doing this are you?
- What do you imagine the result/s might be?

The model and the process are fairly straightforward and it would be possible – but probably not advisable – to establish a coaching programme providing coaches and coachees with nothing more than a model, sample questions and a record keeping template. To coach effectively and become skilled at the coaching process requires at least some training. In a large organisation, where it is important that coachees receive quality coaching and where there should be parity in approaches to coaching, investing in training is vital.

Coaching activities

People can be coached for all sorts of reasons and coaching sessions don't have to be limited to having a lesson observation at the centre of the cycle. As we saw in the first coaching scenario, coaching can help explore and improve organisational skills. In coaching leaders or admin or support staff, a lesson observation would obviously be an inappropriate approach to take. Below are some examples of areas in which coachees might request coaching. There are also 'activities' that could be suggested in the 'what now?' stage.

Preparing a report

A middle leader has to prepare some exams analysis and a detailed report on the results – this is the first time she has done something like this and she decides coaching would help her plan the report effectively.

Giving a presentation

A member of the admin team has been asked to give a presentation to staff on attendance protocols. She thinks coaching might help her feel less anxious and help her deliver the presentation confidently.

Observation

A second in department wants to be coached in observing lessons and giving feedback. Along with the coach, she decides that carrying out a joint lesson observation and (with the teacher's permission) having the coach observe the observation feedback will help her improve her practice.

Problem solving

A Head of Year is having difficulty line managing some of her staff and has encountered some specific problems with one member of staff in particular. She wants to be coached because she thinks it will help her to see things differently and adopt a different and more effective approach to solving the problems.

Research

An NQT might spend some time researching a particular educational theory or reading a recommended book on a specific subject.

Collecting and/or analysing information

The member of staff who has just taken on the responsibility of Key Stage 3 intervention is set a data analysis task. To address an area of underachievement, it might be helpful for a coachee to gather some data and analyse it in order to help them identify strategies or next steps.

Planning

An experienced teacher who has had a career break feels unsure about the planning process. Simply planning and reflecting on the process and effectiveness of a plan could form the basis for a coaching cycle. Between sessions, the plan could be implemented and during the second session its effectiveness reflected upon.

Role change/work shadowing

A middle leader wants to learn more about data management and shadows the data manager for a day. Coachees putting themselves in a different role or shadowing someone's role could help them to gain insights and support them in adapting approaches, developing their own practice or understanding bigger pictures.

Networking

A teacher wants to improve the transition between Key Stage 2 and Key Stage 3 in their subject and is encouraged to network. This could be within the organisation or beyond it. Meeting others who have encountered similar challenges could be a useful part of the coaching process.

What about the paperwork?

As we've suggested, simple, manageable paperwork and record keeping will be better received by staff than anything that is irritatingly complex. Writing while coaching is difficult and we don't see how you can coach effectively if you're simultaneously making extensive notes. There has to be some paperwork because:

- An organisation needs to evidence the work done – not least because the programme has had money spent on it.
- A coaching record will provide a record for the coach and the coachee and support the continuity between sessions.
- A coaching record can be used to show a coachee's progress and the impact of the coaching cycle.

As well as keeping a record of the coaching sessions, it could be useful for both participants to reflect at the end of the coaching cycle on its impact and effectiveness.

How paperwork is collated and what is done with it, will depend on your organisation, but the person responsible for coordinating coaching will likely be the person who collates records so that they can monitor and measure the impact of the programme. Confidentiality will be an important consideration; as with lesson observations and performance management reviews, they are not for public viewing. Some organisations create a coaching contract which covers confidentiality as well as helping to ensure that participants sign up to committing their time and energy to the coaching cycle.

A coaching record could be as simple as the one below. What is important is that all coaches and coachees are very clear about how to use the records. In order that this is the case, introducing the records via a staff meeting, sharing models of completed records and being available to answer questions will all be helpful, as will clear step by step instructions to guide staff throughout the coaching cycle. Everybody needs to be clear about where paperwork can be found, precisely what should be done with it and where it needs to go when it is completed. As with the introduction of any new strategy or programme or change, good management of the process is vital and clarity is key.

Audience	*Methods you might use to engage these stakeholders with your teams' work and achievements*
Other schools in the locality	
Local businesses	• Invite representatives from local businesses to events or performances • Ask them to mentor students • Ask if you can organise a visit for students • Ask if someone can give an inspiring talk to students • Send them copies of a newsletter • Make work shadowing or work experience links.
Local community	
Teacher training organisations	
Nationally	
Globally	

Either the coach or the coachee could be responsible for the completion of a record as long as the approach is simple and consistent. Participants need to know the value of the record, too – coaching records are valuable evidence for staff to collate in their own professional development records.

It might also be helpful to collate coach and coachee evaluations of the coaching process. Evaluation forms are one of modern life's minor irritants, but we think they're great. A good evaluation form can provide useful information to inform future planning, evidence of successes (sometimes to secure future funding) and, frequently, great suggestions or ideas for improvement. Again, they should be simple and easy to use. A paperless survey style system for participants to complete their evaluations could be an effective approach.

Simple evaluations of the coaching cycle could look something like these:

Date *Coach* *Coachee* *Session no.*

Goal / s identified

Reality (brief description of current situation)

Date *Coach* *Coachee* *Session no.*

Options discussed

What next (actions to be carried out)

Date and time of next coaching session

Any other comments

Coachee Evaluation	*Strongly Agree*	*Agree*	*Disagree*	*Strongly Disagree*
The coaching process helped me identify my goals				
I felt well supported during the coaching process				
My coach provided a good level of challenge during the sessions				
My coach encouraged me to be reflective and to explore different ideas and options				
The coaching process helped me plan actions for improvement and development				
As a result of taking part in the coaching programme, my practice has improved / developed in some way				
As a result of taking part in the coaching programme, I feel more confident				
I enjoyed the coaching process and think that it was an excellent form of professional development				

Comments:

Coach Evaluation	*Strongly Agree*	*Agree*	*Disagree*	*Strongly Disagree*
I was successful in helping the coachee identify their goals				
I supported the coachee effectively during the coaching process				
I provided a good level of challenge for my coachee throughout the coaching process				
I was effective in encouraging my coachee to be reflective				
I was effective in encouraging my coachee to plan their actions and next steps				
As a result of the coaching sessions that I led, the coachee has improved / developed their practice in some way				
I feel confident about the quality and effectiveness of my coaching skills				
I enjoyed the coaching process and think that it was an excellent form of professional development				

Comments:

The above are just our suggestions. There are endless possibilities and approaches when it comes to keeping records and evaluating, but we all know that the absolute priority is that paperwork is simple, easy and purposeful.

A good quality programme of coaching serves as an excellent way to develop and motivate staff as well as encouraging them to take ownership of their learning and development. If a coaching programme is well embedded (and tended to carefully with new/refresher training when needed, as well as regular meetings of coaches to discuss developments and changes) it will be a valuable means of continually improving staff and student performance.

Chapter 9 – March

Managing Meetings and Time

"How did it get so late so soon?"
– Dr. Seuss

"Work it harder, make it better, do it faster, makes us stronger. More than ever hour after, our work is never over."
– Daft Punk

Here's a list. It consists of some truths we need to unapologetically speak first:

- Working in schools is fantastic
- Kids are amazing, aren't they?
- Every day is different
- Being a teacher is a privilege
- Teachers hold one of the most important jobs in the country
- The influence of a teacher on a child will be felt for a lifetime
- Kids really are amazing!

If you detect a hint of cliché hanging round those then that would be a real shame because you surely agree with most, if not all, of the above.

You must do, you're reading this book so you're now in (or considering) middle leadership, and so you want to take your expertise and your passion and lead others. However, it seems to us that there exists a crisis in the life of every modern teacher and it is a particularly modern crisis. It's the problem of doing the job you love, and doing it to a standard with which you are happy, while still managing to have some semblance of a life beyond your school's walls. OK, we know teachers get stick for self-important moaning. We know we're not brain surgeons or rocket scientists or firefighters or paramedics or any other very hard and essential job...but your students might be in the future, and your happiness, well-being, personal and professional pride are all factors that could affect those outcomes. You might recognise this as an issue in your own life, or one that affects your colleagues to varying degrees. You may feel that your work/life balance is seriously out of kilter and that moving into middle leadership has done nothing to redress this, in fact it's made it worse. You might feel conflicted at this moment in time, you may even be regretting your promotion, feel guilty that you have neglected something or someone in your personal life or perceive a dereliction of duty in your professional life. The conflict between those two worlds, the professional and the private, is one that needs to be closely managed and monitored. This chapter will show you how. It certainly doesn't promise to fix what could be ultimately unfixable, to hand you back evenings and weekends and holidays, but it does endeavour to show you methods for managing time and organising work, to provide structures and philosophies that might alleviate an over-burdening, ever-increasing workload.

Back in Chapter 2, way back in August, we encouraged you to make some decisions about your team, about how you would delegate responsibility or go further and distribute leadership. Now is the ideal time to reflect upon those decisions you took, to assess the effectiveness of your staff, the progress and impact they have made, the workload being placed upon them, and to make changes. You may need to meet with the most successful and effective team members and look at what challenge they could take on next. You may need to intervene and assist someone with a job they're doing. Or you may need to hold someone to account for his/her inaction or ineffectiveness. It is important to do this now; without this review process, you might discover too late the gaps in your team's work, gaps you yourself will inevitably end up plugging, half-heartedly, resentfully and at the last minute, defeating the object of your decision to delegate in the first place. To help you with this, you can use the table below to make some of your own notes before the relevant staff members meet with you to present their own evidence. In the 'Decision' box, write down how you will proceed from here *eg* change the staff member responsible, put in additional support, schedule further meetings and so on

Team Member	*Area of Responsibility*	*Progress and impact against outcomes*	*Decision and action with any support required*

Your over-arching aim here has been, yes, to relieve you of a series of tasks, but also to build a team capable of leading increasingly complex and increasingly important areas of your work while you employ an increasingly lighter touch. Remember, you will take ultimate responsibility, you will be ultimately accountable, hence the need to review and take action in light of your findings. The continual improvement of your TLR holders is particularly important since succession planning is inherent in this; it is in your interest to mould deputies in your image, coaching them in what constitutes 'your' way so that the smooth running of the team continues in your absence, or even after you've moved onwards and upwards yourself. Everyone will be able to point to a department, a faculty or even an entire school that appeared to implode once an especially dynamic and effective member of staff had moved on, simply because there had been no foresight, no attempt to pre-empt this with the training and development of capable successors who can work autonomously. Some may point to the inevitability of well-trained, skilled and accomplished staff moving on themselves, taking their achievements and record of impact and using them to secure a new post elsewhere. Well, good! You'll have all the benefits of the work they've done for you (long-lasting and embedded if you've managed them properly) and you'll most likely have plenty of time, between them getting another job and actually leaving, to start the whole process once more, identifying likely candidates and starting them on their own route to future leadership. And just because they've moved on it doesn't mean you never have to speak to them again. Maintain as many links as you can; these 'soft federations' between schools (the sharing of resources and ideas, the option to informally sound out a colleague you trust on an issue) are another vitally important component in the effort to reduce workload.

James says…

Allying yourself with another middle leader within school is also a good idea. Find someone who shares your outlook and approach, a critical friend, someone who is willing to share their amazing work, listen to you and collaborate on projects. If you're lucky, this person won't mind you occasionally complaining or dropping by to share some tale of woe, and if you're really lucky this person might keep a secret stash of Jammie Dodgers in their desk drawer.

Let's stop and think for a moment about what exactly is 'your' way and what qualities and abilities you would like to engender in your future leaders. From the list below, choose nine different qualities or abilities and write them in the diamond-nine formation, where the top of the diamond shape is the most important quality you'd like to see in your TLR holders and the bottom is the least. There are three blank boxes to write three of your own:

Qualities and Abilities

Independent	Trustworthy	Creative	Reliable	Meticulous
Strict	Driven	Friendly	Responsible	Intellectual
Brave	Calm	Stays up-to-date	ICT literate	Articulate
Smartly-dressed	Popular	Emotionally intelligent		Well-read
Decisive	Excellent time-management		Prioritises	Interesting
Funny	Delegates			

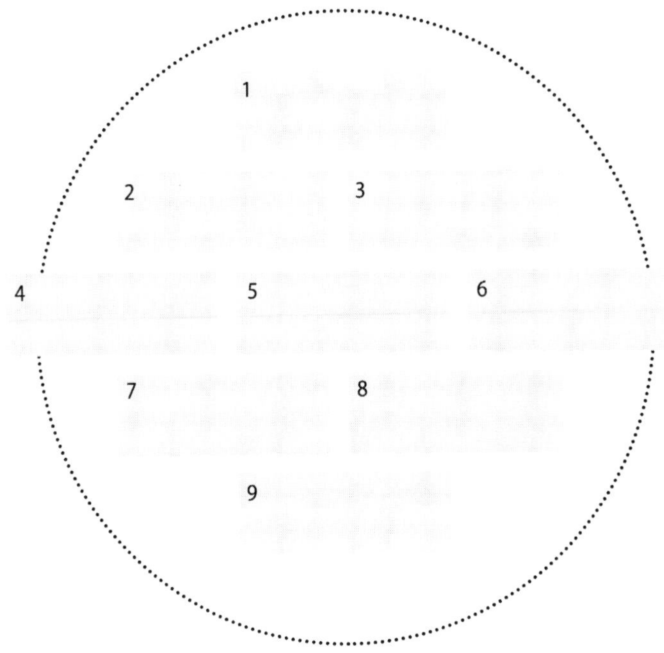

This may be an interesting activity to repeat with colleagues you've identified with leadership potential. It would be a chance for them to think about the necessary qualities of leadership and to reflect on their own abilities, how they measure up to the standards that they themselves might expect to see in a leader. But since this activity has been placed somewhat incongruously in a chapter entitled, 'Managing Meetings and Time', perhaps some qualities in the list above leapt out at you as holding more importance than you first thought (or perhaps not, but go with it). 'Prioritises' could be one such quality. Think about the different contexts in school when this is important: planning and running a meeting, for example, prioritising the content and designing the delivery of different activities so as not to over-run, so conclusions are reached and decisions are made. In turn, we think this prioritises your team's happiness, job-satisfaction, involvement in decision-making and development as teachers and leaders. Model this behaviour so that others in your team work in this way, too, planning and running meetings that are an effective use of everyone's time, energy, skills and knowledge. We have already talked about pre-planning the theme of each of your meetings for the year ahead, assigning different team members to lead each one; thinking about *how* they approach that task is essential, so ensure your own meetings stick to our list of key principles. These are:

- Pre-publish and distribute your agendas – three days before the meeting at the very latest – providing opportunity for any preparation work.
- Time your agenda items and stick to them religiously – have your watch on the table, give one minute warnings when time is nearly up, but ensure a decision is made, a conclusion is reached or an action is detailed.
- Ensure your agenda items are of strategic importance (see activity below). Don't let someone waffle on for 20 minutes about how the music room computer won't connect to the whiteboard.
- Don't allow anyone to hijack your agenda. If someone, usually a member of SLT, says to you, "At your meeting next week, I'd just like you to spend 15 minutes…" say "No!" Whatever it is can be done in a different way – through an email or memo – you've got other, more important, things you'll be doing.

- No AOB – what a waste of time!
- Have action points – 3 max – things that your team need to go away and do and that you return to (briefly!) at the start of your next meeting.
- If your meeting is 3pm to 4pm then finish at 4pm, again ensuring decisions are made and conclusions are reached. Appreciate that people have families and busy lives (we'll come back to this in a bit) or that they may have other meetings to attend, marking to do or parents to phone.
- Make all meetings positive and upbeat – outlaw moaning! – and always finish with someone telling a funny story from the week (this is school after all – something ridiculous happens everyday).
- Finally, ask, "Do we really need to hold this particular meeting?" A grateful team of teachers would love an extra hour of directed time to plan, mark and assess together instead of attending a meeting that, if you were honest about it, didn't need to run at all.

Take a look at the agenda below. It's for an imagined department meeting in a Secondary school. What's wrong with it? How would you improve an agenda like this in light of the list above and the ideas we've discussed on distributed leadership?

Item	*Notes*
Year 9 reports	
Classroom keys	
Corridor display	
Work scrutiny dates and details	

Item	*Notes*
Assessment deadlines	
Year 11 intervention plans	
AOB	

What ideas did you come up with? Hopefully you crossed out AOB straight away. You will also have rejigged the order, placed 'Y11 Intervention Plans' at the top of the list…and then relegated the rest to a couple of emails since they're all information giving, not strategy. Items like 'Classroom keys' are an open invitation to moaners and should be avoided while 'Work scrutiny dates and details' should have been published back in August so only need a gentle reminder email. You could also add timings and a note on the person responsible for its delivery, and a space for action points at the bottom. Your agendas are important for not only signalling what will be under discussion, but how the meeting is going to function, too. Of course, everyone has to be on board if you are to implement a set of rules, but that's the same in any meeting; naysayers or those that love the sound of their own voice will be restricted by rules that might determine what you can talk about and for how long. Maybe these could even be decided upon and agreed as a team. Remember, the aim of these will be to increase the usefulness of your meetings and save you time, surely aims everyone can agree are worthwhile.

Up to now, there have been a couple of occasions where we've suggested emailing instead of meeting, but this extremely useful tool for teachers can have its drawbacks, too, drawbacks you need to consider if you are to prevent counteracting any workload-easing, time-saving measures you're attempting to implement. Firstly, if you feel the urge to send an email after, say, 10pm, save it to your draft box and send it in the morning instead – it can wait. You won't want a reply anyway, particularly one time-stamped after midnight, and what would the quality of this be at this time? No, leave it. Similarly, the quicker you reply to an email, the quicker their reply comes back. Again, leave it, using your judgement to decide when to appropriately respond. Next, beware of emailing on a Sunday night – your recipients will likely read your messages first thing Monday morning when they already have their own to-do list to be getting on with. One of two things will happen here: either any instructions, requests or information sent by you will disappear to the bottom of their pile or, worse, it will go on the top, relegating their own priorities to the bottom, priorities they were organised enough to decide upon in advance. In addition, what does Sunday night emailing say about you as a leader? That you are Mr or Mrs Last-Minute? Give your team their weekend and give them their Monday morning, to work if they need to, absolutely, but to work in their own way and at their own pace on the proviso that your (fair and realistic) deadlines are always met.

Earlier we said you must appreciate that people have families and busy lives, just like you. It isn't a stretch to believe a person's happiness and satisfaction with their home life and their subsequent happiness and satisfaction at work are connected, and vice versa. Who hasn't bounced home like Tigger after a couple of amazing lessons, or smiled through a full day's teaching (plus lunch duty!) because you'd spent an amazing weekend with your significant others? Actively seek to promote a healthy work/life balance for you and your team. After particularly heavy weeks, insist on everyone being out of the door by 3.30 on the Friday (minus the usual 'bag for life' full of marking). You could even hand someone the job of looking after staff well-being, someone who will remember and celebrate your team's birthdays, randomly provide cake and/or coffee, organise a Secret Santa – someone with the emotional intelligence to pick up when a member of your team is struggling with something and make you aware. In Chapter 3, you completed a task that aimed to give you an insight into your team, but now you will have a great deal more knowledge of them than in those early days. Know who works well together, who are genuine friends, who you can turn to for support if a team member arrives at your door in tears (this will happen – have a plan). Know when to step in and relieve someone of work that is becoming a burden. Know the names and ages of your team's children, know where your team live or where they grew up – be sincerely interested. Build relationships. Build a team who will work for *you*. You need to be a 'people person', whether this comes naturally or not – learning to fake it a bit is better than coming across as aloof or curmudgeonly! Lastly, build friendships, too; it's utter nonsense to imagine you shouldn't be friendly with your team. Promotions should not be synonymous with loneliness. Who would you be more likely to go the extra mile for – your respected friend or your antagonist?

That phrase right there – 'extra mile' – contains its own dangers since how you measure that distance is open to interpretation. There have to be cut-off points, points at which you declare, "No more!" For example, take the task of data analysis. Let's imagine it's January and you've been given the job of analysing the progress of Year 4, a year group causing particular concern. This job has the potential to be monumentally vast taking up such swathes of your time that, by the time you've finally completed digging and questioning and observing and meeting, it's July and they're about to go into Year 5. Rather than gluing yourself to a computer screen to pore over endless Excel files looking for answers to leap out at you, make a decision at the outset about how you will approach this task, keeping it simple and focused. Set a time limit and a deadline for yourself that you stick to. A job like this needs a maximum of three weeks. First, get into the classrooms and review the teaching, learning and assessment taking place in this year group, watch a couple of lessons, look at books, identify challenging behaviour, talk to their teachers. The issues will probably reveal themselves at this early stage: disruptive behaviour, an uninspiring curriculum, a core group of underachievers. Next, go to the data. Look at where they are, or where their teachers say they are – does this match your impression? Finally, decide what you're going to do about it, what intervention you are going to implement, how you'll monitor it and how you'll know if it's worked (put some numbers on this). The only thing left to do is communicate all of this to all involved – the students, the Year 4 teachers, the parents, the support staff – being clear what their role is in your plan. And that's it. Don't go beyond your three weeks, but do make sure you revisit to see how they're all doing.

The job described above is typical of the sort of task that comes along every so often, a task you weren't exactly expecting, but one which is certainly important and definitely urgent. Those two words, important and urgent, are ideal for making judgements on the order in which you complete your work in, and out of, school (more on working outside of school in a bit). Use the following grid on an A4 piece of paper taped to your desk to help plan your work. If it sounds old-fashioned, it is. Just because it's not an app on your iPad, doesn't mean it doesn't work. Anything you write in the Important/Urgent box is your priority and shouldn't be put off. For everything else, decide what can be distributed among your team, what could be completed by a member of support staff or what could be rubbed out altogether – if it's not important and it's not urgent, does it even need writing down?!

Area	*Urgent*	*Not Urgent*
Important		
Not Important		

When your grid becomes dog-eared or full, print a new, blank one and transfer over any outstanding tasks. This process in itself will act as a filter where some tasks that seemed important and urgent at the time really aren't and can be shifted around your grid. Some tasks may even disappear altogether. If you get to your second year and some of these jobs are cropping up again, remember them and how insignificant they turned out to be the first time round. Be ruthless otherwise your to-do list risks becoming infinite; remember what we said about cut-off points.

There are particular jobs that demand you complete them away from school in an atmosphere and environment free of distraction or interruption. Be clear with yourself which jobs can be easily completed in school and which would benefit from some distance, sticking to your decisions as far as possible so that you don't find yourself half finishing a task because of interference. Your Senior Team may even be amenable to allowing you to work from home for a morning, an afternoon or even a whole day to allow you to complete a significant piece of work such as a report or a review. There's nothing wrong with asking, but choose days where your teaching load is light, where there is plenty of cover for you in school and where there aren't any after school commitments you'd be missing. And, while you're at home, stick to the timings of the school day, resisting the temptation for a lie-in. If you get chance at the end of the day, check your emails so you're abreast of anything you've missed in the day and so you don't have to do it first thing in the morning. The final obvious benefit is the guarantee you'll definitely be home in time for tea.

The vast majority of your work is, obviously, in school and it is here where you need to ensure you are maximising your available time. We recommend you write yourself a timetable for your week that tightly schedules your entire role. Naturally, your teaching load will come first, followed by identified time for planning, preparation and assessment. You came into this job to teach a subject you love; it would be remiss to allow your teaching to take a back seat now you have been promoted into a position of responsibility, although there is a certain perverse irony in the fact that schools promote all their best teachers and then gradually reduce their teaching commitments. Next, add calendared meeting times, scheduled meeting times you may have with any SLT line manager or TLR holders, and then identify periods you need to keep free for learning walks and scrutinising books. There will need to be some flexibility to account for the unpredictable nature of any typical school day, but your finished timetable should give routine and structure to all aspects of your position and mean all non-contact time is accounted for, never wasted. Over the longer term, determine which 'big jobs' need doing on a regular basis again eliminating surprise and ensuring that the time you need to set aside to complete them is planned for.

Although we have now reached March, it isn't too late to introduce more structure for yourself if you feel it would benefit your working day. Have a go at a draft timetable now, sketching out what could go where. Ours is a pretty generic timetable and might not exactly match your school's day. Cross out or change anything you need to make it fit:

	Monday	*Tuesday*	*Wednesday*	*Thursday*	*Friday*
Before School					
Period One					
Period Two					
Break					
Period Three					
Period Four					
Lunch					

	Monday	Tuesday	Wednesday	Thursday	Friday
Period Five					
Period Six					
After School					
Evening at Home					

Caroline says...

For me, it's all about the list! Lists and sub-lists and lists alongside lists and within lists. In my opinion, producing lists is the number one way to manage your workload and time and essentially your entire life. The very process of writing a list is something I find calming and therapeutic. In my world, it's vital that these lists are written with a Pilot G-2 07 in an A5 lined notebook – nothing else will do! I write lists every morning and they include my work lists which might be subdivided into my areas of responsibility or categories of task (or whatever approach I feel like using to organise the list on a given day). There are also copious lists for 'not work' things so that I don't forget to pick up a child; drop off a dog; purchase a birthday card for a relative; read a meter; turn up at an event; put diesel in the car; replenish the stock of shampoo and conditioner or return a lasagne dish to a neighbour. I know – riveting stuff! I am serious about these lists though. The list is my primary and most important time management tool. When I compose the lists, I am creating an A5 similitude of the day ahead. I visualise myself doing the tasks on the list and consider the order in which they need doing to maximise efficient use of time. During the day, I refer frequently to my lists and add to them or – more satisfyingly – cross tasks out as I complete them.

At the end of every day, I review my lists and assemble a new list of the tasks that need to be carried forward for the following day's lists. What I purposely eschew is giving myself a hard time if I do not carry out every task on the list. This approach is imperative because I almost never carry out all of the listed tasks and that is fine. It is the process of organising, visualising and compartmentalising my tasks that is important to me.

As well as the to do lists, I also have a number of ideas lists on the go at any given time. So often, ideas for solving problems or planning initiatives and events materialise at random moments and capturing them in note form means that I don't have to attempt to remember them, thus creating more room in my head for focusing on the task I am doing.

My other strategy for managing workload and ensuring a work/life balance is what I call 'stop time'. I simply make a decision that at a certain time of day or after a certain number of hours work a week, I will stop work and leave everything. The work will never be complete – there is always more to do and it is easy to keep working and thinking about work unless you are strict with yourself about taking time away from your work. Of course, some people find this easier to do than others.

There is an infinite number of techniques you can use to manage your workload and ensure you have a healthy work/life balance – find the ones that work for you, but don't ignore the issue and assume that it will manage itself because it won't!

We have tried to keep this chapter purposefully short since, unsurprisingly, a chapter on managing time feels like it needs to cut to the chase. With that in mind, let's finish with some final tips:

1. Learn to say no.

   Don't say it all the time, you don't want to appear difficult and obstructive, but just enough so people realise you aren't a pushover. You don't carefully and strategically plan your workload just so someone else can come along and palm off their performance management objectives on you half way through the year.

2. Don't confuse using social media with doing some work.

   Yes, social media is a great place to find out what the weather's doing, who's winning in the Test match or which celebrity has died, but it's also become greatly used by teachers and middle leaders as a place to share resources and ideas. The hashtag function on Twitter, for example, allows for instantaneous corralling of thoughts on a subject and there are many, many generous, clever and inventive Twitter users willing to engage in pedagogical debate, problem-solving or just have a laugh. Social media allows you to stay abreast of all that is happening and developing in schools locally and nationally, particularly at moments of shared significance like exam results day. Be warned, however. Social media can be a deadly time-suck, a black hole into which hours can disappear and, like the real world, populated by a certain proportion of loonies, obsessives and fantasists who think they can say any old guff just because they're behind a computer screen. It can become an echo-chamber, a place where similar viewpoints bounce around gaining more and more false importance, skewing your perspective. Be careful what you say, what you retweet or who you follow or befriend; you are in a socially responsible position and don't want to have your name associated with anything remotely contentious or controversial. By all means use it, as we do, to connect and discover, but don't allow it to become the be all and end all, a distraction from your core purpose. It's a tool to help you with your work, not work in itself. Additionally, if you find yourself habitually browsing social media of an evening for work purposes, when exactly are you planning on mentally switching off, putting some distance between your home and your day job? Once more we come back to cut-off points, knowing when and where to simply stop.

3. Revisit our opening list regularly.

   Here it is again, with some additions:

   - Working in schools is fantastic – and even better when you manage and maximise the time you have properly and strategically.
   - Kids are amazing, aren't they? And they deserve to have their one chance at an education safely in the hands of happy, energetic and enthusiastic teachers.

- Every day is different – but that doesn't stop you having a timetable that structures your day and helps you complete all aspects of your role, one that is flexible enough to adjust for the unusual, unplanned or plain unbelievable,
- Being a teacher is a privilege – and it's easy to lose sight of that if you are buried under six sets of reports, a faculty review or plans for Sports Day…but you aren't alone and there are teachers to whom you can distribute leadership, mould as your successor or instruct to look after everyone's well-being.
- Teachers hold one of the most important jobs in the country – but it's nothing short of a national scandal if teachers cannot be recruited or retained in sufficient numbers. As a school leader, you will play your own part in this, making sure a work/life balance is a realistic aspiration for everyone in your team, especially you.
- The influence of a teacher on a child will be felt for a lifetime – which is why your own teaching must always remain both important and urgent.
- Kids really are amazing! And on that note, we move on to April.

Chapter 10 – April

Enrichment and Community

> *"Why do you go away? So that you can come back. So that you can see the place you came from with new eyes and extra colours. And the people there see you differently, too. Coming back to where you started is not the same as never leaving."*
> - Terry Pratchett, *A Hat Full of Sky*

> *"We don't live alone. We are members of one body. We are responsible for each other."*
> - JB Priestley, *An Inspector Calls*

April is a great month for putting together a great programme of enrichment that you and your team can trial in the summer term. When you put together a programme of curriculum enrichment, you have an opportunity not only to create a fantastic selection of activities and learning opportunities for your students, but also to create a programme that will enable you to really shine as a team. Great enrichment should enable students to develop academically, personally and socially; it should broaden, deepen and, well, enrich not just their learning experience but their lives. Please don't ever view enrichment as yet another time-consuming, red-tape-heavy and costly aspect of your role. It doesn't have to be like that and in this chapter we will guide you through the process of planning and delivering a successful enrichment programme.

The reasons for providing a high quality programme of enrichment activities are many and we think that the following three provide an all-encompassing starting point if you are about to sit down as a team and consider its aims and objectives:

- Enrichment activities provide experiential learning in a wide range of settings and situations.
- Students can develop a range of new skills, broaden their experiences and might raise their aspirations through taking part in enrichment activities.
- Enrichment activities are exciting and fun. If you think back to your own school years, trips, events and visitors to school might form some of the most memorable parts of your learning. Whether it was a ski trip to Austria, a visiting poet or a baking club, everyone will have a memory of an enrichment experience that did just that – enriched their lives and their learning in some way. Sharing these memories with your team could make an excellent starting point for planning enrichment in your department. Think about the kinds of events that were enjoyable and memorable, what made them so and which activities you earnt the most from.

Later in the chapter, we will guide you through the process of planning an enrichment programme, but let's start by looking at the different types of enrichment. What follows is not, of course, a definitive list and there will be overlap, but this can serve as a broad base on which you can consider the different types of enrichment and the ways in which you can develop and improve your current offer. So, in no particular order:

Enrichment within the curriculum

This covers activities that enrich curriculum-based learning and take place within curriculum time. For example, writing workshops with visiting authors; a Spelling Bee with heats delivered in tutor time or a whole school sports day facilitated by a collapsed timetable.

Your school may well have an 'activity week' which is geared specifically to providing a wide range of enrichment activities (both on and off site).

In our experience, an activity week can often result in fierce competition between departments and subjects to provide the most exciting and memorable events, workshops or trips. Subjects like PE often have the edge – or think they do – because they may traditionally provide something exciting like a ski trip or expedition. However, if you're prepared to get creative and put in the time or effort, you can provide memorable trips and experiences linked to any subject area and for any age group, and an activity week may mean you have the opportunity to offer a diverse range of enrichment activities – perhaps a combination of in-school workshops, visitors and trips.

A whole-school enrichment week, perhaps themed, could be a fabulous initiative for primary schools and might work well in the summer term. Timetables can be collapsed, classes can visit different classrooms or teachers and activities can be delivered on a carousel system, leaving each member of staff with just one element to plan. Outdoor learning can be incorporated and the week could culminate in an assembly where learning is shared, displayed and performed with perhaps parents invited.

Within your own curriculum area time, there are opportunities for you to enrich learning without encroaching on the entire school timetable. Perhaps Year 4 are studying the solar system and you amalgamate Year 4 classes for a day, offering a carousel of enrichment activities that culminate in a performance/show-and-tell in front of parents in the afternoon. Or maybe Year 10 are studying a play in English and you arrange for a visiting theatre company to perform to students in the theatre during timetabled English lessons, following this up with workshops on themes and language as part of exam preparation. Although enrichment is primarily about adding to the learning already on offer in the curriculum, enrichment can also be about delivering the learning opportunities in new ways and contexts.

Enrichment before and after school

Traditionally, hour-long after school clubs formed the bedrock of enrichment activities run by teachers at the end of their working day. Increasingly, students attend school before the official start of the learning day and there are breakfast clubs, booster and revision sessions, sporting activities and ICT facilities available for use. What your team can offer students will depend very much on the time commitments of individuals. As a rule of thumb though, we think everybody should offer SOME time before or after the school day for an enrichment activity. Don't confuse revision and enrichment though and, even more importantly, don't just offer revision! Enrichment offered after school has to be particularly well-coordinated. Ideally someone is responsible for overseeing each day's after school timetable of activities and planning is coordinated, too. Work with your team to decide who can offer what on which day/s and then check with other teams or departments that there are no major clashes. You might have a member of staff who can offer a session each week or perhaps someone wants to offer a weekly session that runs for just one half term – you could offer activities on a carousel or work in pairs. The key is to be flexible and plan around what your staff can offer.

Visitors to School

The possibilities here are absolutely endless. Many of these will make themselves known to you through emails and brochures, and will include performers, writers, artists and sportspeople, although it's likely that many of these will charge large sums of money for their services. Often, you and your team will have numerous contacts who have amazing skills that they would be more than happy to share with young people through a workshop or other learning activity. It is always important to communicate to visitors your expectations for the content and style of delivery that your students would require to engage them. They may also need information about student abilities and specific needs. Visits work most successfully when the communication between the organiser and the visitor is clear and detailed. Don't be afraid to ask questions and specify what you require – if there needs to be 20 emails back and forth in order that the visit is planned perfectly, then so be it. Take some time to plan how you will receive visitors, too. It's important to remember the small things – make sure there is someone to greet them and escort them. Be sure to provide tea or coffee and offer lunch if they're there all day. Introduce them to staff they'll be working with and ask the headteacher or other senior leader to pop by at some point during the day to introduce themselves and thank the visitor.

If the visitor is amazing, offers great value for money and an inspired learning experience – arrange to book them again as soon as possible! If the event wasn't so amazing, have a look at what went wrong and decide whether it was the organisation or if the visitor just wasn't quite right for your objectives or students. Learn from any mistakes made – perhaps sessions were too long; perhaps you didn't send enough staff to supervise; perhaps the learning was too easy – all sorts can mean an event won't run perfectly, but the key is to learn from it.

Local community

There will always be local businesses who will have a desire – and a target – to engage with their community to help make a difference to the lives of young people. If you have a large manufacturer in your town, ask them to provide guided tours for budding designers or engineers; theatres can provide guided tours for drama students and football clubs can provide activities on- and off-site as well as provide visits from players and coaches. On a less grand scale, we have both taken trips to a local and independent children's bookshop and given students an allowance to choose and buy their own book. Perhaps not a life changing experience for all, but for some of our students it was the only bookshop they had visited and the first book they had ever bought.

As well as businesses, other learning organisations are excellent for building links. If you have a university nearby, make contact with a relevant faculty and ask how they can help. They may be able to offer visits and tours or perhaps some of their students will come out to your school and deliver workshops and activities, either as a one off or on a regular basis. Often universities will have state of the art equipment and facilities that will be amazing for your students to see in action or to experience using.

Homework and enrichment projects

Project-based learning and research, if well planned and led, can be incredibly enriching and easily facilitated via your VLE. It's also a great way to involve parents and carers. You may well have something in place already. If not, work with your team and use the planning tool to design an online enrichment activity. The activity might link to schemes of work, but it could be totally unrelated, perhaps linked to an exciting area in your subject that isn't on your curriculum. You could base a plan loosely on the approach of project qualifications that schools sometimes offer at Key Stage 4 and at sixth forms and colleges. Students choose their own project (and could work in groups or pairs). They do their own planning and research and keep a log of everything they do – this could include blogs, photos and videos. The project would have an outcome that might be a product or an event, after which students deliver a presentation on their work and evaluate the project. You could, of course, take an entirely different approach and a project could have a focus on something like baking, photography, sport, filmmaking, poetry writing, web design, art history research or sculpture making – the possibilities are endless. It would be fabulous if each year group you work with had the opportunity to carry out a long-term enrichment activity like this. You could have regular meetings with students or you could use your VLE as the primary means of setting tasks, sharing resources and giving feedback.

Planning A VLE Based Enrichment Activity – Initial Plan:

Planning a VLE-based Enrichment Activity - Initial Plan:

Project idea outline	
Learning objectives	
Student outcomes (what will they create or produce?)	
Activity ideas	
Possible resources	

Planning a VLE-based Enrichment Activity - Initial Plan:

Ideas for getting students involved (rewards / competitions / promotion)

Timescales and organisation

Barriers and obstacles

Ideas for overcoming barriers and obstacles

Production and performance

This could include an annual full-scale school production or perhaps showcase performances of music, dance and drama. There are enrichment opportunities connected to productions for students interested in art, design, costume, technical and stage management. There is probably no better way of engaging parents than to invite them to watch their child performing and a production of any kind is fabulous for making links with the community. You can offer VIP seats and free tickets to governors and other key stakeholders. Taking part in a school production as a performer is one of those experiences that becomes a lifelong memory, you might still cherish yours. Where students don't fancy performing, get them involved in designing costumes, producing posters or creating a soundtrack.

Accreditation and competitions

An obvious and popular choice here are the Duke of Edinburgh Awards, but there are all sorts of ways students can be accredited for their learning beyond the classroom. A member of your team might have the ability to teach an interesting subject – Astronomy, Classics, Film Studies or a language that is not on offer as part of the curriculum. It's possible for committed students to gain an additional GCSE as part of their enrichment programme. Project qualifications are also an option as Level 1, 2 or 3 qualifications. However, accreditation doesn't have to be qualification based – sometimes rewarding and recognising participation by handing out certificates and conducting your own awards ceremonies is perfectly adequate and certificates are very useful evidence for students to gather for their college applications and interviews. For Key Stage 1 and 2 children, certificates, badges and awards are fantastic ways of celebrating learning through enrichment. It's important to recognise students' efforts to give up their time to learn a new skill. It is, after all, much easier to go home and sit on the sofa with cake and cartoons!

Supporting students in entering school-based, local or national competitions is an excellent form of enrichment. We have worked with students to enter poetry and writing competitions, such as Poetry By Heart, and as performers in festivals of speech and drama. There will be all sorts of competitions relating to your subjects and the age groups you work with – you just have to make an effort to keep abreast of what is out there.

Trips

If you have never been responsible for a school trip before, start small! Take a few students, keep the activity simple and don't go too far. School trips are brilliant, whether they are a day trip or a longer residential trip. International trips are of course the zenith of curriculum enrichment, but they are not for everybody and they are not the be all and end all. You can create amazing experiences for young people without leaving your county. The bottom line is that trips, visits and off-site activities all provide fantastic experiences and learning opportunities. So, where can you go? Use the list below to generate ideas that are relevant or specific to your subject, curriculum or age group. You don't have to run them all, but the generation of ideas will get your thoughts flowing and motivate and enthuse your team – which is important because they're the ones who will be running these trips!

Trip Planning Task to do with Your Team

Type of trip	*Ideas*
	Don't limit yourself here - think as broadly as possible and don't worry about cost or practicalities at this stage!
Theatre	
Gallery	
Museum	
Factory or business	
University faculty	
Urban landmark	
Rural landmark	
Activity-based	
European	
International	
Other ideas	

Before you start planning your curriculum enrichment programme, spend some time considering who you will involve in the planning, delivery and monitoring and evaluation of the programme. We recommend that you plan as a team and involve students and parents where possible, too. Delivery of curriculum enrichment needs to involve as many people as possible and should include all your staff, support from senior leaders and of course delivery of workshops and activities by visitors. If you plan trips anywhere, there is a wealth of experience and support available when it comes to planning and risk assessing – particularly if you visit anywhere that encourages school visits. Within school too, look for support and guidance from experienced trip organisers and most importantly, follow your organisation's trip protocols and processes to the letter.

Basically, you need to use the same processes as you would for implementing any other kinds of change or strategic development we have looked at throughout the course of the year – and the book. Start with an audit of your current offer. This may well be a five-minute task; you either have an enrichment plan for your subject area or perhaps a list of your current offers – or you don't! If you do have an enrichment programme in place, you will need to ask some questions to ascertain whether it needs tweaking or a total overhaul. We've put together a list of questions that might be useful – add your own of course.

1. Does each Year Group/Key Stage have an equal number of activities on offer?
2. Does your programme contain a range of varied activities?
3. Is there a good balance between in school and out of school enrichment?
4. Do your activities appeal to students with wide ranging interests?
5. How accessible are the activities (this could cover cost/timing/equipment needed etc.)?
6. How many members of your team are involved in delivering your enrichment programme?
7. Do the activities support and develop the learning on your curriculum?

8. Do the activities offer students opportunities to develop new skills and experience new things?
9. Have you considered whether your enrichment offer caters for all the different 'groups' of students?
10. Is the programme of enrichment exciting, innovative and fun?

Check your whole-school enrichment policy, look for an enrichment section on the school development plan and take a look at what other departments are doing. Obviously, if there is a well embedded enrichment programme, there may be a structure to which you will need to work within and/or there may be requirements that you have to fulfil with regards to activities you offer.

April is an excellent time for planning a fresh programme of enrichment activities that you can pilot during the summer term and then review. This doesn't mean that all the activities have to be brand new but the way you organise and deliver them may be different. Think back to Chapter 4 where we looked at leading change and see the process of reinvigorating your enrichment offer as an opportunity to lead more change in a very positive way. What's great about enrichment is that the changes can be led entirely by you and your team – they are not imposed from outside as timetable changes or updates to the National Curriculum – so have some fun owning and leading this type of change. There will be some barriers, the obvious being staff resistance to extra work, lack of time and lack of money – you know, the usual!

When, as a team, you have generated some ideas, your next step is to decide which of those you will work with and map them out across a term or a year. You could start with just the summer term and then create a full year's plan to begin in September.

James says...

Here is an example of an enrichment plan based on one I created with a team of English staff. You will need to add dates and timescales to any plan you create. You also need to show who the lead staff are for each activity or event. You might have more – or fewer – target groups that you want to reach.

Full Cohort	*Extra Curricular Clubs*	*Target Group 1*	*Target Group 2*	*Collaboration*	*Community / Stakeholder Engagement*
Spelling Bee 21 finalists plus whole year group *Impact:* KS3 Literacy	**Film Club** Up to 50 students per showing *Impact:* Develop and widen student knowledge of film.	**BBC School News Report** Y10 - 20 students *Impact:* Give students a taster session as to the life of a journalist. Allow students to practicse non-fiction writing	**BBC Radio 2 500 words Rriting competition** Y7 - selected target students *Impact:* Improve KS3 creative writing and encourage interest in writing for fun	**National Story Telling Week** Y5 / 6 students - visiting event. *Impact:* Encourage reading and ease students in to KS2 / 3 transition	**National Story Telling Week** As many pupils as possible *Impact:* Involve parents in encouraging an interest in reading
World Book Day Whole year group *Impact:* Interest in reading	**Shakespeare Schools Festival** 25 actors and 10 production assistants *Impact:* Experience of large scale performance	**Debating Competition** *Impact:* Improve Speaking and Listening skills in a real life, formal context	**National Blog Posting month** *Impact:* Encourage students to think about different methods of revising for English and in turn show these different techniques to other pupils who read their blogs.		**Shakespeare Schools Festival** In school performance as well as local theatre.

The following templates might be useful, or you can create your own.

*Year Group**	*Half term 1*	*Half term 2*	*Half term 3*	*Half term 4*	*Half term 5*	*Half term 6*

** or different groups of students - more able, pupil premium, boys... whatever your key groups are*

	September	*October*	*November*	*December*	*January*
Curriculum time enrichment					
Before and after school enrichment					
Trips					
VLE Enrichment					
Holiday Enrichment					
Cross-curricular enrichment					
Cross- year group enrichment					

February	March	April	May	June	July

Your plan needs to show who will lead each of the activities and staff need encouraging to do so. Involving them in the planning and creation of an exciting programme will help to persuade them to invest in enrichment. Some activities might span a whole term or even the full school year and others will be one-off events. You will probably find that some events/trips will be made available to more than one group of students. We think it's really important that you map your enrichment plan out in this way because you can ensure there are no gaps. You want all your students to be offered an equal range of enrichment activities. Check, for example, that each year group or other group has at least two trips, one visitor, a homework project, three after school clubs and two competitions they can enter (that's just an example – you may not be in a position to offer that much!) and make sure that the offer is the same for all students. Where there are gaps, look at how you can fill them.

Some of your planning will be detailed, you may know which day of the week a club will run and that is easy to map. However, you may know that you want to offer a theatre trip in December, but you don't know which theatre or show you will be seeing. The important thing here is to know which member of staff will be organising it and which students will be offered the opportunity. Similarly, competitions will appear throughout the year and can't be mapped in detail. It's a difficult balance; if you don't plan, activities may not take place or they may all appear at once meaning that someone is overworked or that trips/events are not well attended. However, if you over-plan and have no room for flexibility, you could later miss out on some amazing opportunities for your students. A final word on mapping – take a close look at the school calendar as you work through the process. There is no point planning a Year 6 residential trip to London during SATs or a Year 10 production during work experience.

Distributing the leadership of your enrichment programme is one of the keys to its success. Everybody should be involved in planning and delivering activities and in doing so they should be able to develop their own skills. For large-scale activities such as a school production or a residential trip, pair staff to work together. Think about who will monitor the success of activities and how they will go about embedding a simple process of quality assurance. You can use quite simple means such as student/staff feedback questionnaires after an event, monitoring attendance and identifying groups of students accessing/not accessing enrichment. You can also get some student feedback on overall enrichment provision in your department.

Good organisation and administration is key to running successful enrichment. As well as mapping and planning, we recommend keeping a file of all your trip letters and risk assessments and other administrative documents. Keep this on a shared area or VLE so that your team can access it and add to it. And keep it tidy and well labelled.

Enrichment is an excellent way in which to raise the profile of your department and get the work of your team noticed and talked about. Make sure that events and achievements are always reported in school newsletters and on the website. For significant events, always contact the local press. Take photographs of everything and add them to pages on your VLE. Keep an evidence file that is regularly updated and demonstrates the work you are doing to enrich your students' education. This could include any letters of thanks or comments from visitors or venues, attendance registers, certificates, photos, newspaper articles and student feedback.

Hopefully the government will be helping you in your efforts: *'we will introduce more support for schools to expand the range of evidence-based, character-building opportunities they provide to pupils and make available funding..."* (*Education Excellence Everywhere*, DfE, 2016).

Community

Your school will be an invaluable asset in your local community: a place of safety and security, continuity and care for some of your most vulnerable pupils; a sporting hub, a venue that hosts netball tournaments, football finals or crucial tennis matches; the setting for live theatre, music and dance and ultimately, the provider of the children of this area's one shot at an education. It is a responsibility that schools take seriously for only in partnership with a community can a school truly hope to realise its ambitions. By 'community', we mean parents, carers and families, local businesses, religious and community leaders, local charities and the local council, a disparate mix who will require different methods of engagement. And by 'engagement', we don't just mean letter writing, providing information about what you've decided to do.

Real engagement means consultation, it means partnership, it requires formality and professionalism and listening, really listening to voices outside of the world of education. In your role, you must endeavour to do this. Not all the time. You got to this position because you're smart, able, you trust your instincts, you make measured, rational decisions – you quite often know best, thank you very much. There's probably a careful balance to find here as you look for ways for the different sectors of your community to support your team's vision without allowing them to fully set the agenda, make demands or change the fundamentals of your team's aims. But being a decent leader means considering other peoples' views from time to time and, if you want to contribute to your school playing a full role in its community, you will need to actively form strong, preferably reciprocated, links.

Being at odds with that community could lead to a whole lot of strife you really don't need. In your area, you will undoubtedly be aware of some bizarre controversy that graced the local headlines for a day or two, some school-based story that got landed with the –gate suffix ('RULERGATE – kids get excluded for forgetting their ruler!', 'SHOEGATE – mum buys wrong school shoes for son!', 'TOILETGATE – kids told by teachers, "Hold it in!!"'). These stories might be unfair and overblown, but they stick, people remember. Watch out for this kind of rubbish and consider the implications of your decisions on the wider community, particularly parents, how they will be perceived or how they could be twisted. Everyone remembers that school where the parents passed chips to their kids through the railings or that one where the head asked the parents not to wear their pyjamas on the school run – you don't want to be caught at the centre of nonsense like that even though we all know the furore surrounding such stories is unfair and overblown. The newspapers, whose default way in to a story these days, on everyone from England cricketers to serial killers, is to talk about which school they attended, can be a useful ally, too, so actively engage with them. Your local newspaper will eagerly fill their pages with stories about your school accompanied by pictures of your smiling, proud students, so for all the significant things you do, both within your curriculum time and as part of your curriculum enrichment, make it your mission to get a good news story out there. In a school where this kind of thing is important, there will probably be a SLT member charged with coordinating these stories, in which case go through him/her; they'll already have the contacts and they'll know how to get your story published. Use your website, too, or even your school's Twitter feed or Facebook page (if they exist) to publicise your efforts, not forgetting the school's newsletter. Lots of schools now have professionally published, glossy newsletters that you should endeavour to use regularly to showcase your work; find someone in your team to coordinate this for you, but ensure you run your eyes over any copy that's produced to check this is the public face you want to show.

In the same way we have given you the opportunity to get to know the key players within your school, it is also essential that you have a keen understanding of your pupils' parents. Now you've got to April, think about whether it is possible to define them as a group, to describe their attitudes, level of involvement in their children's education, the social, racial, cultural blend of your parents – not to be disparaging, not in a judgemental way, just consider what your impressions of them are. How have you come to this understanding? Who has influenced your thinking, what events or interactions with parents have helped to form your judgements? Has your understanding changed through the year? How has this knowledge impacted on your work, if at all?

If you're so inclined, write about them here:

And then having done that, do the following:

Think of an event you could run where parents are invited – to showcase work, to launch a new initiative… – when would you run it, where would you hold it, how would you maximise turnout?

Make a list of all the information particular to your area of the school that would be useful for your parents to know – and how you're going to get it to them (letters, leaflets, website, text message…).

Think of an activity you can get parents involved in, where they might volunteer on a one-off or even regular basis. How would this work, who would run it, what would be the purpose? How would you measure its impact?

You could act on some of these ideas now, implement them before the academic year is out, or decide to use your remaining term to seriously plan your approach to parental engagement to begin the following September.

Your school may already have established links with local businesses. Their choice to engage with the school might not be much of a choice at all, more of a box-ticking exercise, but you shouldn't care too much about their motivations. More likely, their choice to engage with you is borne of simple moral duty, an opportunity to 'give something back' to the community of which they are part. And why not? Larger companies in particular run schemes like this since large portions of their workforce may be your parents, your students their potential future apprentices and employees. They will also probably have someone in charge of making these community links who liaises with schools and other community organisations…but so will your own school. Remember that SLT member with responsibility for liaising with the media? They're probably tasked with this, too, and will already have a contact book with names, numbers and email addresses for you to plunder. Hopefully, there's a large company in your catchment area, but not all schools are lucky enough to have the Nissan factory on their doorstep so it's worth bearing in mind that small businesses and shops are just as viable partners for any burgeoning community schemes you're looking to introduce. Think about what it is you'd like from them – their expertise, their advice, someone to come and give a talk to your pupils, a chance to visit their premises – and what you might be able to offer in return (not money, obviously, it'll never be money). Revisit your development plan from the start of the year to see where establishing business links will help you achieve some of your outcomes, but resist making this a box-ticking exercise of your own. If you believe their reasons are genuine, then yours should be too.

Linking with a charity, in particular, could be a long-term relationship that deepens your pupils' understanding of the real world, gives them experience of an organisation driven by doing good, and possibly offers them a chance to raise money for a worthy cause. Ask pupils to suggest charities they themselves have an interest in, ones that are local, or even ones that are working to support pupils in your school. You could look for charities that provide a natural link to your own subject area – if you're in charge of music, for example, then a quick internet search would show you 'Youth Music', 'Music for All' or 'Live Music Now', all of which look great. An email in the direction of one of these to find out more could be the beginning of a fruitful partnership, one that enriches your pupils' experiences of the curriculum and, indeed, their lives.

Use the table below to record some possibilities:

Name of charity	*Contact details*	*Possible curriculum link or activity*

Now that you've read all about enrichment and community, it's worth pointing out that both of these areas tend to disappear to the bottom of a very large pile of work for middle leaders in schools. And it might be tempting to allow that to happen. They're time-consuming and often complicated, requiring lots of contact with people outside of education who, you'll discover, don't work in the same way that schools do, for better or worse. It's no coincidence that this book has got to April before we've discussed it as a topic. But you should endeavour to make enrichment activities and community engagement activities happen even though we recommend it's just you who does the overseeing – really, another TLR holder within your team needs to be tasked with this, supported by NQTs, RQTs and Teach First staff who are required to plan and run trips as part of their appraisal. Let them get on with creating an exciting enrichment and community plan that supports the vision that you and your team are working towards. Especially for disadvantaged pupils, opportunities like this can have the biggest impact and, it might sound cheesy, when you're sat going over the paperwork for yet another trip, visit or excursion you need only picture their smiling faces to know it will all be worthwhile.

Chapter 11 – May

Preparing for review or inspection

"If your words're true, they're armed."

– David Mitchell, *Black Swan Green*

By the time you arrive at May, you should be assured of having established systems that will make the task of preparing for any scrutiny of you and your work if not easy, then certainly more straightforward. A self-evaluation form is no longer a statutory requirement, but that doesn't mean you shouldn't be doing one. In fact, we highly recommend it. Chances are, your school operates a self-evaluation system and has determined set ways in which they'd like you to collate and present information. The best of these ensure that you aren't producing tome-like documents that, once completed, sit lonely on a shelf, sad, unloved, unread ever again. This is a working, live document that should stand as proud testimony to your endeavours, your successes and indeed your failures; a chance to outline – for YOU and YOUR TEAM primarily – where you are getting things very right *and* very wrong, and therefore what you're doing about it. Yes, your audience will inevitably be a Senior

Leader or some Ofsted official down the line, when you are required to succinctly summarise how amazing you are. Don't be intimidated by the prospect of completing this document, as people new to middle leadership often are; it's not some super top-secret document for super-important people only.

There's nothing wrong with a bit of showing off here – we've all met big-heads who have nothing of substance going on behind all the bragging, whereas the quiet ones, carefully getting on with doing their job, find it difficult to talk up their achievements, seeing it as uncouth. Find a middle ground where you can outline your achievements while also not making yourself seem like arrogance personified. And the style of this is important. Avoid lengthy description – of initiatives, of processes, of people – and stick to evaluation and analysis; if someone wants some more detail of the 'what', they'll have the opportunity to ask, and you can answer, before bringing the discussion back around to impact and effect, the core purpose of completing a SEF. Once again, your school will likely have a way they'd like you to work here, but it's worth summarising our opinion on what makes an effective SEF. It should be:

- In a format that is easily readable by someone who has minimal time in which to make a judgement based on the evidence presented. No waffle, no lengthy description.
- Constantly reviewed – diarise this otherwise it will be forgotten as more immediate pressures take over. Throughout the year, you will probably place this in your Important/Not urgent section of your to-do list (as exemplified in Chapter 9).
- Contributed to by others in your team and used by them too, carefully matching your agreed style and format so that it reads as a unified piece of work, and updated in a systematic way so that sections are not omitted or forgotten. There's nothing wrong with adding or removing something part way through the year as priorities shift or goalposts are moved.
- Chock full of evidence. If it's May and you're scrabbling around for this, then something has gone wrong. In both Chapters 5 and 6, we have advocated systems for the collection of evidence across your area of responsibility and in a variety of formats. Together,

> this will form a substantial base upon which your SEF can be built, data-rich, full of personal observation and referenced against the standards upon which you are to be judged.

You'll need a structure, too, a way to hang all your evidence together so that it is accessible and it's easy to navigate – especially for you. You don't need something so complex that it can even outfox you, its creator, when faced with the task of using it to support your judgements in meetings with your senior team or an inspector. Indeed, use the inspectorate's four areas of assessment to build your SEF: Leadership and management; Teaching, learning and assessment; Personal development, behaviour and welfare and Outcomes. This approach should allow you the breadth of coverage required while also organising your evidence into a logical system.

Preparing for an Internal Review

There's plenty of overlap between the requirements of an internal review versus an external inspection. You would hope that any internal review of your work would be done in a supportive and constructive manner, delivering feedback and advice that is diagnostic. Your reviewer(s) will most likely have already established a working relationship with you so you shouldn't be expecting anything confrontational or antagonistic in tone, a perception of the typical Ofsted inspection that still persists. There may be a great deal of collaboration where you are helped to find the evidence required to fulfil a particular standard. If you have been religiously following your own QA calendar, then a senior leader, maybe even one involved in your internal review, will have participated on some level in monitoring teaching and learning, marking and feedback, behaviour and anything else that will prove relevant here, and so will bring knowledge of your methods, efforts and accomplishments. This will prove useful in your discussions. If they are doing their job right, they should be challenging you, too, to look beyond the evidence you have compiled in your SEF and explore where your next foci should be.

So, what sort of stuff should you be covering in your SEF? Let's think about this a different way and consider what sort of questions you may be expected to answer about your work, using your responses to build a comprehensive analysis. Along the way, we've chosen one question from each section and explored how you might go about answering it.

Leadership and management

How are you supported and challenged as a middle leader?

How have you created a culture in which students and staff can excel?

How would you describe the relationships between staff and students? How do you know?

Can you demonstrate how you focus on outcomes for students, especially disadvantaged students?

How do you use the views of pupils, parents and staff to inform your understanding of the school's effectiveness in key areas?

How do you review and monitor your actions and their impact?

How do you use performance management to challenge your staff and to develop them professionally? How do you encourage them to work collaboratively? Do teachers feel like they can take risks and work independently?

What's teaching like in your department / area of responsibility? How do you know?

> *Is your curriculum broad and balanced?*
>
> For this you'll want to talk about the learning journey that pupils take through your curriculum, highlighting your most successful and creative units of work. Talk about what makes them successful using evidence from assessment data, pupil voice analysis and your own observations including book scrutinies and learning walks. You need only choose relevant quotations from your records or even photographs of pupil work. Describe the inclusive nature of your curriculum and emphasise how it is carefully crafted to take account of the National Curriculum, future examination requirements, the interests of your pupils and their prior attainment, the strengths of your teaching staff and advances in current pedagogical thinking.

How do you promote 'British values' and pupils' SMSC development?

How do you ensure that you have effective safeguarding systems, a culture of equality and universal intolerance of prejudice and extremist views?

Do your pupils feel safe?

Teaching, learning and assessment

Do your teachers have a deep understanding of the subjects that they teach? How do you know? Do teachers have any particular specialisms?

How is questioning used in lessons? Do teachers intervene effectively to address misconception and offer support that allows those who've fallen behind to catch up?

Do teachers plan lessons effectively, managing resources and time? How do you know?

Do teachers manage pupil behaviour effectively? How do you know?

Do lessons contain adequate time and opportunity for pupils to embed skills and knowledge?

Do you see teachers checking pupils' understanding? Do they offer incisive feedback in line with the school's assessment policy? Do pupils use this feedback effectively?

What's homework like? Does it make a difference to learning and progress? How do you know?

Here you will need more real evidence of the homework pupils do – again, photos are a great way to show the range and quality of homework being completed. If your school has formalised a homework timetable for pupils, include this. Some schools also have longer term, pre-published homework projects that you could include while other schools use their VLE to set and monitor homework, a great way to get lots of accurate data. You will need to provide your homework policy which should demonstrate the rationale behind what is set and how often, as well as the ways in which it should be assessed.

What is the teaching of RWCM (Reading, Writing, Communication and Maths) like?

Can you demonstrate that teachers have high expectations and that pupils take pride in their work?

How would you describe your pupils' approach to learning? Do they take part in extra-curricular activities?

How well do you keep parents informed about their child's progress and the content of their curriculum?

Do teachers' lessons and resources seek to deepen pupils' experiences of the world around them, its diversity, the people and communities beyond their immediate experience?

Personal development, behaviour and welfare

How would you describe your pupils and their attitudes to learning? How do you nurture and develop them? How can you demonstrate pupil pride in their work?

How can you demonstrate that pupils show respect for others and their beliefs?

How do you help pupils prepare for the next stage of their education? Does the education they receive provide them with the behaviours and attitudes required to be successful in the world of work or further education?

What is attendance like? How do you promote regular attendance?

> *How would you describe pupils' behaviour?*
>
> You will need to spend some time raiding your school's information management system for the required data here that you will need to back up your observations and assertions. If you're lucky, you might already be provided with, probably monthly, updates from a member of the support staff whose job it is to collate and distribute data on behaviour, both positive and negative. If you aren't, revisit chapter five and the section on monitoring behaviour for some more tips. Finally, this isn't the place to be negative about your own pupils (as if you would!); anything of this sort will be given short shrift, quite rightly, and dismissed as excuse-making. If you do work in a school where challenging behaviour is a feature, then only your efforts to counter-act it are important here, and a good idea would be to present case studies of pupils who have really turned it around – together, how did you achieve this?

How have you tackled incidences of bullying, whatever form it takes?

Do pupils feel safe? How do you know? Can you demonstrate that, as a leader, you have taken swift and decisive action to maintain pupil safety?

How do you contribute to pupils' understanding of how to be healthy – healthy eating, fitness, emotional well-being?

How do you ensure that pupils understand how to stay safe online? How are you contributing to their SMSC (Spiritual, Moral, Social and Cultural) education?

Outcomes

Are pupils making substantial and sustained progress? How do pupils develop their knowledge, understanding and skills? How are disadvantaged pupils, the more-able, lower attaining pupils and SEND pupils doing?

Are students able to articulate their knowledge and hold thoughtful conversations? How do you know? Have you had any conversations like these yourself?

Do pupils read widely and often? How can you evidence this in your area?

Is progress and attainment broadly in line with national averages?

Key here is your use of RAISEOnline. If you don't know how to use this, demand some training. If you think you do know how to use this, get some more training because it's likely changed. Once you get used to the progress scores and all the scatterplot graphs, you should find it all quite straightforward.

If your school doesn't already have a pre-agreed SEF for you to use, then take our simple *pro forma* on the following page. Use it as it is or adapt it to suit you.

Ofsted Area	*Summary of Strengths & Evidence**	*Areas for Development:*	*Led by:*
Leadership and Management Grade 1 2 3 4 5 A	B	C	D
Teaching, Learning and Assessment Grade 1 2 3 4 5			
Personal Development, Behaviour and Welfare Grade 1 2 3 4 5			
Outcomes Grade 1 2 3 4 5			

Key

A: Highlight your current grade

B: Bullet point what you are doing well with plenty of evidence to back up your claims.

C: Bullet point what you know you need to improve, how you will do it and by when.

D: Assign responsibility to show how you have distributed leadership

** with reference to files and key documents:*

In assembling your responses to these questions, your over-arching aim is to build a positive picture of you and the work that is being done by your team. You need to be honest, but this is not the place to make excuses or lay blame for any failures or short-fall. You may work in challenging or difficult circumstances, in a school situated in an area of high social deprivation, for example, but it is your task to analyse how your actions negate the effects of any influencing factors. You may have heard, unfortunately, colleagues in your current school or in previous employment lament the pupils they teach, the attitudes of their parents, the aspirations of the community – "Oh, well, the thing about our pupils is they just can't do something or other." What a lot of awful, awful rubbish. This tainting of your pupils by naysayers cannot, must not, be ignored or shrugged off; this kind of talk is pervasive, corrosive. So the thing about this kind of talk is that, when it's heard by any decent leader, it needs to be stamped upon, challenged, refuted – "And if you really believe that to be the case, what have you done to counter-act it?" If you keep repeating this, like a mantra, they will either change their ways, simply shut up, or, best case scenario, pack up and leave.

Preparing for an Ofsted Inspection.

In reality, you will have only a short period of time to prepare for the arrival of a team of inspectors, probably about half a day. But due to the nature of the cycle of inspections, your school will only be too aware of a window in which their next inspection is likely to occur; if it's imminent, then they'll be in a near permanent state of 'Ofsted Alert', some poor PA nervously anticipating the phone ringing everyday at high noon, deliberately chosen no doubt to invoke the showdown nature of the following day's visit. Before the inspectors eventually ride into town (apologies – this is where this metaphor will end since it is overly romanticising a group of people who, let's face it, are more likely to prefer a silver Vauxhall Insignia to *Silver*, trusty steed of The Lone Ranger!), there are a great many things you can do to be ready. Your work shouldn't live and die on the fear of an Ofsted judgement, ensuring you never begin a sentence with, "Well, Ofsted expects this so..." But nor should misplaced bravado cause you to dismiss them either. When it arrives, a person in your position will undoubtedly be called upon to play a direct role in meeting with inspectors. They'll have their questions, absolutely, and not dissimilar to the ones we've provided above. However, this is *your* opportunity: take it. It's your moment to do some of that showing off that we talked about earlier, and certainly not the place to air any grievances.

Your SEF plays an important role here in presenting your sense of optimism and pride in your school. Instinctively, you will want it to demonstrate how your leadership in particular is impacting upon all areas of school life, but it must also talk up how a collective responsibility is driving forward change and improvement. If you're a secondary Head of Department, you will need to draw upon your team to assist in the collection of evidence, the evaluation of their impact and to gather their input and ideas for next steps, how to keep moving things forward. As a primary middle or senior leader, a lot of this may fall to you to assemble, collate and analyse if you don't necessarily have your own 'team' to call upon. But in both sectors, be aware of or seek out other colleagues writing similar documents, making similar assessments, forming similar judgements, so that you can organise yourselves to work together to shoulder the burden.

Before we move on to handling the meetings themselves, spend about 10 minutes on this activity. Think about the three proudest elements of your work to date in each of the four Ofsted categories from above. They could be from your current role or from a previous role, but they should demonstrate your impact on the school and its pupils. For each, think carefully about how you know they were a success, ensuring your evidence is concrete, not based on a feeling or impression or something intangible.

Leadership and Management

Teaching, Learning and Assessment

Personal Development, Behaviour and Welfare	*Outcomes*

You may have had a slow start to that activity, but once you got going ideas should have come pouring out, possibly prompting an internal struggle over what to omit. This is good. Go back and write the rest down anyway. You may find it helpful to chat with someone else about this, too, since the act of discussion will open your eyes to things you may otherwise have overlooked or downplayed. Put a ten-minute item on your agenda for any team meeting, talk with your SLT line manager or even ask your husband/wife/partner/best friend; they'll have heard all about it, believe us, and might surprise you in how much they can talk knowledgeably about your work!

To any meeting with an inspector, you will feel obliged to take with you, maybe even comforted by, a folder of evidence like your SEF. Even if their questions don't necessarily lead into something you want to talk about, a bit of skilful side-stepping can guide the discussion back to something you're desperate to put in their hands, so have your key documents (a curriculum plan, a data summary sheet, analysis of pupil voice activities…) at your fingertips. Put this all in a big, shiny folder and leave it behind for them to flick through after you've finished. Answer questions at length and truthfully, ensuring any statements you make can be supported by hard facts or by subsequent observation of good practice by the inspectors. Don't tell them that everyone consistently marks to a high standard, for example, if they don't; highlight where excellent marking is taking place and outline how you are addressing any deficiencies. Avoid excuse-making as well.

Harsh though it may be, no one cares if your faculty has been full of non-specialist teachers or long-term supply all year – the only thing they'll be interested in is how you counter-acted these challenges, how you foresaw problems and pre-empted any negative effects on pupils and their learning. If you are conscientious, if you are consistent, if you are organised and follow your own systems, you will genuinely have nothing to worry about. If you don't consider yourself great at talking in interview situations like this, then why not practise? You need only be yourself, albeit a hyper-vigilant, hyper-corporate, armour-plated Ofsted-killing machine version of yourself.

Typically, these meetings will last for as little as 15 minutes and may involve a group of you who hold similar roles. Don't fight to talk over each other, work together, even gently prompting colleagues who may not have spoken much or have missed some details in their contributions to the discussion if you truly know they have something significant to add that they've omitted. Chances are that the final report, if it finds room for you at all, could give you a couple of sentences here or there. Validation of your work, scant though it might be, but validation nonetheless.

It is a stronger measure of leadership to acknowledge weaknesses and know how to deal with them than to pretend they don't exist in the first place. No school, department or leader is perfect, but it is about knowing your strengths and areas for development, and having a clear idea of how you are tackling this.

In this next task, we'd like you to think of the three questions you really, really hope won't be asked. Because, inevitably, they will be, so you will need to be sure how you will go about answering them. Choose three from our list from earlier or come up with three entirely new questions that are specific to you and your role, or a mixture of both:

1.

2.

3.

When your school eventually receives notification of an inspection, perceived wisdom would suggest to just carry on doing what you do, since why wouldn't that be good enough for someone to come and look at? But human nature will inevitably lead you down a different path, one where you insist on triple-checking lesson plans (not needed), the progress of your Year 4 reading scheme (don't worry about it – they're doing great, remember that report you did two weeks ago?) or the condition of classroom displays (they're wonderful, and your support staff will have been drilled not to even think about removing even one staple if there isn't something equally wonderful completed, laminated and ready to replace it). The point is, if you've been the strong leader you want to be, if you've initiated procedures and policies that mean you can confidently point to impact, difference, improvement, then there'll be no problem. People will know their roles and, where you've distributed the leadership of particular areas, should be trusted to get on with it.

James says…

At this crucial moment in your leadership, you may be tempted to resort to micro-management, ignoring many of the practices and systems you have painstakingly established over your time in charge. It might be that you don't catch yourself doing this, but that someone else does, and they might just have a quiet word. Listen to them, if this is the case. Trust your instincts. You're doing a good job.

You'll need to gather people together as soon as you can and lead a short, positive and clear briefing that lays out your expectations, possibly preceded by a brief meeting with your own line manager to clarify the messages that need to be delivered. You might not find out until after lunchtime that an inspection is imminent and you might then be teaching all afternoon followed by a parents evening that night. So you'll have to fit that meeting in somewhere. No matter how much you might have been sent into a frenzy by the news of an inspection, you can't let your team see this. They need you to be strong and confident – remember how we've talked about modelling the leadership you expect to see in others. Be ready to listen to peoples' concerns ("I've got my difficult Year 10 class last lesson!"), solve potential issues they foresee ("I've got a leave of absence tomorrow to attend my youngest's nativity play!!"), and extinguish mini-meltdowns ("Aaaaaarggh!!!"). Pay special attention to your NQTs and trainee teachers; they'll need quiet reassurance and maybe a chance to talk through their plans for the day. While any observation of them by an inspector might not be officially included in the overall judgement of teaching and learning, their development as teachers and the support they receive from the school could still be scrutinised, and a partial observation of their teaching might form part of a different judgement. A good ten minutes with any support staff you line manage is also advisable, including teaching assistants and admin staff. Make sure they know that their contribution is extremely valuable, and that they are also certain of where they are supposed to be, when and who with.

Check classrooms, corridors and other learning spaces that fall under your area of responsibility. Now clearly isn't the time to start ripping down displays and replacing them with ones you hope to magic up, but the overall impression the learning environment gives cannot be underestimated. Your only focus should be on ensuring the basics are right, like tidiness, freedom from clutter and junk and wires neatly stored away.

If you've only been in the job 10 minutes, then that's a different prospect – by all means you should get your head around all your teachers' planning, see with your own eyes the current state of pupils' exercise books and spend a good hour fixing key data in your head. Be sure about what the state of play was before you arrived in post (and put this across diplomatically if asked – remember the need to remain corporately loyal), what you have done since and your vision for the future of your area of responsibility, something you would have formulated in August alongside your team. Ensure your action plan is complete and up to date, that you know what your key priorities are, a particularly important requirement if you are new in post or in a school which may be struggling. Way in advance of any inspection, you and your fellow middle leaders should be pressing your SLT to take you through different aspects of an inspection as a team, even employing external consultants to put you through your paces. This should be a standing item on your middle leadership meeting agendas.

We can probably all agree that the inspection system we have isn't perfect, that surely a co-operative, collaborative and supportive approach to school improvement would be better than antagonism, confrontation, criticism without advice. But it's the system we've got. It's a high stakes game you will have to play, probably more than once in your career. Know the rules. Practise. Revise, even. Be determined that, when the moment arrives, you can hold your nerve and demonstrate the outstanding middle leadership skills you have developed, the impact you have had on your pupils and your commitment to education. The feeling of elation and relief that will come with a positive judgement, one that you earned the hard way and the right way, will be worth it.

Chapter 12 – June

Designing a Creative Curriculum

> *"Creativity involves breaking out of established patterns in order to look at things in a different way."*
> - Edward De Bono

By the time you get to the June of your first year in post, you'll know what is working in your curriculum and what most definitely isn't. Some of this may be beyond your immediate control or could be outside your sphere of influence; for example, the number of periods a week of maths allocated to your Year 10 pupils will have been set long before you arrived as the Head of maths back in September, fitting tightly as it will into a curriculum model designed carefully by your senior team alongside a meticulously organised timetable. You could have been operating a legacy curriculum this past year, one you were stuck with, designed by your predecessor and too late to change when you began the job because of the upset and increase in workload it would have caused your team. Or you could've changed it when you started, or even part way through the year, but it was a half-hearted change or a reactionary one, necessary because of worrying data, unhappy children, inferior planning, unfocused assessment or inadequate coverage of a specification or the National Curriculum.

Your share of curriculum time might not be directly within your control, nor the length of lessons, nor necessarily the staffing of those lessons (although this is something you definitely should be controlling, placing the members of your team fairly, equitably and appropriately), but you most definitely will control the content of your curriculum…we hope. Any interference in this area from above, any questioning of your autonomy on curriculum design, on your ability to make the final call on what it looks and feels like, should be actively repulsed. And this is why. By the time you have settled on your ultimate curriculum model, you will have followed a rigorous consultation process, reached out to a network of colleagues, read up on the key literature, crunched the numbers, empowered your team to lead on different aspects of its creation and triple-checked the mechanics. After launch, there'll be inevitable tinkering, but it will be just that, nothing that can't be fixed by the tightening of a few screws here and there. You won't require anyone to come along and second guess your decisions, especially when the process to arrive at those decisions will have been so thorough and conscientious.

James says…

I suppose I've always been fortunate to have been trusted when it came to making decisions about the curriculum, and to be listened to when pointing to something that isn't working, as long as I had a solution or alternative. I've also (mostly) enjoyed consistency in my staffing so that I could distribute teaching loads across all year groups and levels of ability. I found it especially useful to create, for myself and my team, a separate document that provided an overview of where staff were placed so that all could see the logic behind my decisions and, hopefully, the fair-mindedness of them, too. It would look something like this:

Year 7 (4 periods per week)

Class	7En1	7En2	7En3	7En4	7En5	7En6
Staff	Mr Ashmore	Mrs Clay	Mrs Atkinson	Mrs Greenwood	Mr Rees	Mrs Weston

Year 8 (4 periods per week)

Class	8En1	8En2	8En3	8En4	8En5	8En6
Staff	Mrs Greenwood	Mr Rees	Mrs Weston	Mr Ashmore	Mrs Clay	Mrs Atkinson

...and so on. Not a timetable, just a summary of who was teaching which class that could be kept updated throughout the year to take into account any changes you had to make.

And one more thing – please don't give yourself all the top sets!

So this chapter is all about getting to that point. We'll do this by starting with some key principles of curriculum design, and thinking about what it takes to make a curriculum outstanding.

Your curriculum should provide your pupils with truly memorable experiences and opportunities.

This is where you have to be clear about your definition of memorable. We certainly remember particular lessons from our school days like they were yesterday – the one where someone put a condom on the drama room door handle, the one where the art teacher locked herself in the storeroom in tears, and so on – but (and sorry for the facetiousness) that's not what you're looking for here, obviously. Think about how you'd like pupils to remember your lessons, picture them leaving your classrooms buzzing about what they've just experienced, desperate to return for more. How can your curriculum create that? Think about the impact 'memorable experiences' will have on behaviour, on take-up of subjects at GCSE and beyond, on pupils' willingness to return after school, to volunteer for activities, clubs or performances, on results even as the positivity pupils feel towards their learning is translated into efforts to revise and prepare, maybe even (unconsciously) prioritising your subject over others. In Chapter 10, we discussed the importance of enrichment, another key part of ensuring your curriculum lives long in the memory.

Make a list of your own positive memories from your school days. Think about why you hold them in such high regard. How can you be active in delivering these opportunities for your pupils?

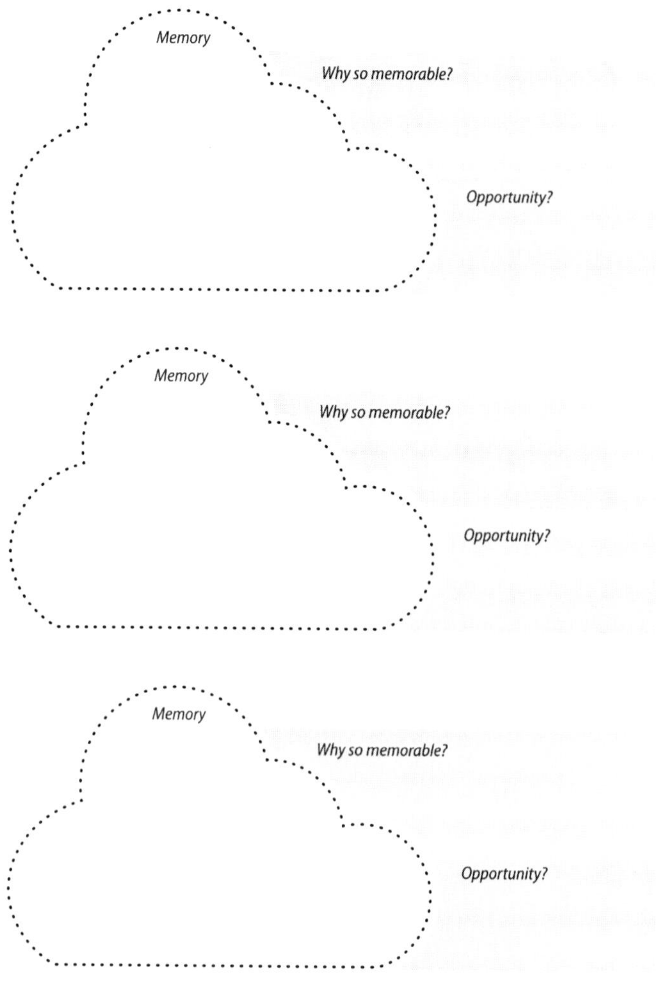

You should be looking to innovate and take calculated risks.

True innovators in any field of human endeavour may give the impression that it all just comes so easy, that it was a spark of genius that led to their trailblazing, but that notion belies the deep, deep thought that will have preceded their eventual success. You too can innovate, *must* innovate if you want to create those memorable experiences. But a revolution in your curriculum will need careful handling. What if the unit of work you despise and want to dump is much beloved by the rest of your team? Well, why is it? Find out. Do they have good reason to want to retain it? Has it led to proven results? What do the kids think of it? If it stands up to these tests, you may need to keep it. If it doesn't, and you can replace it with something creative, new, modern, that you believe will bring freshness to what was stale, it's got to go. Along the way, you may need to trial your innovations, gradually transitioning from the old to the new. Egos may need gently massaging, too, but you'll handle that in and amongst.

Think for a moment about risk. What, in the world of curriculum redesign, might you consider risky? Make a list here, and then think carefully about the measures you would take to counter each risk.

Risk	*How I would counter it*

You should create breadth and balance while also meeting the needs of individuals and groups.

Those two words, breadth and balance, are all very well, but only if you carefully manage just how broad you want to go and consider the outside pressures that could tip the balance towards one particular aspect of your curriculum over another. Too broad and you risk spreading the work pupils do too thinly, forcing your team to race through units of work or skim the surface of topics without giving pupils the chance to explore them in depth, to write extensively or to embed knowledge and skills. By balancing your curriculum, you will need to think about the weighting given to individual assessment foci, for example, or the weighting given to particular facets of an examination. This will already be happening on a whole school level as national performance measures inevitably squeeze out subjects, raising the prominence of some subjects (the EBacc at secondary level) while diminishing others, pushing the likes of drama and music to the side-lines so that they may even exist only as extra-curricular options. This is a sad consequence of a seemingly ideological drive to narrow the curriculum, to re-balance it in favour of only a limited number of subjects. And what are senior leaders meant to do here? Does this meet the needs of individuals and groups? What, in your role, can you do about it?

A great deal, is the answer, because whether you are a subject coordinator in a primary school or a Head of Department in a secondary school, or even a senior leader in either, you'll need to fight the good fight. Your pupils deserve to benefit from a curriculum that provides them with scope, opens the eyes, ears and minds to a world beyond their local community, so ensure yours gives each and every one of them the chance to broaden horizons and bring balance to their learning.

So, how are you going to do this in practical terms? Think now about your own personal aims when it comes to providing both breadth and balance, and write these as targets now:

Breadth: ______________________________

Balance: ______________________________

And, therefore, to achieve these what will you need to actually consider teaching your pupils?

You should ensure reading, writing, communication, numeracy and ICT are well-served by your curriculum.
The key here is to make sure your team understand the difference between reading a bit of a book, spending five minutes on a few sums or getting the kids to create a revision Powerpoint, and *actually teaching* literacy, numeracy and ICT, something they may not be comfortable with. If they aren't, this is an immediate and obvious professional development need. Likely there are a number of people within your school tasked with the monitoring of these areas on a cross-curricular basis, but the monitoring of them is perhaps as far as their role extends. You may be lucky to have more proactive staff members whose role is to develop the teaching of literacy, numeracy and ICT, but their reach and influence can only extend so far, and it is really you as a middle leader who needs to drive how they fit into your curriculum. You need to ensure their inclusion isn't tokenistic either and that their significance is recognised in the schemes of work your team create.

You should make sure it is planned very, very well and that your schemes of work build towards productive outcomes.
Your units of work must be characterised by their ability to interweave ideas and concepts so that there is a clear sequencing of learning, a journey through your curriculum that anyone could follow by picking up a pupil's exercise book and leafing through its pages. This sequencing, this step by step approach to planning, will require attention to detail from you and your team, but will also require you to be influenced by what students have learned previously, particularly at the KS2 to KS3 transition point. Here, you will need to take into account the impact on Year 7 of the KS2 programme of study and its successful (or otherwise) application in your primary feeder schools. We make no apology for

constantly name-checking the secondary Heads of English and Maths in this book since so much external policy-making impacts so significantly on their work in particular. And here, again, is another area where they will be expected to act decisively, identifying gaps in prior learning to shape their Year 7 curriculum. Necessarily reactive, their choices here will ripple outwards across all the other subjects within a secondary school, probably with literacy and numeracy coordinators using the data, too, to inform the foci for the year ahead. Like we said, planned very, very well, at an almost micro level on this occasion.

As we've pointed out on numerous occasions throughout this book, Ofsted, quite rightly, have stated they don't expect to see a particular way of teaching, that all they're looking for is effective teaching, in whatever form, having measurable impact on pupil progress. But in the planning of your units of work, desirous features of lessons will likely be variety, creativity. Being creative in teaching is sometimes misinterpreted (please, don't make kids do loads of drawing unless you teach art – the art department won't appreciate this since it devalues the skills they are expertly teaching pupils in their lessons), so you have to be clear as a team with how you define something which can be a little abstract. Learning activities and teaching approaches that you collectively consider creative must lead to high-value outcomes and high-quality work. At the same time, in order to be accessed across your team and maybe even delivered by non-specialists, they will need to be well-resourced, easy to interpret, but also customisable so that individual teachers can match lessons and resources to the needs of their own class. This, of course, must never be at the expense of high expectations; a teacher can't drop an extended writing activity because "My class could never do that." The mission must always be to adapt your planning while maintaining aspirations, and it's surely the job of every teacher to push pupils to achieve something they themselves may have thought beyond their reach before they stepped through that classroom door.

There will be all sorts of talents within your team of teachers so allow them to explore these in their planning. Although we are saying meticulous planning is important, teachers shouldn't necessarily see it as a straitjacket. Good teachers know they need to adapt their planning regularly (a week later, a lesson later, a minute later!) to react to misunderstanding, misinterpretation or plain old "We just don't get it, sir!" Conversely, poor teachers who stick too rigidly to the plan and who plough on through their unit of work regardless of the pupils, who see lessons of a series of tasks to get through, will need to be shown how to break free of something that just isn't working…as long as you reinforce that it is the end point, always the end point, that is the most important element, that this does remain fixed. A productive outcome of a unit of work, probably through standardised assessments of some kind, is an inflexible red line in planning. Designing those assessments is also paramount since you have to know what the end point is first before you even consider lesson content. That's not teaching to a test – that's having a clear understanding of the ultimate destination of the learning journey on which you will take your pupils.

By now, you are clear about who your team are, what qualities they bring to the table and where their strengths lie. Think about this purely from the position of their teaching for the moment. Write down the names of some of your team below and note down their standout skill that comes through in lesson after lesson. How, through professional development, peer coaching or team meetings, could you exploit these skills to benefit your whole team?

Team member

Skill

Team member

Skill

You should continuously renew and improve your curriculum. The world doesn't stand still and, for good or bad, this is particularly true in the world of teaching. Once again, in stating that you should 'continuously renew and improve', a diplomatic balance will need to be achieved. The frustration that follows some sweeping change instigated by the DfE, the moving of the goalposts by Ofsted, the inevitable switch of priority or approach that accompanies the appointment of new senior leaders in a school are all deeply unsettling so you don't want to be yet another contributor to this narrative of change. Change is good, necessary even, but never for the satisfaction of ego, or because of personal ideology. The renewal and improvement of your curriculum should always be seen as an opportunity and never a burden: so you're introducing a new text because five Year 4 boys won't stop talking about it and they think it should be law that everyone reads it; you're investing in brand new athletics equipment for PE because the school is buzzing from seeing Team GB's Olympic exploits and you're considering switching exam boards in History to take advantage of a new, exciting specification.

In making these decisions, consider who you should consult. Fill in the circles below with as many individuals or groups who deserve to have an input into the redesign or renewal of your curriculum, and its delivery:

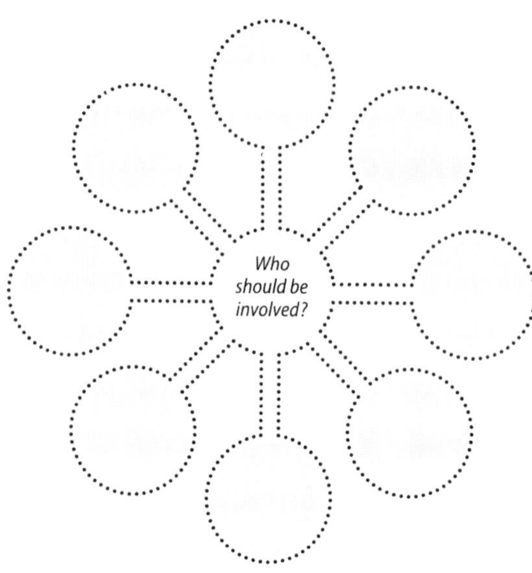

You should look to make independent learning a cornerstone of your plans.

In the final analysis, your pupils will be judged on how they perform independently – in an exam, a performance, a practical – so their ability to learn independently should be central to your thinking when designing a curriculum. To some, this will come naturally, but to most it will need to be taught. Creating independent learners, a phrase often regurgitated by staff when they are asked about their school's mission, as they often are in those PD sessions where you are asked to visualise your ideal pupil, repeated so often now it may already have passed over into empty-phrase territory…is a worthwhile, decent objective. For us, this is where an effective homework policy comes into its own. Ensure homework is fully incorporated into your planning and ensure that all homework tasks are meaningful. They must complement and contribute to the learning taking place during curriculum time, while also being designed to encourage independent learning outside of school hours. Think carefully about how you will go about monitoring that homework is being set regularly, that it fulfils your brief to be important, maybe even substantial, and that it is being completed to a good standard. But watch out, too, because you can't just expect to magically create a culture of independent learning just by making sure you've got a working homework policy. There are dangers attached to having an ambitious homework policy, dangers you will need to think about cancelling out via your actions as a middle leader: homework adds to the marking load of your teachers; its completion, if erratic, can quickly lead to the bureaucracy of homework collection taking over lessons or your team's time as they chase non-completers around school. Pupils may find homework tasks from a range of subjects clashing on a weekly basis with the deadlines for each task also overlapping, thus becoming impossible to meet, leaving kids ragged and stressed or simply opting out, ignoring that they have it to do and so not doing anything, somehow a worse, more depressing option.

Address potential issues with homework head-on:

- Is homework creating extra marking? Can it be assessed in lesson using peer- or self-assessment, can you employ software on your VLE (some, like Frog, certainly have this sort of thing built in, although it's far from perfect) to lessen the load, can you suggest teachers carefully plan when homework is given so that three pieces of homework aren't all due in on the same day, can tasks always be extensions or development of classwork so their assessment is bundled up into the teacher's regular marking cycle?

- Are pupils not completing homework? Could you set up a homework club, could you have an open-door policy for students at break and lunchtimes to come and complete homework, could you ensure that homework tasks are achievable and accessible (*eg* not reliant on internet access if not all pupils have this), could you insist on all teachers displaying their weekly homework tasks on a dry-wipe board on their door for each class, could you implement a clear system of sanctions for continued non-completion of homework?
- Do your homework tasks clash regularly with other subjects? Can you coordinate this better, creating a homework timetable with other middle leaders that you adhere to, can you ensure your team are allowing plenty of time for students to complete homework, can you tell your team to be on the lookout for signs of undue stress and worry amongst their pupils because of homework?

We aren't trying to pretend that doing all of this will make pupils into independent learners overnight. This is just one area in which you can place time and resources in the hope of making a difference. There are inevitably a range of other influencing factors in play here – the pupil's attitude to school, their friendship groups, their outside hobbies and interests, the level of parental support, their ambition and maturity… and so on – some of which are beyond your control. But, time and again, we hear that the biggest influence on a pupil's academic success or otherwise is the teacher in front of them day in and day out, a trained, knowledgeable and conscientious operator. So your decisions about *how* they operate, in this case with regards to how decent homework can contribute to the creation of independent learners, are particularly significant when placed in that context.

Chapter 13 - July

Reflection for Long-term Strategic Planning

> *"By three methods we may learn wisdom: First, by reflection, which is noblest; second, by imitation, which is easiest; and third by experience, which is the bitterest."*
> - Confucius

It's July, commonly the month where – if you work in a school – you are exhausted or elated or a combination of the two. You perhaps feel a huge sense of achievement when you look back on your first year as a middle leader. Reflecting on some of your less glorious moments in the past year may induce cringing and disbelief as you confront yourself with your own stupidity. Those moments when you have felt like you're at the top of your game, an inspirational trailblazer and the type of leader others would aspire to be will be more pleasant to reflect on. There will also be times when you felt despair, frustration, anger or perhaps as though you are lost at sea...and sinking. All of these are absolutely to be expected and experiencing such feelings is entirely normal; in fact, they're a positive sign of percipient self-awareness.

In this chapter we will guide you through the process of reflecting honestly on aspects of your year, looking closely at successes and areas for improvement. You will create a solid foundation on which you will be able to build strategic plans for the coming academic year.

In order to adapt and improve, we are required to reflect well. It's not enough to chew something over with a colleague and kid yourself that you have reflected deeply and honestly when what you have actually done is moan about systems and people and blame a problem on someone else. It's also not helpful if your method of reflection is to ruminate endlessly about your performance and other's perceptions of your performance. Beating yourself up over each and every minor blunder is never an effective way to reflect. A healthy measure of self-doubt is ok, but don't let too much creep in.

We think that good reflection should be structured and should always involve writing things down. You need notes that you can use to inform planning and they will also serve as a record and a measure of your progress as a leader. Writing on actual paper helps organise your thinking – don't carry out all the reflection in your head!

This chapter is comprised almost entirely of reflective tasks for you to carry out. We're not apologetic about this and we absolutely recommend that you should take it seriously and spend lots of time on it! The reflection you do now will be invaluable as you begin to plan the coming year. At the very least, you will have a wonderful list of action points to help inform your strategic planning. There will be other areas that we have missed that are relevant to your particular role. Use our model to reflect on these if you find it helpful but whatever you do – do reflect!

As a profession, we always encourage teachers to reflect on their teaching practice and support them in doing so and it is similarly vital that we reflect on our leadership. It's possible that you will find it helpful to consult others as you reflect on some areas; your line manager or members of your team might be able to support you in reviewing your performance. Ask people who will be honest and commit seriously to supporting your reflection process. It's no help just being told you're doing a great job and that everybody admires you; as pleasant as it might be, it is not good reflective practice just to amble around fishing for compliments! You could team up with another middle leader and work through the process together if that helps. If time is an issue, share your plan with your line manager and insist politely on having some additional time to carry out this important process.

These are what we think are the key questions you should ask which will help you reflect constructively on any aspect of your work or leadership. Of course, they might need adapting at times but the general structure is – we think – helpful.

What precisely am I reflecting on?

Be precise about what you are reflecting on and also be clear about whether you're reflecting on the state of that area within your team OR your leadership of that area. Both are important but keep them separate as you reflect.

How do I feel about the thing I am reflecting on?

How you feel is important. We all have gut feelings about our performance and sometimes those gut feelings or instincts are right, but sometimes they need to be challenged. As a busy middle leader, you may rarely indulge yourself with the opportunity to describe or discuss your feelings. In fact, as a leader, you may find that you spend an inordinate amount of time concealing them! We're not well versed in theories of psychology, but we do know that expressing – or at the very least identifying and acknowledging – your feelings is important. Some people find it comes naturally, for others it will be more of a challenge.

How would I describe my performance objectively?

Reflection also requires that you adopt a dispassionate, uninvolved and neutral mind-set. It can be helpful to ask for help here, but not vital. You're looking at the facts and need to describe it as it is.

What really happened here? What worked or didn't work and why?

Now you need to become analytical and dig deeper. Multiple, interconnected factors may have led to a failure or success. What were they? What/who affected outcomes? Why did this happen?

What do I need to do now?

Plan your actions for improvement or development or change. Some things will need a drastic rethink and overhaul, others will need tweaking and some can run successfully exactly as they are. Be judicious and don't set yourself up to fail by planning too many big changes at once.

Begin by using our structure to reflect on your leadership to date:

What am I reflecting on?	*How do I feel about this area?*	*How would I describe my performance?*
	Your honest gut feeling in a few words	What do / might others say?
My leadership skills and knowledge		
My leadership style		
My management skills		
My organisational skills		
The way I motivate my team		
The way I support my team		
The way I challenge my team		
The way I develop my team		
The ways in which I have utilised the talents of members of staff		
My openness to feedback and advice		
The ways in which I respond to challenges		
The ways in which I deal with and lead change		
The level of support and challenge I have been given		
The ways in which I have celebrated successes with my team		

What really happened here?	*What now?*
What worked or didn't work and why?	Actions I might need to take to improve / develop

At the beginning of the year, you graded yourself 1-5 in each of the following areas. Repeat the task now and then look back at the first time you did it. Have you made progress in some areas? Where have you not made progress? Why is this? How will you address this?

Circle your grade

I have created a culture that enables pupils and staff to excel. 1 2 3 4 5	Relationships between staff and pupils are exemplary. 1 2 3 4 5	I am uncompromising in my ambition to improve outcomes. 1 2 3 4 5
I focus on consistently improving outcomes for all pupils. 1 2 3 4 5	I use incisive performance management that leads to professional development that encourages, challenges and supports teachers' improvement. 1 2 3 4 5	I have a deep and accurate understanding of the school's effectiveness. 1 2 3 4 5
I have created a climate in which teachers are motivated and trusted to take risks and innovate in ways that are right for their pupils. 1 2 3 4 5	I promote equality of opportunity and diversity exceptionally well. 1 2 3 4 5	Our broad and balanced curriculum inspires pupils to learn. 1 2 3 4 5
Pupils' spiritual, moral, social and cultural development is at the heart of what we do 1 2 3 4 5	Work to protect pupils from radicalisation and extremism is exemplary. 1 2 3 4 5	Safeguarding is effective. 1 2 3 4 5

We spent some time in Chapter 7 working on developing a strong ethos for your team. You were asked to describe the departmental ethos that you would like to foster and develop. Reflect honestly on the ethos of your department now and then compare it to the description of the **ethos you wanted to create**:

What am I reflecting on?	*How do I feel about this area?*	*How would I describe my performance?*
The current ethos of my department		
	What really happened here?	*What now?*

In Chapter 10, we looked at ways in which you might develop and raise your team's profile and engage with key stakeholders. Reflect on how this went:

What am I reflecting on?	*How do I feel about this area?*	*How would I describe my performance?*
The work my team ...	- Your honest gut feeling in a few words	- What do / might others say?
has done to engage with staff throughout the organisation		
has done to engage with SLT		
has done to engage with parents		
has done to engage with schools in our learning community		
has done to engage with colleges and universities		
has done to engage with local businesses		
has done to engage with the local community		
has done to engage with teacher training organisations		
has done to raise our profile nationally or globally		

What really happened here?	*What now?*
- What worked or didn't work and why?	- Actions I might need to take to improve / develop

In reflecting on your leadership of teaching and learning (Chapter 5), you might like to involve or consult with other members of your team in reflecting on teaching and learning. Working on this as a team could serve as a useful exercise. Staff will be much more open to changes that take place if they have been involved in identifying the need for that change:

What am I reflecting on?	*How do I feel about this area?*	*How would I describe my performance?*
	- Your honest gut feeling in a few words	- What do / might others say?
Achievement		
Progress		
Curriculum		
Planning		
Display		
Tracking, monitoring and intervention		
Observations		
Learning walks		
Student feedback / voice		
Marking scrutinies		
Standardisation		
Moderation		

What really happened here?	*What now?*
- What worked or didn't work and why?	- Actions I might need to take to improve / develop

Reflect on your performance in managing meetings and time – we looked at this in Chapter 9:

What am I reflecting on?	*How do I feel about this area?*	*How would I describe my performance?*
	- Your honest gut feeling in a few words	- What do / might others say?
How I have managed meetings		
How I have managed and led departmental communication		
How well I support my team in managing time and work / life balance		
How well I manage my own work / life balance		

What really happened here?	*What now?*
- What worked or didn't work and why?	- Actions I might need to take to improve / develop

How well have you dealt with and used data? There are tasks you completed in Chapter 6 that might help here:

What am I reflecting on?	*How do I feel about this area?*	*How would I describe my performance?*
	- Your honest gut feeling in a few words	- What do / might others say?
My departmental trackers		
How effectively staff in my team use data		
The design of intervention strategies		
The delivery of the intervention strategies		
The impact of the intervention strategies		
Shared leadership of intervention programmes and activities		

What really happened here?	*What now?*
- What worked or didn't work and why?	- Actions I might need to take to improve / develop

Now reflect on your work at devising an enrichment programme and engaging with the community – you can refer to Chapter 10 here:

What am I reflecting on?	*How do I feel about this area?*	*How would I describe my performance?*
	- Your honest gut feeling in a few words	- What do / might others say?
The quality and variety of enrichment opportunities my team provided		
How I have ensured shared leadership of enrichment activities		
The impact of the enrichment activities		
My leadership of the monitoring and quality assurance of enrichment activities		

What really happened here?	*What now?*
- What worked or didn't work and why?	- Actions I might need to take to improve / develop

In Chapter 12, we looked at the designing of a creative curriculum. Reflect on your work in this area:

What am I reflecting on?	*How do I feel about this area?*	*How would I describe my performance?*
	- Your honest gut feeling in a few words	- What do / might others say?
The curriculum provides memorable experiences		
We innovate and take risks		
Our curriculum has breadth and balance		
The curriculum is well-planned the focus of the curriculum is on progress and outcomes		
RWC, numeracy and ICT are well served by our curriculum		
Our curriculum helps foster independence and resilience		

What really happened here?	*What now?*
- What worked or didn't work and why?	- Actions I might need to take to improve / develop

You may or may not find it useful to use some of Ofsted's criteria for outstanding leadership and management in your reflection process. We've included it as an optional task:

What am I reflecting on?	*How do I feel about this area?* - Your honest gut feeling in a few words	*How would I describe my performance?* - What do / might others say?
Leaders and governors have created a culture that enables pupils and staff to excel. They are committed unwaveringly to setting high expectations for the conduct of pupils and staff. Relationships between staff and pupils are exemplary.		
Leaders and governors focus on consistently improving outcomes for all pupils, but especially for disadvantaged pupils. They are uncompromising in their ambition.		
The school's actions have secured substantial improvement in progress for disadvantaged pupils. Progress is rising across the curriculum, including in English and mathematics.		
Leaders and governors have a deep, accurate understanding of the school's effectiveness informed by the views of pupils, parents and staff. They use this to keep the school improving by focusing on the impact of their actions in key areas.		

What really happened here?	*What now?*
- What worked or didn't work and why?	- Actions I might need to take to improve / develop

If you've completed everything we have suggested, you'll have fifty plus items under the 'What do I need to do now?' heading. We recommend typing up this list, prioritising it, streamlining it, reflecting upon it some more and ultimately **using it** to plan strategically for the coming year.

We're aware that this chapter has been an easy ride for us and that you have done all the work but we do promise that the work you have done will be invaluable. We think that any time you spend developing your reflective skills will be time well spent.

Chapter 14 – August

Results

"History is a wheel, for the nature of man is fundamentally unchanging. What has happened before will perforce happen again."
- George R.R. Martin, *A Feast for Crows*

"It's fine to celebrate success, but it is more important to heed the lessons of failure."
- Bill Gates

A year ago, you undertook the analysis of a set of results of which you had little to no ownership. But that was a year ago. Now, your task is to analyse *your* results, a set of facts and figures that you have been able to directly influence. Over the past twelve months, your changes, ideas, initiatives and decisions have cumulatively led to this point. You may be nervous, and rightly so. A good set of results will not only stand as justification that your way has been the right way, but will also potentially be vindication for your many choices, some of which may have been unpopular, doubted or even openly questioned by those above or below you. The chance of any future resistance will be greatly lessened in the face of such strong evidence of your success. Additionally, you will instantly gain the power to push for more – more money to spend, more time for your team, more staff, more resources, more rooms, more whatever-is-your-priority – since a strong set of results is the answer to any question you might now be asked about why a change you want to make is required. Remember your plan, however. You mapped out your vision for your team 12 months ago, too, the endgame of which is not being played this August, but three, five or seven years from now, or longer if you're here for the real long haul, and so you need to be crystal clear where these results sit within that plan. You will need to be even clearer than that if these results have been not as good as expected, or indeed, not good as expected. If your results are a disappointment, we'll come on to what to do about this in good time. First, though, we'll look at how to approach your analysis.

In Chapter Two, we directed you to ask six questions:

1. What did the students achieve and what progress did they make?
2. What should they have achieved and what progress should they have made?
3. How accurate was forecasting?
4. Who has over-performed/underperformed/done as expected?
5. Can you identify any patterns or trends?
6. Which 'groups' of students have done well and which haven't?

Do this again, but this time you are going to extend each prompt with the tag question of 'How and why is this different to last year?'

1. What did the students achieve and what progress did they make? How and why is this different to last year?

   Previously, you were required to investigate how the standard of teaching had impacted on your results, whether the curriculum was fit for purpose and whether there had been any staffing issues. All this still stands, but now you must also outline what changes you have put in place and the impact they have had. Draw contrasts between the two Augusts, talking up your achievements and gently reminding your audience how far you, your team and your students have come in a year. Sure, not everything will be fixed; emphasise that this is a work in progress and discuss the plans specific to making gains in pupil achievement that you have for the coming year, and then demonstrate how these will continue to positively push up results.

2. What should they have achieved and what progress should they have made? How and why is this different to last year?

   Do a full comparison to targets first and then you need to show how you have narrowed or even eliminated the gaps between expected achievement and actual achievement.

3. How accurate was forecasting? How and why is this different to last year?

   You should be able to show improved accuracy in your team's forecasting abilities, especially if you have implemented the systems of moderation and standardisation we have recommended elsewhere in this book. However, recent years have been characterised by some kind of national 'story' (think about those controversies in secondary English and maths) that has usually come about because of tinkering with grade boundaries, changing how final grades are calculated by combining external and internal assessments, changing specifications, changing expectations in terms of level of challenge, the removal of controlled assessment, the double-barring of qualifications, the adjustment from modular to linear assessment or the removal of opportunities for early entry...and so on and so on. This instability, this turbulence, it has to stop some time, right? But what if this year the 'story' as applied to your school happens to have you as its main character? How will you deal with this? Until there is a period of stability and consistency, then truly accurate forecasting is going to prove very difficult. Your leadership team will know this, but you still have to endeavour to address how you will do everything you can to counter the effects of changes like these (such as higher internal grade boundaries for mock exams or using the most challenging past papers). Looking back, some of these things could never have been pre-empted, so ridiculous, unfair or from completely out of nowhere have they been, but you have to be optimistic and hope those days are gone.

4. Who has over-performed/underperformed/done as expected? How and why is this different to last year?

   Get your long lists of students together and meet with your team again. This time, pupil names will be familiar; you will know their stories, you will be aware of where there are real successes and where there are catastrophes, you will have directed and guided teachers to take specific actions and you will also know all you did to intervene since your intervention strategy this year will have been your own. In the planning of intervention, we encouraged you to include a review process to systematically evaluate its effectiveness as you went along, adjusting and renewing your strategies throughout the year. Now, in your final review, summarise the effectiveness of each of the groups of students involved, including a breakdown of what you've already put in place for the next year group coming up – and your rationale for this. Just because something worked for this year group, it might not again. Tailored and personal intervention means figuring out what will work for a whole new set of pupils every year, and what works for you and your team, too.

It's worth spending time right now evaluating the effectiveness of your initiatives, interventions and strategies from this year. Complete the table below with your ideas, noting which ones contributed to results, which ones had some impact but need work and which ones, in retrospect, were a complete waste of time.

Initiative, intervention or strategy employed by you and your team.	*Observations on its effectiveness with evidence or data.*	*What will you do differently next year?*

James says...

I know you've just read a chapter that has encouraged deep and honest reflection, but it really is worth spending time on the activity above, even if it feels repeated, because now you've got a new set of results in front of you. And they may cast your intervention strategies in a very different light.

5. Can you identify any patterns or trends? How and why is this different to last year?

   Once more, consider these results as part of a three year set. If there has been improvement, highlight this with a graph or table (it's relatively simple to create these in MS Excel or get your data manager to help out) that visually demonstrates the impact you are having. If there's been a decline, this shouldn't be coming as a shock to anyone – but you have to be prepared with your explanations, never excuses.

6. Which 'groups' of students have done well and which haven't? How and why is this different to last year?

   There will most likely be a difference between this year and the previous year since no two year groups are ever going to be the same. That said, it's highly possible that your school has had a relentless focus on particular groups of students this year – White British, boys, disadvantaged students – and so, inevitably, you will have had this focus, too, because they have caused concern for a number of years and their attainment needs addressing. Foreground the achievements of these focus groups in your analysis. You will undoubtedly come back to your intervention strategies here, highlighting the many ways you have gone about engaging these students, tracking their progress and, in the end, narrowing the gap between them and the achievement of the rest of the student body or their peers nationally. Here's a reminder of the list we suggested in Chapter Two for which groups to consider:

   - Gender
   - Ethnicity

- SEND status
- More Able
- Form/Tutor/Year group
- Pupil Premium
- Free School Meals status
- Prior attainment (KS1, KS2, KS3, or previous year's end of year result) – usually broken down into low/middle/high attainers
- Summer born children
- Looked after children.

Revisit last year's report that you wrote to remind yourself of the structure and format required. Here it is again, briefly:

1. **Trends**: Three-year trend of improvement
2. **National Context**: Comparison with national averages
3. **Team Performance**: Detailed breakdown of each class/subject
4. **Groups**: Performance of key groups
5. **Other Year Groups**: Summarise end of year performance of other year groups
6. **Next Year**: Next year's key cohorts
7. **Intervention**: Early intervention ideas.
8. **Action Points**: Summarise 3-4 action points that will feed directly into your development plan.

Once more, check your work thoroughly. If anything, this should be a much more accomplished document to last year's, reflecting your year in post and your increased familiarity and understanding of the school, its pupils and its systems. In turn, the process of producing this report should be much more straightforward, but there's no harm in once again running it by a trusted counterpart and hearing their views. On the flip side, you're no longer the new guy, so any goodwill or understanding from your senior leaders, any leniency they might have shown you in last year's meeting, may have mysteriously evaporated somewhere in the last twelve months; expect tougher, more challenging questioning, deeper probing of your record and increased scrutiny of your actions and decisions. These can be easily and comprehensively answered if you've done your homework, and you've got the results to back you up. But what about if results this year have been nothing short of disastrous? What to do then?

A poor set of results, especially if unexpected, can seem catastrophic. You will inevitably take this news to heart, a personal indictment of your work so far and your capability as a leader. Like grief, you may initially feel denial closely followed by anger, real rage at what you see as the injustice in these events. It's easy to say, but this would be a mistake. Yes, you have to address very openly what went wrong, reflecting honestly on the year you've had, but you should be careful of the path down which this will lead you. You should be looking to move towards conscious incompetence (knowing what you're rubbish at) and then how to fix it rather than wallowing in self-doubt. Besides, it won't be all bad, but it might take a while before you come to accept that. Grieving over a set of results (and this isn't hyperbole – you will feel real loss over these results) may last some time and, in all seriousness, for your own well-being, you really will need to talk about it with someone. Your senior team will expect total openness from you when you're given the chance to present your analysis, but more important to them is the future; what steps are you intending to take to ensure this doesn't occur again? Be forensic in your breakdown of the steps you will need to take, anticipating obstacles, enlisting support, requesting resources or allowances that you believe will counteract any recurrence. Hopefully, your SLT have shown faith in you this year – they employed you in the first place – so they aren't about to hang you out to dry (and if they did, it would say more about them as leaders than you). Repay that faith by not chucking it all in at the first sign of trouble. Show them that you have learned from this experience and how, as a new leader, you have enough energy and ideas to ensure, twelve months from now, there will be no repeat.

Chapter 15 – Moving on to Senior Leadership

"By faithfully working eight hours a day you may eventually get to be boss and work twelve hours a day."
– Robert Frost

When you first embark on a role as middle leader, aspirations to ever become part of a senior leadership team may seem a mild improbability or a totally preposterous notion. Or it could be that that's exactly where you plan to be in a few years and you're constantly working towards achieving that goal. Or, as is probably the case with many of us, you will work as a middle leader for a year or two and either feel content with the role and position or you will begin to ponder whether senior leadership could actually be for you.

In this chapter, we will look at the differences between middle and senior leadership and the reasons that you might wish to move into a senior leadership role. We'll also look at the practical steps you will need to take in order to prepare for applying for a senior leadership role. Even if you're unsure about whether you would like to become a senior leader, or you think you might but not just yet, there are things you can do to ready yourself for the possible next stage in your career. Sometimes opportunities present themselves – the perfect SLT role in the school you currently work in, for example – and it makes sense to be at least somewhat prepared for such eventualities.

A leader, regardless of where in the pecking order they are operating, is a leader and innate leadership skills can be observed in action in every setting where people come together. Some people are natural leaders and, as we have seen, much can be taught and learned about leadership theory and practice. While the core attributes of a great leader remain a constant, there are many differences between the roles of middle and a senior leader. The characteristics and behaviours of good leaders are what are vitally important at all levels. For that reason, we will revisit the attributes that we looked at in Chapter 1. As you read through these, consider how your time as a middle leader has contributed to you developing these personal attributes. Imagine a before and after for each of the eight attributes. Was that attribute evident in your work and behaviours before you became a middle leader and is it more evident now that you are a middle leader? What does that characteristic look like to others and what does it feel like to have those characteristics? A middle leadership role will have, without doubt, required you to develop and hone your organisational skills. What is your experience? How have you developed and expanded your skills and knowledge as a middle leader? How do you think or feel this has prepared you for a move into senior leadership?

Attributes of great leaders	*Before you embarked on your middle leadership role*	*Now that you are an experienced middle leader*
A sense of purpose: The best leaders we have worked with are always going somewhere. This might be somewhere long term or an ultimate goal, but it's also just the way they do their day-to-day thing. They move and talk with a sense of purpose and resolve.		
An explorer: We think that good leaders are open to exploration. They are eager to explore new avenues and possibilities. They might have a clear sense of their ultimate goal, but they are always aware that there are new things to see, do and learn along the way and they're open to their own new learning. Where there are problems, they probe and analyse.		
Positive: On the whole, the best leaders are positive people. That doesn't mean that they are at all times smiley and amenable, bright and cheery, but their take on life is positive. The way they approach challenges and barriers is with the old cliché of a 'can-do' approach. You don't hear good leaders sighing and whinging.		
Creative: We could write an entire chapter on creativity and creative approaches to problem solving but the bottom line is that leaders create. They create all sorts of things: the right atmosphere for success, opportunities, challenges, great trackers, great resources, interesting and varied schemes of work and of course hardworking and successful teams - of learners and of staff. A really good leader is not precious about their creations and encourages opinions, input and adaptations from others.		

Attributes of great leaders	*Before you embarked on your middle leadership role*	*Now that you are an experienced middle leader*
A learner: Good leaders are learners whether they are working in an educational setting or not. They can be seen learning new skills and knowledge and delight in it. They're also comfortable with being seen to be learning. Leaders who lead us all to believe that they are infallible, all-knowing demi-gods don't impress anyone.		
Great communicators: Whether they are supporting, building teams, chatting, praising, debating, presenting or explaining - they do it well. They communicate clearly and with confidence.		
Organised: It's easy to get carried away on the tide of leadership and focus on the inspirational and creative nature of great leaders, but the bottom line is that day-to-day management and organisation are integral to good leadership. Great leaders will be seen spinning their own plates, and ensuring that everyone else's plates keep spinning too. They will be there when plates break, fixing them, replacing them, asking why they fell and making sure nobody has too many or too few plates on the go at once.		
Inspirational: We have talked at length about just what it is that makes a person inspirational. We have agreed that it is a combination of characteristics and behaviours, some of which are difficult to define and fugacious in nature. What inspires some may well be different to the traits that we find inspirational. Above all, leaders who are authentic and original inspire us. They forge their own path and have a healthy, but reflective and well-reasoned, disregard for trends and obvious choices. We are also inspired by those whose focus is on others. Folk who have an innate yearning to improve the lives of and help other people, in any way, are an inspiration. We are not inspired - or even mildly impressed - by relentless self-promotion thinly disguised as strategic school improvement!		

When you have reflected on how your leadership characteristics and skills have developed, it might be helpful to reflect on how you feel about your leadership. Use the table below to make some notes as you reflect on your experiences as a leader to date. Be as honest as you can and take the time to consider each question thoroughly.

How do I feel about my leadership?	
What do you enjoy about the leadership elements of your role?	
What do you really dislike about the leadership elements of your role?	
What do you find challenging about the leadership elements of your role?	
What elements of leadership do you find really easy?	
Where are there gaps in your leadership skillset? How could you fill these gaps?	
As a leader, what do you do best?	
As a leader, how do you think others perceive you?	
As a leader, how do you feel about having a wider sphere of influence? How would you feel about leading more people?	

Obviously, as a senior leader you will be responsible (and accountable) for the leadership and development of many more staff than you are as a middle leader. You will also have a much higher profile within (and perhaps beyond) your organisation and a wider sphere of influence. Whichever key strand of school development becomes your responsibility, you will likely deliver training and CPD to staff and you will be responsible for the implementation and development of all role-related initiatives across the organisation as well as monitoring, quality assuring and measuring impact. The work that you'll do will be larger scale, which, while challenging, is also great fun. Suddenly the boundaries that once confined you to a single corridor, that meant you engaged predominantly with the same staff each day, are gone. Being a senior leader can feel so much more sociable as you find yourself out and about and interacting with all sorts of people who have previously been confined to their own corridors.

Middle leaders often bemoan the lack of time that they have to be strategic and lead effectively; from where they are sat, a senior leadership role can have the illusion of being laden with free time where you can work quietly on meaningful and strategic projects, analyse data in peace and schedule meetings and appointments to suit you. Obviously, it doesn't pan out quite like that, but senior leadership does feel a tiny bit less like the relentless treadmill of five lessons, a break duty and departmental detention followed by marking and planning and then some more marking. If you have ever taught all day and not had time to visit the toilet, you will be pleased to know that as a senior leader you can be a whole lot more flexible with your bathroom visits.

There is of course a downside to this – you will have a lot more responsibility for managing your own workload, prioritising tasks, allocating time to tasks and organising meetings. You are already great at all of this – you have to be as a middle leader – but a SLT role will take your time-management and organisational skills to a whole new level.

A team of senior leaders might well differ in lots of ways from the teams you have worked in in the past. If you're a subject leader, you'll have worked in the main with a group of like-minded folk who love that subject as much as you! If your middle leader role is pastoral or involves responsibility for a Key Stage, Year or whole school initiative, you may have worked alongside and led a greater number of staff than a subject leader. However, your team will have common goals and student interests at the centre of what they do. Whatever your role, you have built a relationship with a team and worked closely with them.

Should you join a team of senior leaders they may seem like a somewhat disparate band with a wildly varied set of qualities and characteristics, each with distinctive leadership styles and characteristics and perhaps their collective presence gives the impression of divergent mismatch. We think that having a senior leadership that appears a diverse and eclectic formation is a great thing. A brilliant senior leadership team will be composed of leaders with different skills and attributes and an assortment of leadership styles, as well as having likely come from different subject backgrounds and different career pathways. Some of the team will be teachers and some will have different professional roles within the organisation. While all these differences are a good thing, we think it is vital that members of a senior leadership team have in common:

- A strong and shared commitment to the vision for the organisation
- The ability to operate as a highly functioning team
- The ability to present themselves as a united and harmonious squad at all times

The ways in which senior leadership teams are structured are many and varied and, of course, each organisation will structure its leadership team in order to best serve the needs of the organisation. Each member of the team will have areas on which they lead and areas that they manage. Like a middle leader's role, a senior leader's role will combine leadership and management and you will be expected to adopt a range of leadership styles as appropriate. If you look at advertisements for senior leadership roles such as Assistant Headteacher or Assistant Principal, you'll find that some give a very clear outline of the role that they are looking to fill. Others, however, may be a little more non-specific. Often an organisation will look for a person who will make a great leader in their school or college and, after they have appointed, will decide how leadership is shared across the team depending on skills and experience of those that make up the team. In days gone by, some senior leaders might lead on the same project forever and ever – if you were the timetabling guy, then you timetabled every year until you retired, eternally revered for your timetabling artistry. These days, leadership is usually shared much more strategically with a focus on building the skills of the team and succession planning.

We think that, ideally, you take initial steps to prepare for a senior leadership role about a year before you arrive at application stage. If you're thinking about a move in this direction, plan to spend a full school year readying yourself for the application process. We've put together some suggestions that might support you in this process but – as is always the case with this book – adapt and amend to suit you. Hopefully your continued professional development is supported by your organisation and you have access to training and development programmes.

The following is a list of areas for which you should gain evidence of having succeeded or (if there has been the occasional misstep or full-blown catastrophe) evidence that you are on a learning journey and are in the process of developing the necessary skills and knowledge. You didn't rock up to your middle leader role knowing everything you needed to know; you have learned and are still learning on the job. In this respect, it will be exactly the same if you commence a role as a senior leader.

Collect evidence that:

You are amazing in your current role

It goes without saying that you need to feel confident that you are doing an awesome job as a middle leader and are ready to take the next step. Evidence of your success will be easy to source because you have to collect it all the time. Just evidencing great results or progress is not enough; gather evidence that demonstrates how you have had a positive impact on staff, students and other stakeholders. Evidence changes you have implemented, your leadership skills and the effective day-to-day running of the area for which you are responsible.

You can deliver whole school training/CPD

If you haven't done yet, deliver something whole school. It doesn't really matter what it is, but find out whether you can engage a hundred exhausted teachers and get them on board with your ideas, plans or initiatives. Practising this will not only help you hone skills, but you will be widening that sphere of influence and gauging how that feels.

You can plan and lead large-scale intervention strategies and evidence impact

We're not talking classroom intervention and small group stuff here. We're talking mammoth scale coordination of intervention programmes and strategies across year groups and key stages and with many staff and other stakeholders involved. We're also talking data and impact – measurements!

You have developed an effective leadership style

Your leadership skills will have developed hugely and you should identify successes and areas for development. No doubt you lead a complex and sometimes challenging team of people and lead them in different ways at different times. You'll have a predominant leadership style and unique approaches to leadership – what matters here is that you are reflective about your leadership and develop a strong self-awareness. Be able to describe and explain what you do and also what you are learning.

You have experience of coaching and mentoring

You may be working in an organisation that has an established programme of coaching and/or mentoring or perhaps you have set up a small-scale programme within your team. It could be that you mentor an NQT and informally coach someone. Whatever you do, ensure you evidence the work you do and the impact it has.

You are an effective line manager and you are aware of your strengths and areas for development

Again this requires you to be reflective. It could also be productive to ask for support here – discuss with your own line manager your strengths and areas for development. If a particular area – or indeed a particular person – happens to be challenging and difficult for you to make progress with, set yourself targets with help from your line manager and keep evidence of the progress that you make. This could be a simple notebook where you jot down observations and reflections on a regular basis. We think that you will be able to look back at these notes and use them to prepare examples you might discuss during the application process.

You are skilled at implementing quality assurance

Whether it's lesson observations, learning walks, book scrutinies or display inspection, you need to demonstrate that you are methodical and follow protocols. You also need to be super organised at record keeping and you must also be skilled at giving constructive feedback. Consider the way you use your findings to inform future planning and to make improvements.

You can engage with external partners

If you are working hard but are somewhat confined to your corridor of day-to-day operations and detached from the rest of the school – or the rest of the world – you need to make a concerted effort to engage with others. We know that this is a seriously tall order given the amount of work you have to do and the time constraints you work under, BUT you will need to do it a lot as a senior leader. Start getting some experience now. To make things easier, involve your whole team. Find opportunities to work with other learning providers, local businesses and politicians, minor (or major) celebrities, sports people and experts in your field. Engaging with external partners needn't be an additional and arduous task if you ensure projects target specific points in your development plan. A large-scale in-house event will take a lot of organising and coordination, but it will be an excellent development opportunity.

You are passionate and motivated

Yes, it's hard to quantify and measure passion and motivation, and the impact they have on your leadership. However, you're going to need to demonstrate these attributes so show your passion. Join some working parties; become a staff governor; organise trips and events; support other staff and departments in their events and ask senior leaders if you can help and support with initiatives on which they are leading. They're not going to say no because they will be delighted to have help. In return for help, you learn new skills and gain experience. You will probably have gaps in your skill set and experience, but if you plan in advance, you have time to address the gaps and impress at interview when you talk about the work you have put in to preparing yourself for a role in senior leadership.

Topics you may be asked to discuss at some point during the application process

This is not, of course, the definitive list and we are deliberately not reducing this to a list of sample questions. Our advice is that for each area you discuss, you should be able to give examples of successes – and times where you didn't succeed but learned something and changed – in your current role and/or talk about how you would implement something in your new role.

Current developments in education

Basically, you need to know what's going on in the world of education. What are the burning issues right now? We recommend being prepared to talk about something that is a little outside your area of expertise. If you're currently a Head of maths, don't just talk about the latest maths curriculum and the latest maths GCSE specifications; be able to talk about the debate surrounding Multi-Academy Trusts or the latest research on revision techniques or new government initiative. Show that your interests and knowledge are broad. Have opinions, but don't be too opinionated!

Your current leadership role and responsibilities – successes, failures, strengths and weaknesses

We think that a candidate who declares they have had no failures and has no weaknesses is cause for concern. They're either lying or utterly lacking skills in self-reflection – either way, we wouldn't be impressed. The key is to have a realistic balance when you talk about your achievements. Aim to come across as 85% successful and 15% failure (we don't mean walking disaster scale failure, just things that didn't work out). Talk honestly and openly about the mistakes you have made or the things you find challenging, but most importantly, demonstrate your self-awareness and resilience. As a senior leader, you will need an ability to see the bigger picture and this can be an eye opener for those new to senior leadership because the scope of the role can be quite wide-reaching.

Your contributions to whole school policies or initiatives

To help demonstrate your awareness of the bigger picture, it's great to talk about your contributions to whole school policy and initiatives. What have you worked on that is beyond your remit or subject area? Perhaps you've joined something like a behaviour or curriculum working party and learned about and contributed to the bigger picture in some way.

What motivates you to be a leader?

Why do you do your current job and what do you love about it? Why do you want to do the job you are applying for? What is it that makes you want to lead others? Whatever your personal motivations are, our advice is to focus on the students and making a difference. We do this stuff for the same reasons as we began teaching in the first place. We're passionate about helping others in learning and achieving.

Impact of your work as a leader to your school's performance – with data

During the application process, you will need to be mindful of referring constantly to impact. While it's marvellous that you have introduced a well-attended holiday revision programme and got your whole team on board with the planning and delivery of an exciting series of workshops, what people will really want to know is what impact the programme had. Reduce everything to progress and achievement and quote clear and simple data to demonstrate impact.

An example of a time when you have worked sensitively with staff in a coaching or mentoring role and the impact your work had

You will almost certainly, as a middle leader, have come across and dealt with difficult people and difficult situations that required you to act sensitively. As a middle leader you will have coached and mentored both formally and informally. Be prepared to talk about the impact of the work you did and show that you have the ability to act with empathy, have difficult conversations and can take a creative approach to problem solving. Demonstrate your emotional intelligence here and how you are able to skilfully manage relationships – both those between you and others, and those between members of your team. Finally, show that you can be persuasive, how you adeptly bring others round to your way of thinking.

An example of a time when you inspired, motivated or challenged staff and the impact this had

This is important because as a senior leader you need to have influence. You will not only be credible and respected, but also be a source of motivation and inspiration to others. How have you done this in your current role? We recommend preparing solid examples and anecdotal evidence that you can tell and back up with explanation of the impact your inspiring or challenging had. Be careful to talk about how what you did ultimately impacted on students' learning and achievement as well as the member/s of staff. Often, we find it hard to talk about ourselves as motivational and inspirational – it feels a tad braggy – but it needs to be done and, if you prepare carefully, you can come across as passionate and inspiring whilst still being humble and down to earth.

Your thoughts about what makes a good senior leader

Quite simple, but be prepared to talk in some detail about leadership and always use examples. Talk about people you have worked with and observed and the ways they led well or not so well. Balance your detailed knowledge of leadership theory with real life anecdotes or tales of leaders who have inspired, challenged, developed and supported you. Talk about who/what has influenced your leadership style, about how you will further develop your leadership style and skills as you make a transition from middle to senior leader. What support do you perceive you might need in doing this?

Community engagement

All schools belong to part of a community and it goes without saying that strong and successful links with your community will help raise the profile of your organisation. You will also, as an organisation, be able to offer support to these partners and community members in the form of knowledge, expertise, resources or volunteers. Have you introduced or led on any initiative to engage the community? This could include local schools and colleges, parents or volunteers. Talk about the work you have to done to engage parents or involve the community. This could be something simple like inviting parents to a revision master class or working with a local business to deliver learning programmes in or outside your school. Have you increased attendance at parents evening or developed a volunteer reading programme?

How you will go about establishing yourself in your new role

A new senior leader role might be in the organisation in which you are a middle leader or you may move somewhere new. Either way, establishing oneself as a senior leader has its challenges. The way you are perceived by others will change, as will your sphere of influence. Think about the way senior leaders are viewed in the organisations you have worked in. Remember yourself as an NQT and the encounters you had with senior leaders and how you – rightly or wrongly – perceived them. Even if all your encounters were positive, it is likely that at times you were awestruck by these beings who patrolled corridors with a regal air. They appeared to make things happen with minimal effort and talked knowledgeably about aspects of education that were beyond your current level of understanding. As well as being awestruck on occasions, we recall times when we were nervous about approaching senior leaders because they seemed so incredibly busy and important and we didn't feel worthy of their time. As a senior leader you will, purely because of your position, have similar effects on people and you need to think about how you will manage this. That's just one example of the possible effect you might have on others – think about other situations and scenarios, how you want to be perceived and how you can achieve that. There are all sorts of other things to consider in establishing yourself in this new role and some people find the transition easier than others. What is certain is that you will need support; perhaps this will be in the form of a designated mentor or more informal support from other members of the senior leadership team.

Money and budgets

You may be in control of a small budget now, but as a senior leader you may look after larger or multiple budgets. How will you do this? Have you done it successfully as a middle leader? Show that you can work accurately with attention to detail, but also that you can be creative with a budget and successful in getting value for money.

Your ideas for improving an aspect of a school (teaching and learning, behaviour or attendance, for example)

Are you creative and do you have an ability to think 'outside the box'? Can you take innovative approaches to problem solving? Could you introduce a new initiative and bring colleagues along with you? You will have done some of these already so cite examples, but also be prepared to talk about how you might initiate, develop and embed improvements in a new role.

Monitoring and quality assurance you have carried out and its impact

Any effective organisation will have slick systems for monitoring and QA. The processes will run like a well-oiled machine; policies and protocols and responsibilities will be clear and transparent. Most importantly though, monitoring systems and quality assurance processes will be purposeful and effective. They will have impact. They will exist in order to ensure that progress and achievement are the best they possibly can be. When this is the case, the majority of staff will be happy and comfortable with these systems. Look carefully at the systems that you have put in place and be prepared, as ever, to explain their impact and talk about the successes you have had. Consider how well prepared you feel to widen the scope of QA to an entire organisation rather than a small team.

A time when you implemented a significant change

What significant changes have you brought about in your current role? Why did you make the change? How did you implement and lead the change? How did you deal with staff who were resistant to change? What was – as usual – the impact of the change? Are you ready to lead larger scale change?

Create a simple action plan to help you ready yourself to apply for a more senior leadership role.

Area for development	*Action and timescale*	*Support and / or resources required*

You can take all sorts of practical and planned steps in order to develop professionally and further your career. We think the three most important are:

- Observe
- Listen
- Reflect

And in your own practice, always keep your focus. Remember why you are here.